Floorplan Manager:
The Comprehensive Guide

James Wood

Bowdark
PRESS

Disclaimer

Contents

Preface

As luck would have it, my first exposure to the floorplan concept occurred around the same time that my wife and I decided to build our first house. Whether by coincidence or fate, the serendipity of encountering a framework based on building metaphors at the exact moment that I was neck deep in architectural blueprints helped me look past some prior bad experiences with web development frameworks and approach the Floorplan Manager (FPM) framework with an open mind. Several years later, I've moved from being a cautious skeptic to an advocate for what has become the de facto technology for building web-based enterprise applications in the SAP landscape. As you read through this book, we believe that you'll develop a similar appreciation for what the FPM framework brings to the table.

When you peel back all of the various layers of the FPM framework, you'll quickly discover that there's a lot to material to cover. To address this complexity, we've endeavored to organize the contents of this book in such a way that there's a healthy combination of theory, nitty-gritty details, and practical hands-on examples. We hope that you'll find our approach conducive to learning. If we've done our job right, we think that you should be ready to hit the ground running on FPM development projects as soon as you finish reading this book.

Target Group and Prerequisites

This book is geared towards seasoned ABAP developers who have at least some experience working with Web Dynpro ABAP (WDA) technology. Since the FPM framework is based heavily on WDA technology, there's simply no skating around this requirement. So, if you're new to WDA technology, we'd recommend that you first spend some time coming up to speed before approaching this book. A good resource here would be *Web Dynpro ABAP: The Comprehensive Guide* (SAP PRESS, 2012).

Besides the core WDA requirement, there is a general expectation that you have some understanding of object-oriented programming (OOP) concepts in general and ABAP Objects in particular. Though we'll do our best to provide a gentle introduction here, there are certain aspects of the FPM API that will be difficult to understand if you don't know how to create new ABAP Objects classes, inherit from existing ones, and so forth. A useful resource here is *Object-Oriented Programming with ABAP Objects* (SAP PRESS, 2009).

Finally, though this book is chock full of practical examples and screenshots that should help guide you through the learning process, we cannot stress enough the importance of getting hands on with the development tools. Therefore, if you have access to an ABAP development system, we recommend that you use it to follow along with the book's examples. As the saying[1] goes, "nothing ever becomes real 'til it is experienced".

How This Book Is Organized

Anytime you write about a complex technology framework like the FPM, one of the major challenges is figuring out how to organize the material so that the concepts build on top of each other in an organic and intuitive way. A real pet peeve of ours is finding technical books which are a tangled mess of circular references. We find these kinds of circuitous journeys exhausting, leaving us with a sense that we need to go back and re-read the book to pick up on things we might have missed. It is our sincere hope that this is not your experience while reading this book.

Instead, we endeavored to divide the content up into three distinct sections that build on top of one another. As such, our intent is for readers to read the chapters in order, though more experienced developers may naturally want to skip over some of the introductory material. After you grasp the main concepts, you may want to periodically come back to various chapters to refresh your memory about how to utilize particular framework elements, etc.

---

[1] This famous quote came from the English poet John Keats.

Part 1: Getting Started

In this first part of the book, we'll introduce the FPM framework and its core concepts. This foundation sets the stage for more advanced concepts introduced later on in the book.

Chapter 1, *Introduction*

In this chapter, we introduce the FPM framework and identify some of the features that set it apart from other web development frameworks you might have come into contact with outside of the SAP landscape (e.g. Jakarta Struts, Tiles, and so forth).

Chapter 2, *Tutorial: Creating an FPM Application*

Since the FPM is all about developing UIs, many of its core concepts are best explained by example. With that in mind, this chapter walks you through the development of a working FPM application so that you can see how the various framework elements come together in a real and tangible way. At this stage in the book, the goal is to simply see the big picture; we'll fill in the details in the chapters to follow.

Chapter 3, *Floorplan Overview*

In this chapter, we'll take an in-depth look at the various floorplan types provided by the FPM framework. Here, we'll observe the various floorplan page types, custom features, and so forth.

Chapter 4, *Working with the FPM Development Tools*

This chapter concludes our introduction by showing you how to work with the editor tools used to develop FPM applications. Here, we'll highlight differences between tool functionality in various SAP NetWeaver releases.

Part 2: Developing Application Content

In part two of the book, we'll dig deeper into FPM application development concepts by looking at different ways to develop application content.

Chapter 5, *Freestyle UIBBs and the FPM Event Loop*

This chapter introduces the UIBB concept and shows you how to create freestyle UIBBs using custom WDA components. During the course of this introduction, we'll also introduce the FPM event loop which provides the necessary hooks for a given UIBB to be able to communicate with other UIBBs.

Chapter 6, *Generic and Reuse UIBBs*

> Having looked at the makeup of UIBBs in the previous chapter, this chapter picks up with the concept of *Generic UIBBs* (GUIBBs) and *Reuse UIBBs* (RUIBBs). Here, we'll discover that SAP has provided some highly configurable UI components which can really speed up the UI development process.

Chapter 7, *Working with the Wire Model*

> In this chapter, we put the finishing touches on our UIBB discussion by showing you how to supply UIBB components with data using the *wire model*.

Part 3: Putting it all Together

In the final part of the book, we'll look at FPM application development at the macro level, focusing on framework elements which influence behaviors at the application level. Once these concepts are generally understood, we close by showing you how to enhance pre-existing FPM applications.

Chapter 8, *Influencing Application Behavior*

> In this chapter, we turn our attention towards those elements of the FPM framework which affect the overall application behavior. Specifically, we look at the notion of application controllers. We also look at a handful of APIs used to apply changes to floorplan layouts, etc.

Chapter 9, *Interactive Elements of the FPM*

> This chapter explores some of the various elements of the FPM framework which make FPM applications more interactive. Here we look at toolbars, dialog boxes, messaging, quick helps, and so forth.

Chapter 10, *Enhancement Concepts*

> In this final chapter, we look at some of the various options we have for enhancing pre-delivered FPM applications (such as the ones delivered by SAP). Here, we'll learn how to enhance both the UI and the backend application logic.

Conventions Used in This Book

This book contains many examples demonstrating programming language syntax, etc. Therefore, to distinguish these sections, we use a monospaced font type similar to the one used in many integrated development environments to improve code readability:

```
METHOD process_before_output.
  CASE io_event->mv_event_id.
    WHEN if_fpm_constants=>gc_event-save.
      "Handle save event...
  ENDCASE.
ENDMETHOD.
```

When new features are introduced in the code, the selected sections will be highlighted in bold-faced font as shown in the WHEN clause above.

Example Content

At various points throughout the book, we make reference to a code bundle that contains example FPM applications and so forth. This code can be downloaded from the book's companion site at http://www.bowdark.com/books.html#fpmbook. There, you will find instructions for how to install the content as well as the necessary transport files.

How to Contact Us

If you have questions, comments, (or even complaints!) about this book, we'd love to receive your feedback. You can e-mail the author directly at jwood@bowdark.com.

We will post errata, updates, and any additional information out on the book's companion site at http://www.bowdark.com/books.html#fpmbook.

Acknowledgments

Writing a book like this requires a lot of time, research, and dedication. This in turn requires quite a bit of support from the people that you care about. Therefore, a hearty thanks goes out to my wife Andrea, and kids Andersen, Paige, Parker, and Xander. You guys are the best and I couldn't do any of this without you.

Chapter 1
Introduction

Since the advent of the World Wide Web, we've seen many web development frameworks come and go - both within the SAP development landscape and beyond. Whether they're based on the well-known Model-View-Controller (MVC) paradigm or something else, the raison d'être for each of these frameworks is to overcome barriers inherent in a web infrastructure that was not designed with interactive applications in mind. In other words, such frameworks have endeavored to port the familiar rich client application models from yesteryear onto the web, thus extending the reach of applications to a myriad of devices that connect from all over the world.

Fundamentally, web development frameworks provide us with a layer of abstraction that allows us to focus on business requirements and not worry so much about lower level technical details such as HTTP protocol handling, stateful processing, HTML/CSS/JavaScript support, and so on. In practice, this layered approach has been shown to provide several important benefits:

➤ If the framework is designed correctly, the framework layer and the application layer can vary independently. In other words, we can change the business logic without having to change the core user interface and vice versa.

➤ It eliminates many of the traditional barriers to web development by:

❖ Providing an abstraction which makes it possible for developers who are not well-versed in common web-based technologies (e.g. HTML, JavaScript, and so on) to still be able to participate in the development process.

❖ Reducing the time it takes to get a web application up and running.

❖ Taking most of the guesswork out of user interface (UI) design. Here, developers can simply work with abstract UI constructs such as labels, input fields, and buttons and let the framework figure out how to render these widgets at runtime. If you've ever sat in front of a CSS editor and obsessed over what color a particular UI element should be, then you probably have some sense of what we're talking about here.

➢ It promotes standardization and predictability in the UI design process. This in turn makes it easier to backfill features into existing web applications in a consistent manner.

In this chapter, we'll show you how SAP's latest innovation in the web development framework space, the *Floorplan Manager for Web Dynpro ABAP* (or FPM), kicks things up several notches when it comes to the development of web-based user interfaces. For now, our focus will be on fundamental concepts so that you can see the forest through the trees. Then, once we get the basics out of the way, we'll hit the ground running in Chapter 2 by seeing just how easy it is to create an FPM application from soup to nuts.

1.1 What is the FPM?

Before we begin unpacking the FPM and looking at all of the features it has to offer, we first need to come to a basic understanding of what it is. Here, an excellent place to start is to look at the definition provided by SAP within the FPM online help documentation[2]: *Floorplan Manager (FPM) is a highly configurable user interface (UI) framework for easy and efficient application development and adaptation based on Web Dynpro ABAP.* If we start at the end of this definition and work our way backwards, there are several key aspects of the framework that stick out:

➢ First of all, the FPM framework is based on *Web Dynpro ABAP* (WDA) technology. This is an important distinction to note since many developers see FPM and WDA as *competing* as opposed to *complementary* technologies. We'll explore the nature of this relationship further in Section 1.2.

➢ Secondly, we can see that the FPM is a framework designed to speed up and simplify the application development process.

➢ Finally, use of words like *configurable* and *adaptation* give us a clue that the framework brings a lot of flexibility to the entirety of the application development lifecycle, not just the development phase.

---

[2] This definition was taken from the SAP Help Library which is available online at *http://help.sap.com/saphelp_nw73ehp1/helpdata/en/fa/a222ce95ea454d9671b18ad191649a/frameset.htm.*

When we put all this together, we arrive at a framework which promotes consistency and standardization in UI development (based on SAP UI standards and best practices) as opposed to the loosey-goosey sort of results that occur whenever developers are left to their own devices. Of course, the FPM is about more than just standardization. Having a consistent model for UI development also promotes rapid application development (RAD) through the reuse of UI building blocks, a common API and event model, and repeatable design patterns. We'll see all of these concepts on display in the chapters to come.

1.2 FPM and WDA: Complementary Technologies

As we alluded to in the previous section, WDA provides the technical foundation for the FPM framework. Therefore, it's appropriate to think of the FPM and WDA as *complementary technologies* which can be used in tandem to rapidly create web-based user interfaces.

In order to put the relationship between the FPM and WDA into perspective, let's consider the basic architecture of an FPM application as shown in Figure 1.1. Here, even though there are quite a few moving parts, you can see that technically, FPM applications are just WDA applications that are assigned one of three SAP standard floorplan components delivered with the FPM framework: `FPM_OIF_COMPONENT`, `FPM_GAF_COMPONENT`, or `FPM_OVP_COMPONENT`. Therefore, from a runtime perspective, there's no real difference between an FPM application and a custom-built WDA application. At the end of the day, both application types use the same underlying technology stack (i.e., the WDA runtime environment).

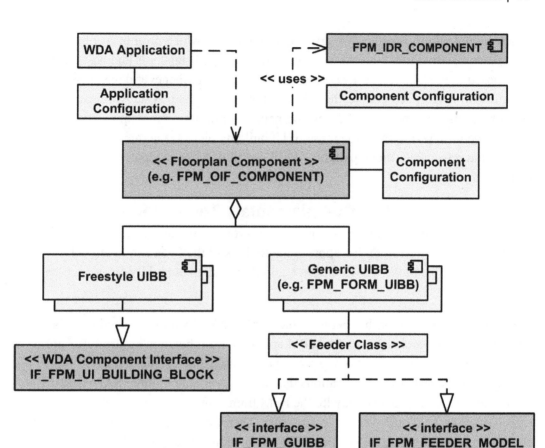

Figure 1.1: Anatomy of an FPM Application

From a design perspective though, FPM applications definitely have a different makeup than most traditional WDA applications. This starts with the main floorplan component that forms the basis of the application (i.e. the FPM_OIF_COMPONENT depicted in Figure 1.1). Unlike other WDA components that you might be accustomed to working with, these floorplan components are like abstract templates that define the basic structure and layout of the application; they do not provide any real application functionality in and of themselves. Instead, the core application functionality is delegated to a series of aggregated WDA components that are referred to within the framework as *user interface building blocks* (UIBBs).

If we think of floorplan components as being like the canvas in a "paint-by-number" kit, then UIBBs would be the media with which we fill in the enumerated content areas. In other words, the floorplan components provide the rough outlines, but we're basically free to fill in between the lines with whatever UIBB content we like. Here, we have three different UIBB types to choose from:

> **Freestyle UIBBs**

Freestyle UIBBs are standalone WDA components that implement the IF_FPM_UI_BUILDING_BLOCK component interface. Besides this base level requirement, there are no other restrictions imposed by the framework concerning how the WDA component is designed (hence the term *freestyle*). Therefore, freestyle UIBBs represent a fairly low-level entry point for integrating pre-existing WDA components into FPM applications.

> **Generic UIBBs (GUIBBs)**

Generic UIBBs (or *GUIBBs*) are pre-defined UI building blocks that are based on a series of generic WDA components delivered with the FPM framework: FPM_FORM_UIBB, FPM_LIST_UIBB, and so on. Unlike freestyle UIBBs, the basic layout/behavior of GUIBBs is specified through *configuration* (in the form of WDA component configurations). Of course, this functionality can be extended further on an as-needed basis using a special kind of ABAP Objects class called a *feeder class* (see Figure 1.1).

> **Reuse UIBBs (RUIBBs)**

Reuse UIBBs (or *RUIBBs*) were introduced with the SAP NetWeaver 7.03 release. These UI building blocks encapsulate business logic within the view layout in order to provide an even higher level of abstraction/reuse.

Component architectures like the one shown in Figure 1.1 are achieved primarily through *configuration*. Here, features of the WDA configuration framework are used to declaratively define component usages and tweak the reusable UIBBs to meet the needs of a particular application scenario. This plug-and-play approach to UI development is illustrated in Figure 1.2.

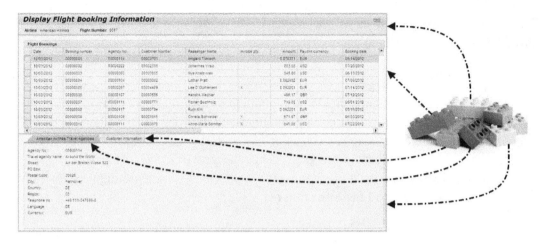

Figure 1.2: Integrating UIBBs into a Floorplan Layout © Copyright 2013. SAP AG. All rights reserved

Though we'll have more of an opportunity to unpack the various architectural components that make up an FPM application in the upcoming chapters, the important takeaway for now is that FPM applications are nothing more than WDA applications that happen to be based upon a set of pre-defined WDA components provided by the FPM framework. This implies that we have the full arsenal of WDA functionality at our disposal when developing FPM applications.

1.2.1 Why Do We Need the FPM?

Anytime you adopt the use of a new development framework like the FPM, there is an upfront cost associated with learning the basic mechanics of the framework and its touch points with the technology it abstracts (WDA in this case). For ABAP developers who have only recently invested the time to learn the basics of WDA, it's only natural to wonder if the additional time investment to learn the FPM is warranted. After all, it's not as if the WDA framework is exactly unproductive when it comes to the development of web applications within the enterprise.

As we progress through this book, we'll see many places where the FPM can improve developer productivity. However, to really understand the value and positioning of the FPM, we need to look at what the framework brings to the table from SAP's perspective. For SAP (or a 3rd-party partner), it's not enough to deliver a functional application. Customers want to be able to enhance, tweak, and customize these applications in all kinds of different ways. Sometimes these enhancements can be implemented using the configuration/adaptation/enhancement features that are built into the WDA framework. More frequently though, customers come up with enhancement ideas that extend beyond the boundaries of what can be achieved in WDA without requiring modifications.

With applications based upon the FPM, it's a completely different story. In the upcoming chapters, we'll see that the flexibility of the FPM framework makes it possible to achieve just about anything using customization/configuration techniques. So, as you invest the time to learn the FPM framework, we would encourage you to be mindful of the fact that the FPM is not just about improving developer productivity; it's also about building flexibility into application designs. Unless you happen to work for a customer who never changes course when it comes to defining business requirements, who couldn't use a little more flexibility in their application designs?

1.3   Understanding the Floorplan Metaphor

In the previous section, we've talked about how the FPM provides a layer of abstraction on top of Web Dynpro. With that in mind, let's take a closer look at the nature of this abstraction by exploring the notion of *floorplans* within the FPM.

1.3.1 Moving Towards a User-Centric Design

Historically, one of the knocks on SAP software products has been that the user interfaces are too complicated for the average user. Though we could debate the merits of such accusations in some cases, such charges are not completely unwarranted. Alas, despite their best efforts to the contrary, there have been times that where SAP has fallen into the trap of "trying to serve everyone and ending up serving no one" with their UI designs.

In recent years, SAP has launched several initiatives whose goal is to remove this negative stereotype from the minds of customers. These initiatives are collectively headed up by the *SAP User Experience Team* which is comprised of a large group of user researchers, interaction designers, and visual designers who work hand-in-hand with customers and developers all over the world to come up with solutions that meet users where they are[3].

One of the many by-products of the efforts of the SAP User Experience Team is a set of UI guidelines documents which keep a record of best practices and recommendations for developing UIs. As you might expect, compiling all this design experience into a usable

---

[3] You can find out more about the SAP User Experience Team online at *http://www.sapdesignguild.org*. This website also offers tons of reference materials, UI best practices documents, and perhaps most importantly, the official UI guideline documents published by SAP.

style guide is no easy task. Recognizing this, the SAP User Experience Team elected to adopt a patterns-based approach to UI development. The basic idea here is to document solutions to common UI design problems in context as opposed to just putting together a handbook that says "all buttons shall be fuchsia", etc. Naturally, the former approach makes it much easier for developers in the field to reuse successful designs. Plus, it also leads to consistency in the UI design process since UI patterns eliminate a lot of the guesswork that normally causes developers to head off in different directions.

Understanding the Pattern-Based Approach

If you've worked in the software field for very long, then you've probably heard the term "design pattern" used (or misused) a few times. This term was made popular in the software field by the classic software engineering text *Design Patterns: Elements of Reusable Object-Oriented Software* (Addison-Wesley, 1995). Within this book, the authors describe design patterns as being a "solution to a problem in context". This is to say that design patterns:

❖ Put a name on a particular design problem so that we can build up a sort of design vocabulary.

❖ Describe the types of problem(s) where the use of a particular design approach makes sense.

❖ Characterize the primary components that make up the design, their interaction points, and so on. Here, it is important to note that design patterns are not intended to provide a comprehensive solution. Rather, their purpose is to define a template that can be used to solve similar problems.

❖ Document consequences and trade-offs that should be taken into account when applying the pattern.

Overall, the basic premise with design patterns is to catalog design experience so that developers don't set out to reinvent the wheel each time they go to solve a particular problem. In essence, they provide the basic framework for building a solution which has been proven to work in a given problem context.

As you read through the UI guidelines documents, you'll see that floorplans figure largely in SAP's adaptation of the pattern approach to UI design. In the next section, we'll take a look at the origins of the floorplan metaphor and see how it provides a holistic solution for modeling UIs.

1.3.2 The Floorplan Abstraction Concept

The term *floorplan* is borrowed from the building industry. In this context, a floorplan is a drawing (or sketch) which outlines the boundaries of a physical structure. For example, the floorplan shown in Figure 1.3 defines the layout of a single-story home. Here, you can see how the floorplan not only specifies the dimensions of the individual rooms, but also illustrates various technical details such as fixture placement, and so on.

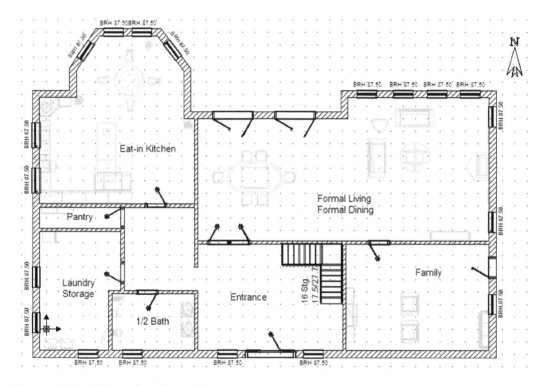

Figure 1.3: A Floorplan Example

Within the building industry, floorplans are used as a guide to help builders navigate through the construction process. Having such a plan in place is particularly important for larger projects where multiple sub-contractors may be working in parallel. Here, as long as everyone follows the plan, the building process should run smoothly and the final product should match customer expectations.

So what does all this have to do with the design of web-based UIs? Well, once we get past the differences in physical media (i.e. brick and mortar vs. pixels on a screen), we can see that the process of constructing web UIs bears a lot of similarities with traditional building processes. After all, whether we're building a single-story home or a

UI to process sales orders, the most fundamental questions that we need to answer before we get started are basically the same:

➢ What are the different rooms/compartments that should be included in the finished product?

➢ Where should these rooms/compartments be placed in relation to one another?

➢ What are the basic dimensions of these rooms/compartments?

➢ How are the rooms/compartments connected with one another?

Relating these concepts to UI development, we can see that floorplans provide a model which helps us to identify the various UI components that contribute to an application design, visualize the boundaries between the components, and understand how the components are interconnected.

While much of this may seem like common sense, you might be surprised to learn how many UI development projects are kicked off before these basic details are ironed out. Naturally, such projects are consumed by many false starts and rework, but those toils only account for part of the productivity losses; the rest is lost in missed opportunities for innovation which can only be discovered when we look at the big picture of UI design. It's here that the application of the floorplan model to UI development begins to take shape.

In practice, builders use floorplans as patterns (or *templates*) for creating an entire class of structures that have a similar shape or style. As opposed to starting from scratch with a new design each time out, the advantage of the template-based approach is that builders can incorporate innovations discovered during the building process back into the template (which is a living document). For example, at some point a builder might discover that it is more cost effective to purchase a sub-structure from a business partner than it is to manufacture the sub-structure in-house. In this case, all the builder has to do is update the floorplan and the design knowledge will be carried forward to the next building project. Over time, such innovations lead to a streamlined building process with shorter build cycles and reduced costs.

Similarly, in the context of UI development, floorplans define a class of applications which share a common UI layout. For example, consider the floorplan illustrated in Figure 1.4. This floorplan divides the UI up into three distinct sections: a top-level identification region, a toolbar region, and a main content area. By using this floorplan as a template for creating other applications that have a similar look-and-feel, we can achieve the following benefits:

➢ We can shorten the duration of the development cycle by identifying and incorporating reusable components that can be leveraged by other applications based on the same floorplan (e.g. a generic identification region or toolbar).

➢ If we need to change the look-and-feel of a suite of applications, we can apply the changes to the floorplan itself and then all of the applications that are based on that floorplan will be updated automatically. (This is an advantage that the digital world has over the physical world).

➢ The definition of clear component interfaces allows us to develop higher level APIs/frameworks which control common application functions such as messaging, navigation handling, personalization, and so on.

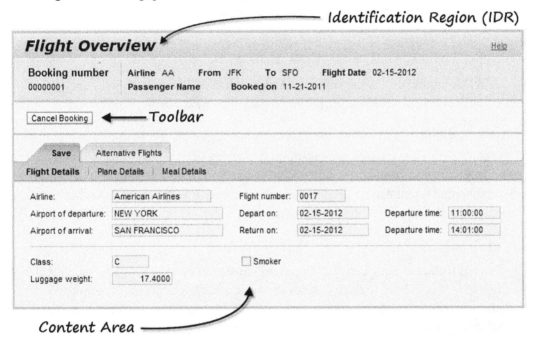

Figure 1.4: A UI Floorplan Example © Copyright 2013. SAP AG. All rights reserved

When we look at floorplans in this light, it's plain to see that they are more than just some 2D sketch of what a UI is supposed to look like. In effect, they can be used to define the backbone of an entire suite of applications that have a similar look-and-feel. This particular point will become clearer when we see how the selection of a floorplan within the FPM influences just about every aspect of a WDA application design. This leads to a highly streamlined development process.

1.3.3 FPM as a Model-Driven Architecture

In the previous section, we characterized floorplans within the FPM as being like models that define the structure of WDA applications. Typically, we think of software models as being inanimate objects. In other words, even though we may reference them repeatedly during the development process, they only contribute indirectly to the final product. This is not the case with floorplans, however.

As we learned in Section 1.2, floorplans in the FPM are implemented in the form of WDA components. Therefore, in order to apply a floorplan towards the creation of a WDA application, we must create several WDA-related development objects:

➤ A WDA application which is based on the desired floorplan component.

➤ A WDA component configuration which specifies how the various compartments within the floorplan layout will be implemented.

➤ A WDA application configuration which ties the WDA application to the component configuration for the target floorplan component.

If you're not familiar with some of these development object types, don't worry; we'll cover each of them at length in the upcoming chapters. The point is that, collectively, these development objects provide the FPM framework with what amounts to an executable model that can be used to generate a working WDA application at runtime. Here, we can distinguish between *floorplans* and *floorplan instances*:

➤ **Floorplan**

From a technical perspective, a floorplan within the FPM is a WDA component (e.g. `FPM_OIF_COMPONENT`) which defines the basic structure of a class of applications. To some extent, it's appropriate to think of the FPM floorplan components as being like *abstract components* whose implementation details will be provided at configuration time via application/component configurations.

➤ **Floorplan Instance**

A floorplan instance is the application of a floorplan within a given FPM application. In other words, floorplan instances take an abstract floorplan component and fill in all of the implementation details required to create an FPM-based WDA application. Examples of such implementation details include which UIBBs are used to fill in specific content areas within the floorplan layout, application-specific behaviors, and so on.

If all of the requisite WDA components exist already, then there really isn't any development that has to be done. Instead, we simply need to define the appropriate configuration objects that weave these components together. Then, once the configuration is in place, the FPM framework will take over at runtime and load the finished product onto the screen. We'll see how this works firsthand in Chapter 2.

1.4 Summary

In this chapter, we provided you with a brief introduction to the FPM framework and its relationship to WDA. We emphasize the term "brief" here because we feel that FPM concepts are best learned by example as opposed to rhetoric. Still, without some basic orientation, it's difficult to jump right into an FPM application design and understand what you're looking at.

Anyway, now that we've gotten some of the basics out of the way, we're ready to move on and see how FPM applications come together in a real and tangible way. So, if you're concerned about your understanding of certain concepts covered in this chapter, don't worry; help is on the way. Once you see how the various components fit together on the screen, things will become much clearer.

Chapter 2

Tutorial: Creating an FPM Application

Compared to traditional WDA applications, FPM applications have a lot of moving parts. As a result, learning how to develop FPM applications can present a bit of a challenge since it's hard to know where to begin. For the purposes of this book, we decided that a top-down approach makes the most sense. Therefore, in this chapter, we're going to roll up our sleeves and see how FPM applications are built from a hands-on perspective. Here, we'll take apart a working FPM application and then rebuild it from the ground up.

At this early stage of the book we'll stick to the basics and concentrate on getting a working application up and running. This implies that we'll defer some of the nitty-gritty details of FPM application design to later chapters. For now, our goals are two-fold: to reinforce the basic concepts described in Chapter 1 and build a visual frame of reference to draw upon as we approach more advanced topics later on in the book.

2.1 Requirements Overview

In keeping with tradition, our first FPM application will be based upon the familiar "Hello, World!" demo program that has been used to introduce programming environments for nearly 40 years. To put an FPM twist on things however, we'll create the "Hello, World!" application using the *Guided Activity Floorplan* (GAF) floorplan type.

Since we haven't yet had an opportunity to explore the various FPM floorplan types in depth, a brief introduction to the GAF floorplan type is in order[4]. As the name suggests, the GAF floorplan is used in scenarios where we want to *guide* users through a process which consists of sequential steps (i.e. like a roadmap). In our contrived "Hello, World!"

---

[4] We'll swing back and cover all of the available floorplan types in great detail in Chapter 3.

example, we'll create a couple of steps to capture the user's first and last name and a confirmation step to display a "Hello!" message on the screen. You can see what each of these steps will look like in Figure 2.1, Figure 2.2, and Figure 2.3, respectively.

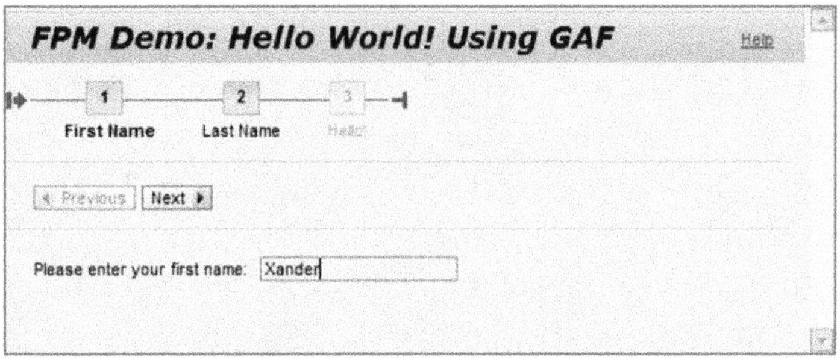

Figure 2.1: Hello, World! Demo - GAF Step 1

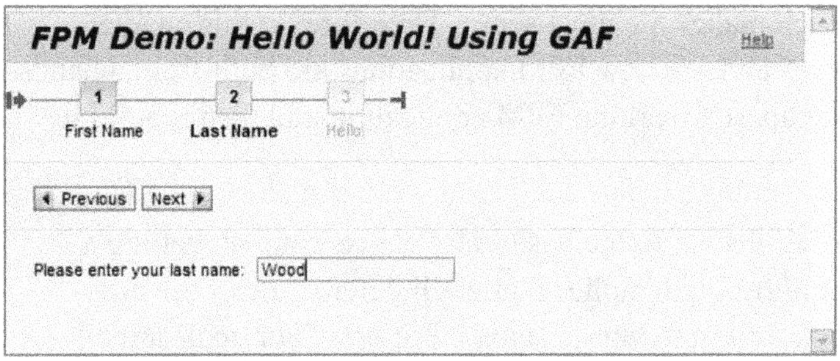

Figure 2.2: Hello, World! Demo - GAF Step 2

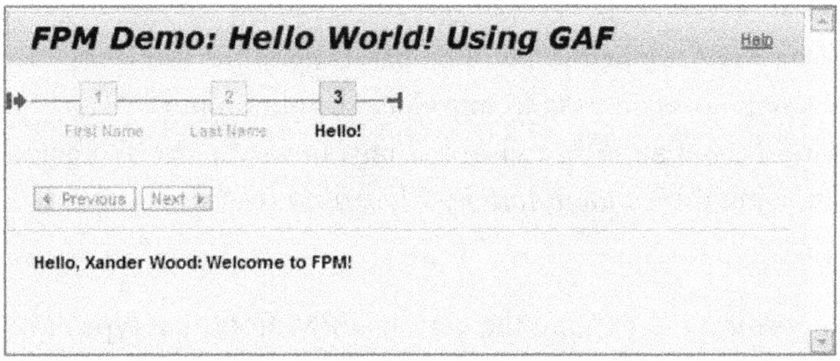

Figure 2.3: Hello, World! Demo - GAF Confirmation Step

From a usability perspective, GAF floorplans are quite intuitive. As you can see in Figure 2.4 the basic GAF floorplan is split into four distinct content areas:

➢ At the top of the screen, there is an identification region (IDR) which is used to display the page title and additional header-level details (as needed).

➢ Next, there is a roadmap (based upon the WDA RoadMap UI element) which helps users orient themselves within the process flow. Here, notice how the process is split into discrete steps which are ordered sequentially.

➢ To enable navigation within the roadmap, a toolbar is provided with buttons to allow users to move forward or backward between steps.

➢ Finally, underneath all that, we have the main content area which contains the UI content for a particular step. Unlike the other three content areas, this content area is freeform and can vary greatly between step types.

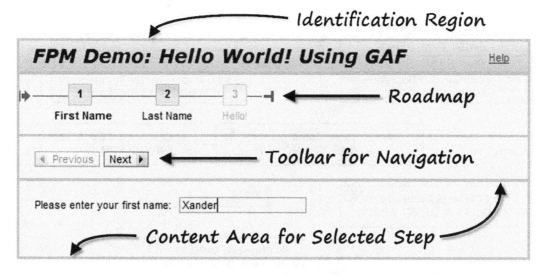

Figure 2.4: Basic Layout of GAF Floorplan © Copyright 2013. SAP AG. All rights reserved

The first three content areas shown in Figure 2.4 are provided automatically by the GAF floorplan component (though they do require some configuration). However, it's up to us to lay out the individual roadmap steps. So, with that in mind, let's turn our attention towards application design issues.

2.2 Design Approach

Now that we have a basic understanding of the application requirements, we can put our architect's hat on and begin formulating a design approach. As we mentioned in the previous section, the GAF floorplan component provides a good portion of the base functionality out-of-the-box; we just have to configure it. However, before we kick off the configuration process, there are a few missing pieces that we have to fill in from a development perspective: namely, the components that make up the step content areas.

Since this is our first FPM application, we're going to take a methodical approach and build the application from the ground up, starting with the development of the user interface building blocks (UIBBs) that make up the step content areas. Then, once these UIBBs are in place, we can transition over into the configuration realm and link everything together. Figure 2.5 shows what the final component diagram will look like when we're done. For reference, we have annotated the component diagram with numbers to help us determine the order of operations within the development process.

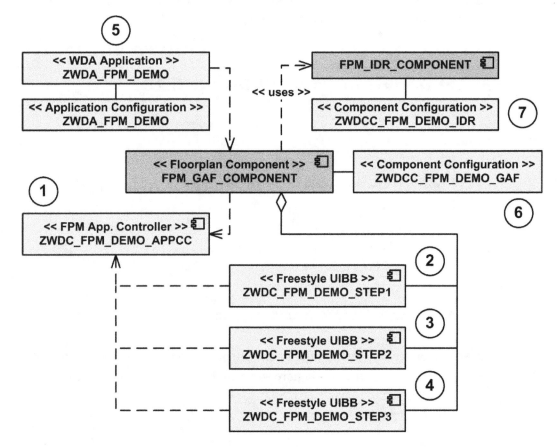

Figure 2.5: Component Diagram for Hello, World! Application

Before we move on from the subject of application design, we need to take a closer look at a couple of UIBB design points. Looking at Figure 2.5, you can see that we'll be defining 3 freestyle UIBBs: one for each of the steps within the roadmap. As you may recall from Chapter 1, freestyle UIBBs are nothing more than regular WDA components that happen to implement the `IF_FPM_UI_BUILDING_BLOCK` WDA component interface. Other than that, it will be WDA development as per usual.

However, since each of the freestyle UIBB components are standalone components, we do have a dilemma on our hands: how do we feed data from one step to another? As ABAP developers, we can probably conceive of a number of different ways to solve this problem (e.g. using shared memory, singleton classes, and so on). As it turns out though, the FPM framework defines a cleaner (and more standardized) way of handling this problem. Here, we define a separate faceless WDA component that implements the `IF_FPM_SHARED_DATA` WDA component (tag) interface, model the shared data within that component's interface controller context, and then map the data over to the UIBB components (via component usages). With this approach, we don't have to do anything to synchronize the data; the FPM event loop will take care of it automatically.

2.3   Building the Application Components

With our component piece list in place, we're ready to proceed with the development of the custom application components which are required to implement our "Hello, World!" application. So, without further ado, let's get started.

2.3.1 Defining the FPM Application Controller

The first component that we'll be building is a standalone WDA component that will supply data to the individual step UIBBs. For this simple application scenario, data sharing is the only thing that this particular component will be tasked with. However, since we're going to the trouble of creating the component in the first place, it makes sense to go ahead and build the component out as a full-fledged *FPM application controller*.

Though we won't have an opportunity to cover application controllers in detail until we get to Chapter 8, suffice it to say that they are used to implement functionality that spans an entire FPM application. Examples of such behaviors include global consistency checks, coordinated event handling, and dynamic changes to a floorplan layout. In general, if you have a need to implement any kind of centralized application behavior, it's a good idea to go ahead and stub out an application controller. That way, if we need to implement any custom application-wide features down the road, all of the basic elements are in place to do so.

To get things started, we'll create a brand new WDA component (in the book's source code bundle, we called the component ZWDC_FPM_DEMO_APPCC but you can name the component whatever you like). Then, once the component is created, we will implement the following WDA component interfaces:

➤ IF_FPM_APP_CONTROLLER

This component interface makes it possible for the WDA component to be positioned as an application controller.

➤ IF_FPM_GAF_CONF_EXIT

This optional component interface provides hooks for allowing the application controller to intercede whenever certain events are triggered within the FPM event loop. Much like a user exit, this component interface allows the application controller to override certain behaviors as needed.

➤ IF_FPM_SHARED_DATA

This tag interface informs the FPM framework that the component is a shared data component so that it will flush data changes to interested components as needed.

To implement the component interfaces, we need to open up the application controller component in the Web Dynpro Explorer and select the IMPLEMENTED INTERFACES tab. Then, we can plug in each component interface into the IMPLEMENTED WEB DYNPRO COMPONENT INTERFACES table and click on the REIMPLEMENT button in the ACTION column as necessary. Figure 2.6 shows what the component looks like after the component interfaces have been implemented.

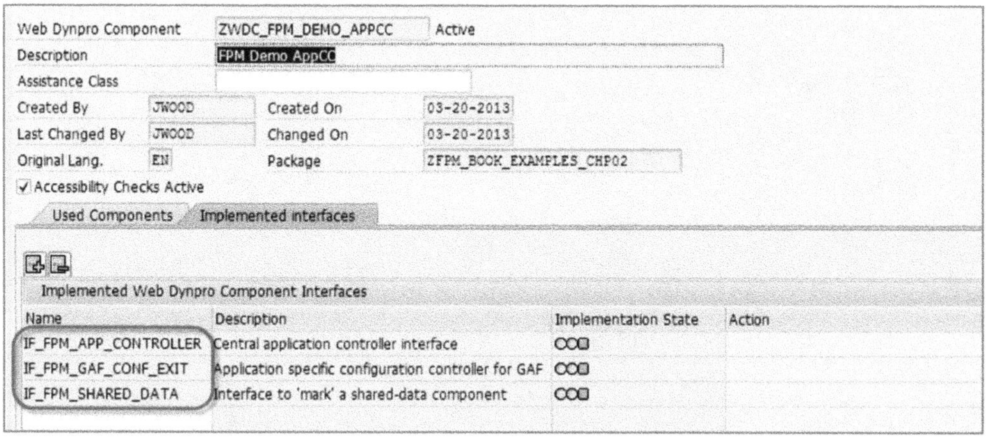

Web Dynpro Component	ZWDC_FPM_DEMO_APPCC	Active		
Description	FPM Demo AppCC			
Assistance Class				
Created By	JWOOD	Created On	03-20-2013	
Last Changed By	JWOOD	Changed On	03-20-2013	
Original Lang.	EN	Package	ZFPM_BOOK_EXAMPLES_CHP02	

✓ Accessibility Checks Active

   Used Components   Implemented interfaces

Implemented Web Dynpro Component Interfaces

Name	Description	Implementation State	Action
IF_FPM_APP_CONTROLLER	Central application controller interface	○○▣	
IF_FPM_GAF_CONF_EXIT	Application specific configuration controller for GAF	○○▣	
IF_FPM_SHARED_DATA	Interface to 'mark' a shared-data component	○○▣	

Figure 2.6: Defining the FPM Application Controller - Part 1 © Copyright 2013. SAP AG. All rights reserved

After the requisite component interfaces have been implemented, the next thing we need to do is model the shared data within the interface controller context. For this task, we need to open up the application controller component's component controller in the Web Dynpro Explorer and navigate to the CONTEXT tab. As you can see in Figure 2.7, we have defined simple context node called USER_DETAILS which contains two string attributes used to capture the user's name information: FIRST_NAME and LAST_NAME, respectively. Finally, in order to add the USER_DETAILS node to the component interface, we must select the INTERFACE NODE property as highlighted in Figure 2.7.

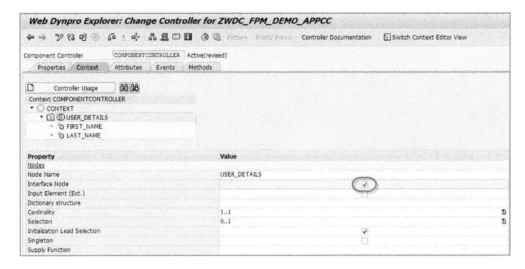

Figure 2.7: Defining the FPM Application Controller - Part 2 © Copyright 2013. SAP AG. All rights reserved

2.3.2 Defining the Step UIBBs

With our application controller now in place, we're now ready to start developing the freestyle UIBBs that will make up the steps in our GAF application floorplan. We'll implement these in step-wise order.

Creating the UIBB for Step One of the GAF

Looking back at Figure 2.1, we can see that the first step of our GAF floorplan contains a simple form which allows users to fill in their first name. To define this form, we'll need to create a new WDA component (we called ours ZWDC_FPM_DEMO_STEP1). In order to use this WDA component as a UIBB, we must implement the IF_FPM_UI_BUILDING_BLOCK component interface (see Figure 2.8).

Web Dynpro Component	ZWDC_FPM_DEMO_STEP1		Inactive/revised
Description	FPM Demo: QAF Step 1		
Assistance Class			
Created By	JWOOD	Created On	03-20-2013
Last Changed By	JWOOD	Changed On	03-20-2013
Original Lang.	EN	Package	ZFPM_BOOK_EXAMPLES_CHP02

✓ Accessibility Checks Active

Used Components | Implemented interfaces

Implemented Web Dynpro Component Interfaces

Name	Description	Implementation State	Action
IF_FPM_UI_BUILDING_BLOCK	IF_FPM_UI_BUILDING_BLOCK	○○▣	

Figure 2.8: Creating the Freestyle UIBB for Step 1 of the GAF © Copyright 2013. SAP AG. All rights reserved

Besides the implementation of the IF_FPM_UI_BUILDING_BLOCK interface, our UIBB also needs to define a component usage to our application controller component. As you can see in Figure 2.9, this usage can be configured on the USED COMPONENTS tab in the component editor.

Web Dynpro Component	ZWDC_FPM_DEMO_STEP1		Active
Description	FPM Demo: QAF Step 1		
Assistance Class			
Created By	JWOOD	Created On	03-20-2013
Last Changed By	JWOOD	Changed On	03-20-2013
Original Lang.	EN	Package	ZFPM_BOOK_EXAMPLES_CHP02

✓ Accessibility Checks Active

Used Components | Implemented interfaces

Used Web Dynpro Components

Component Use	Component	Description of Component
APPCC_USAGE	ZWDC_FPM_DEMO_APPCC	⊡M Demo AppCC

Figure 2.9: Defining a Component Usage to the Application Controller © Copyright 2013. SAP AG. All rights reserved

With the component usage in place, we can now map the shared data node from the application controller. For this task, we need to open up the component controller for the UIBB component and navigate to the CONTEXT tab. Before we can map the data, we must first define a controller usage to the interface controller of the used application controller component. This can be achieved by clicking on the CONTROLLER USAGE button and selecting the corresponding used controller (see Figure 2.10).

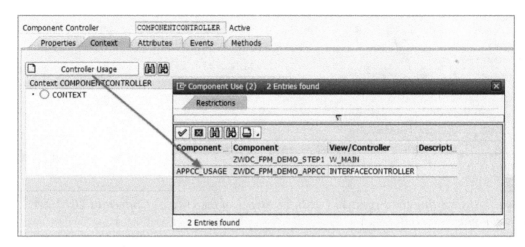

Figure 2.10: Mapping the User Data - Part 1 © Copyright 2013. SAP AG. All rights reserved

Then, we can map the shared USER_DETAILS node by simply dragging-and-dropping it over onto the component controller context (see Figure 2.11).

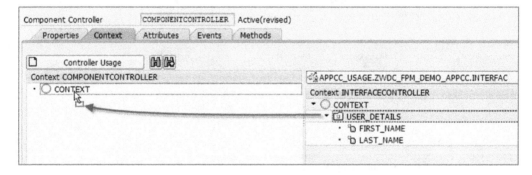

Figure 2.11: Mapping the User Data - Part 2 © Copyright 2013. SAP AG. All rights reserved

In order to carry the shared data down to the view which will contain the data entry form, we must map the shared USER_DETAILS context node from the component controller over to the target view. This can be achieved by opening up the target view in the View Editor and dragging the shared node over to the view controller's context (see Figure 2.12).

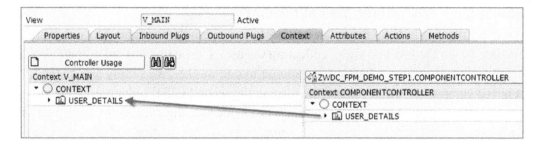

Figure 2.12: Mapping the User Data - Part 3 © Copyright 2013. SAP AG. All rights reserved

Finally, once the data mapping is in place, we can build out the form from Figure 2.1 using the View Designer tool as per usual (see Figure 2.13). After the form is laid out, our work here is done. Note that no custom controller coding is required since the GAF component handles eventing/navigation and our application controller component takes care of synchronizing the data entered on the form.

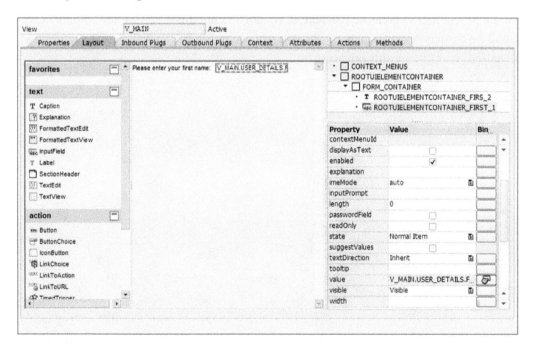

Figure 2.13: Building the Form for Step 1 of the GAF © Copyright 2013. SAP AG. All rights reserved

Creating the UIBB for Step Two of the GAF

The second step in our GAF floorplan is almost identical to the first one. The only real difference lies in the fact that we're collecting the user's last name instead of their first name. So, since these two UIBBs are so similar to one another, we simply copied the first UIBB component and reworked the form in the second UIBB (which we called ZWDC_FPM_DEMO_STEP2) to capture the user's last name (see Figure 2.2). As contrived as this may seem, our intent here was to demonstrate a GAF application with several steps so that you could see what this floorplan looks like in real life.

Creating the UIBB for Step Three of the GAF

The last (or confirmation) step in our GAF floorplan collects the user data entered in steps 1 and 2 and displays a "Hello!" message on the screen (see Figure 2.3). So, we'll create yet another UIBB, repeating the steps described earlier (e.g. implementing the IF_FPM_UI_BUILDING_BLOCK component interface, defining a component usage against the application controller, and so on).

Once the new UIBB is created, we need to model a context node to capture the message that will be displayed on the screen. As you can see in Figure 2.14, we created a context node called MESSAGE for this purpose.

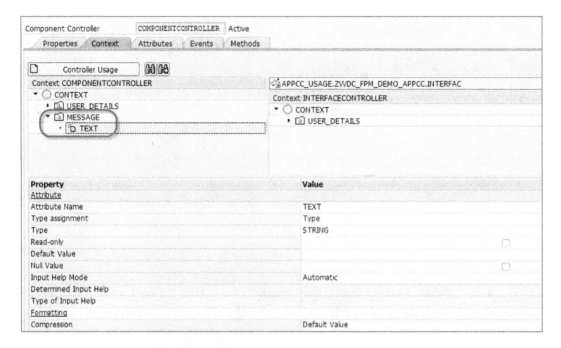

*Figure 2.14: Modeling the Context Node for the Message Display © Copyright 2013.
SAP AG. All rights reserved*

To populate the message text for display, we must implement the
PROCESS_BEFORE_OUTPUT() callback method defined by the
IF_FPM_UI_BUILDING_BLOCK component interface as shown in Figure 2.15. If you're
familiar with the classic Dynpro programming model, then the nature of this callback
method should be pretty intuitive. If not, suffice it to say that this callback method is
invoked by the FPM framework right before the UIBB is rendered on the screen. Thus,
it provides us with an opportunity to retrieve/derive the model data that is to be
displayed on the screen.

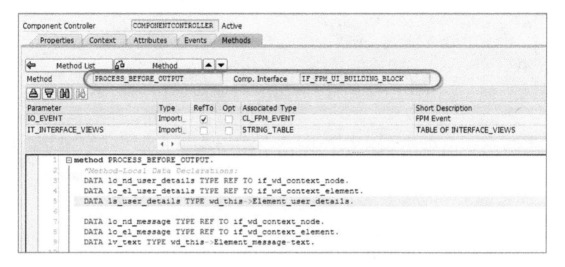

Figure 2.15: Populating the Message Text © Copyright 2013. SAP AG. All rights reserved

Listing 2.1 demonstrates how we've implemented the PROCESS_BEFORE_OUTPUT() method. As you can see, the logic is pretty straightforward. Basically, we're querying the controller context to retrieve the user details (which are automatically mapped via the application controller), building the "Hello!" message, and populating the MESSAGE.TEXT context attribute. To build the message string, we're using the new string template functionality added in the SAP NetWeaver 7.02 release.

```
method PROCESS_BEFORE_OUTPUT.
  DATA lo_nd_user_details TYPE REF TO if_wd_context_node.
  DATA lo_el_user_details TYPE REF TO if_wd_context_element.
  DATA ls_user_details TYPE wd_this->Element_user_details.

  DATA lo_nd_message TYPE REF TO if_wd_context_node.
  DATA lo_el_message TYPE REF TO if_wd_context_element.
  DATA lv_text TYPE wd_this->Element_message-text.

  "Read the current user details from (shared) context:
  lo_nd_user_details = wd_context->get_child_node(
    name = wd_this->wdctx_user_details ).
  lo_el_user_details = lo_nd_user_details->get_element( ).

  lo_el_user_details->get_static_attributes(
    IMPORTING
      static_attributes = ls_user_details ).

  "Build the hello message:
  lv_text =
```

```
      |Hello, { ls_user_details-first_name } _
       { ls_user_details-last_name }: Welcome to FPM!|.

   lo_nd_message = wd_context->get_child_node(
     name = wd_this->wdctx_message ).
   lo_el_message = lo_nd_message->get_element( ).

   lo_el_message->set_attribute(
     name =  `TEXT`
     value = lv_text ).
endmethod.
```

Listing 2.1: Preparing the Confirmation Step Output

To display the "Hello!" message on the screen, we've defined a simple view which contains a single TextView UI element as shown in Figure 2.16.

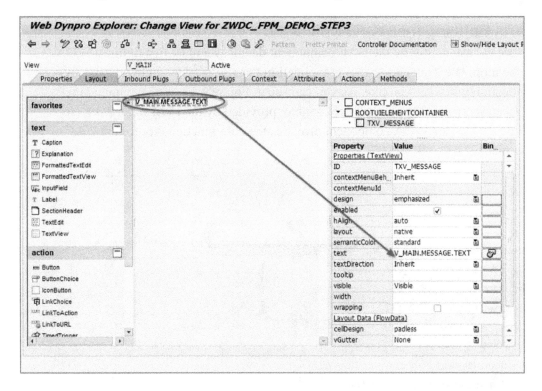

Figure 2.16: Displaying the Message Text © Copyright 2013. SAP AG. All rights reserved

2.4   Putting it All Together

Looking back at the annotated component diagram from Figure 2.5, you can see that we've now completed steps 1-4. These steps comprise the custom development stage; from this point forward, our focus will be on *integration*. We hesitate to use the term configuration here since the objects we'll be creating are in fact workbench objects from a CTS perspective. Nevertheless, the experience is much the same as if we were defining configuration objects in the IMG.

Depending on the version of SAP NetWeaver you are currently working with, the look-and-feel of some of the screens that we will be working with may vary somewhat. We'll have an opportunity to cover these screens in detail in Chapter 4. For now, our focus will be on creating the objects themselves so that we can see how all of the various pieces fit together.

2.4.1   Defining the WDA Application

Before we can configure the GAF component details, we must first define a WDA application. We decided to call our application ZWDA_FPM_DEMO, but you can call your application whatever you like. As you can see in Figure 2.17, we have bound the application against the FPM_GAF_COMPONENT provided by the FPM framework (see Figure 2.17). This WDA component provides the core functionality for the GAF floorplan.

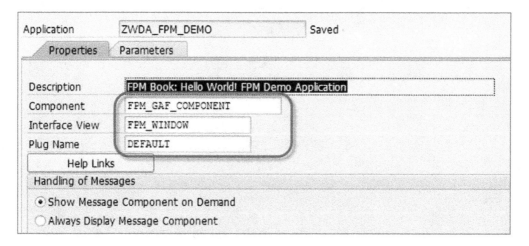

Figure 2.17: Creating the FPM Application © Copyright 2013. SAP AG. All rights reserved

Since floorplan components like FPM_GAF_COMPONENT are, for all intents and purposes, abstract components, we must provide configuration details in order to use them. The glue that ties all this together is a WDA application configuration. Such application configurations can be created by right-clicking on the WDA application in the Web Dynpro Explorer and selecting the CREATE/CHANGE CONFIGURATION context menu option. This selection will open up a WDA-based editor screen like the one shown in Figure 2.18.

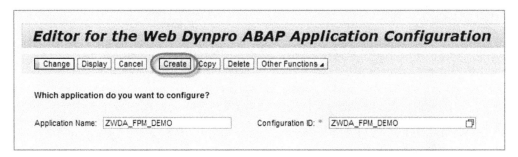

Figure 2.18: Creating a WDA Application Configuration – Part 1 © Copyright 2013. SAP AG. All rights reserved

To create the application configuration, enter a configuration ID[5] in the CONFIGURATION ID field and click on the CREATE button (see Figure 2.18). This will take you to a screen like the one shown in Figure 2.19. For now, simply click on the SAVE button to save the configuration. We'll start filling in the configuration details in the next section.

---

[5] As you can see in Figure 2.18, we have chosen to give the application configuration the same name as the WDA application. Though this convention is not required, it does offer the advantage of not having to physically specify the target application configuration via application parameters. For further details about configuration determination, consult the online help documentation.

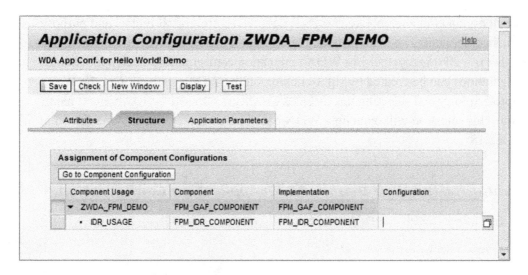

Figure 2.19: Creating a WDA Application Configuration - Part 2 © Copyright 2013. SAP AG. All rights reserved

2.4.2 Configuring the GAF Component

WDA application configurations like the one we created in the previous section are kind of like mapping objects. Basically, they tell the WDA runtime environment which component configurations to apply to leveraged WDA components at runtime. It's here that we'll transcend from a generic GAF floorplan template to an actual floorplan instance that matches our application requirements.

The first step towards connecting these dots is the specification of a WDA component configuration for the FPM_GAF_COMPONENT. We can create this component configuration from the application configuration screen by selecting the FPM_GAF_COMPONENT usage, plugging in a component configuration name in the CONFIGURATION column, and clicking on the GO TO COMPONENT CONFIGURATION button as shown in Figure 2.20.

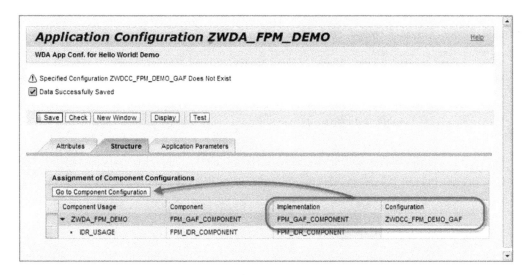

Figure 2.20: Creating a Component Configuration for the GAF Component - Part 1

This will open up a screen like the one shown in Figure 2.21. Here, you will receive an error indicating that the component configuration doesn't exist. In this case, simply click on the CREATE button to go ahead and create the component configuration.

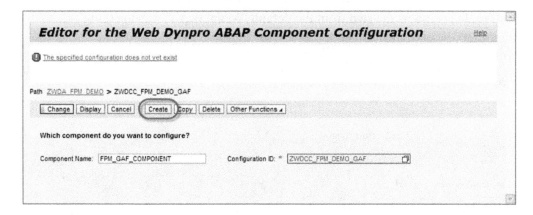

Figure 2.21: Creating a Component Configuration for the GAF Component - Part 2

Once the component configuration is created, you'll arrive at a screen like the one shown in Figure 2.22. As you can see, the initial component configuration contains a shell of the GAF floorplan. From here, we can begin configuring the individual steps and so on. Be sure to save your changes.

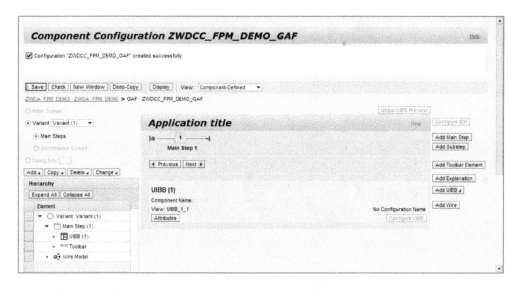

Figure 2.22: Creating a Component Configuration for the GAF Component - Part 3

Configuring the Step Definitions

Since the GAF floorplan defines a default first step in the roadmap, we'll use that main step definition as the starting point for configuring the application. Here, the first thing we want to do is rename the step from the default "Main Step 1" to something meaningful to the user such as "First Name" (see Figure 2.23).

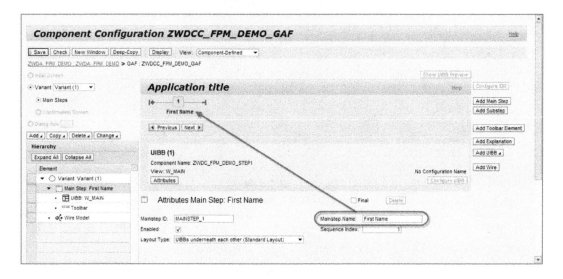

Figure 2.23: Configuring the First GAF Step - Part 1

Next, we need to plug in the UIBB that we want to use to fill the step's content area. For this task, we can simply expand the main step definition on the left-hand side of the configuration editor and choose the UIBB sub-node. Then, in the UIBB attributes, we'll plug in the name of our UIBB for step 1 (e.g. `ZWDC_FPM_DEMO_STEP1`) and the corresponding interface view (see Figure 2.24).

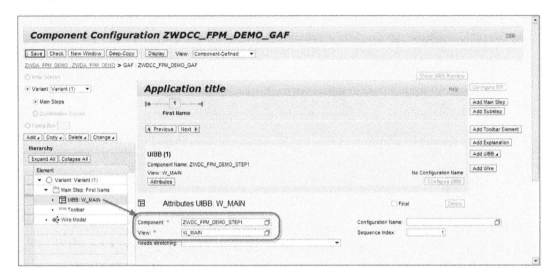

Figure 2.24: Configuring the First GAF Step - Part 2 © Copyright 2013. SAP AG. All rights reserved

To add the next step, we must click on the ADD MAIN STEP button on the right-hand side of the configuration editor. Then, once the new main step is created, we can repeat the configuration steps we used before to select the step name and target UIBB (see Figure 2.25).

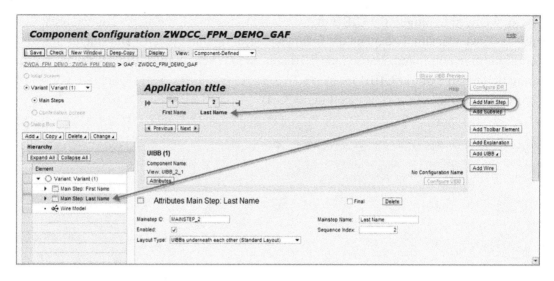

Figure 2.25: Configuring the Second GAF Step © Copyright 2013. SAP AG. All rights reserved

The last step within our "Hello, World!" application is a bit special. Whereas the first two steps are used to collect information from the user, the last step marks the end of the roadmap. In other words, once we get to the final step, there's nothing left to do (except maybe start over). In order to define this kind of behavior within a step, we must configure it as a *Confirmation Screen*. We can set up confirmation screens using the following steps:

1. First, we need to add a confirmation screen to the floorplan layout. This can be achieved by selecting the ADD • CONFIRMATION SCREEN menu option on the left-hand side of the configuration editor as shown in Figure 2.26.

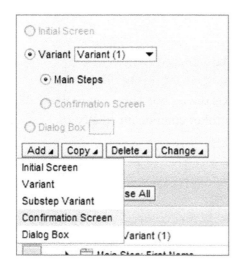

2. Then, once the confirmation step has been created, we can fill in its content area and label text as shown in Figure 2.27.

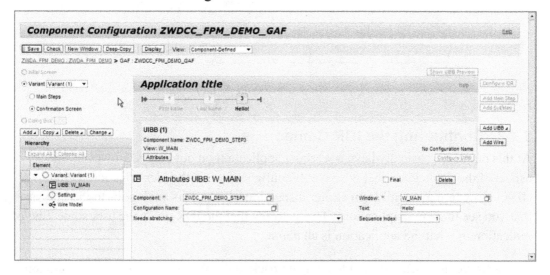

At this point, all three of our steps are configured and ready to go, so now is a good time to save your changes.

Configuring the Application Controller

Before we move on from configuring the GAF component, we need to do one more thing: configure our application controller. This can be achieved by selecting the CHANGE • GLOBAL SETTINGS menu option on the left-hand side of the configuration editor screen. This will open up the GLOBAL SETTINGS dialog box shown in Figure 2.28. Here, all we have to do is plug in the application controller component created in Section 2.3.1. Once again, be sure to save your changes.

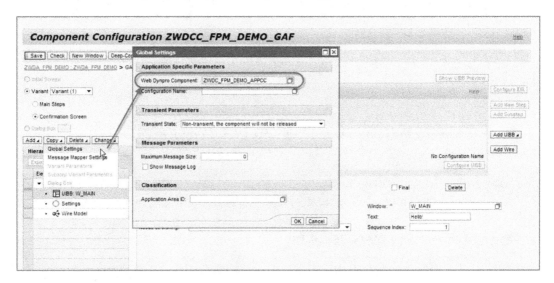

Figure 2.28: Specifying the Application Controller © Copyright 2013. SAP AG. All rights reserved

2.4.3 Configuring the IDR Component

At this point, we basically have a working application on our hands. However, one aspect of the application that we haven't configured yet is the identification region (IDR). As you may recall from earlier discussions, the IDR is analogous to the title bar that you see in many applications. This is to say that the IDR gives the user some kind of indication of what the application is all about.

To configure the IDR, we need to navigate back to the WDA application configuration for our application. If you still have the configuration editor open for the GAF component configuration, you can use the breadcrumb trail at the top of the editor to navigate backwards (see Figure 2.29).

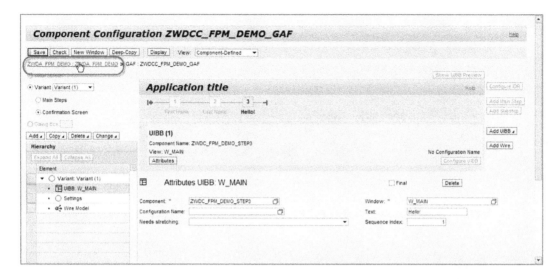

Figure 2.29: Navigating Back to the Application Configuration © Copyright 2013. SAP AG. All rights reserved

Then, to configure the IDR, select the IDR component usage in the application configuration, plug in the component configuration ID, and click on the GO TO COMPONENT CONFIGURATION button (see Figure 2.30). As was the case before with the component configuration for the GAF component, you will be prompted to create the component configuration.

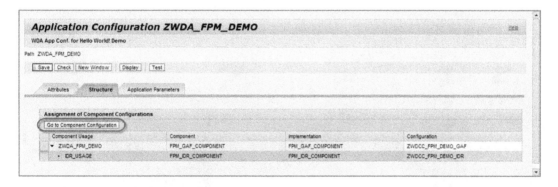

Figure 2.30: Configuring the IDR - Part 1 © Copyright 2013. SAP AG. All rights reserved

Once the component configuration is created, we can plug in an application title in the correspondingly named field on the configuration editor screen (see Figure 2.31). Here, there's not much else to configure since IDRs are, by default, pretty simple. Be sure to save your changes (both here and within the application configuration).

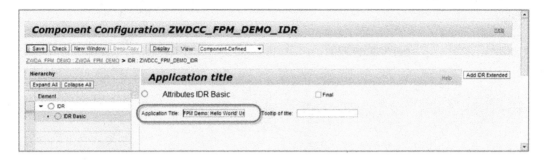

Figure 2.31: Configuring the IDR - Part 2 © Copyright 2013. SAP AG. All rights reserved

2.4.4 Testing the Finished Product

After the final configurations are in place, we're ready to fire up the application and see how it works. For this task, we can simply open up the WDA application definition and click on the TEST/EXECUTE button (see Figure 2.32). If all goes well, you should end up with an application whose screens match the ones shown in Figure 2.1, Figure 2.2, and Figure 2.3, respectively.

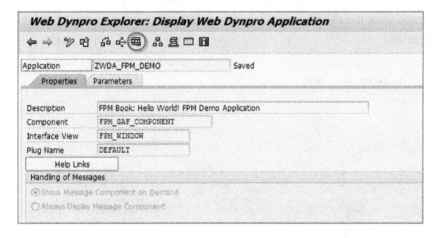

Figure 2.32: Testing the FPM Application © Copyright 2013. SAP AG. All rights reserved

2.5   Summary

As the saying goes, a picture's worth a thousand words, so hopefully this hands-on tutorial helped you visualize how FPM applications come together. At the same time, we recognize that a hands-on tutorial at this stage may have raised just as many questions as it answered. So, in the next chapter, we'll go back to square one and take an up-close look at floorplans within the FPM framework.

Chapter 3
Floorplan Overview

In the previous chapter, we got our first glimpse at an actual floorplan within the FPM whenever we built a simple GAF application. Of course, such a simple demonstration barely scratches the surface of what the GAF floorplan has to offer. Plus, we still haven't seen the other floorplan types offered by the FPM framework. So, with that in mind, we thought we'd devote this chapter to looking at each of the floorplan types provided by the FPM framework up close.

3.1   Object Instance Floorplan (OIF)

The first floorplan type that we'll be looking at is the *Object Instance Floorplan* (OIF). As the name suggests, the OIF floorplan provides a template for constructing UIs that are used to edit business object instances. Therefore, the OIF floorplan is normally used to create UIs for performing basic CRUD operations (i.e. **C**reate, **R**emove, **U**pdate, and **D**isplay) on business objects such as sales orders or products.

Most SAP users will find themselves right at home with the OIF floorplan since it has a similar look-and-feel to many of the common classic Dynpro-based transactions in the SAP® Business Suite. For example, a sales order application based on the OIF floorplan will definitely bear a resemblance to the familiar VA01, VA02, and VA03 transactions used to edit sales orders in an SAP® ERP system. In the upcoming sections, we'll dissect the OIF floorplan and see how it's used to build transactions around business objects.

3.1.1   Structure of the OIF Floorplan

In order to understand how the OIF floorplan is structured, it helps to be able to look at a live example. Figure 3.1 contains a screenshot of a sample OIF application used to maintain sales orders. Here, we have marked up the screenshot so that you can see how the various content areas are laid out within the floorplan.

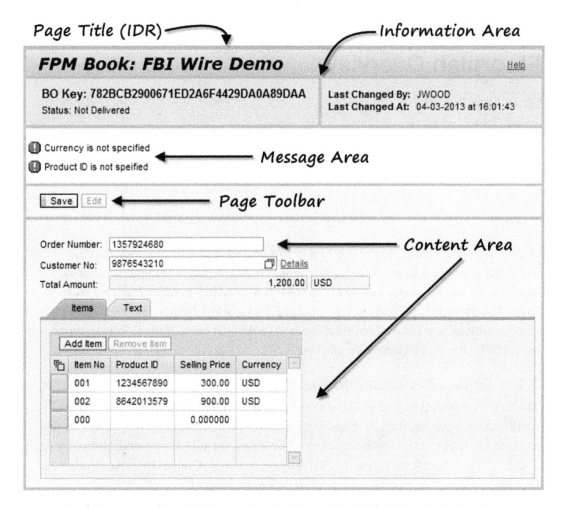

Figure 3.1: Anatomy of an OIF Floorplan © Copyright 2013. SAP AG. All rights reserved

As you can see in Figure 3.1, the OIF floorplan layout is split into 5 distinct content areas:

➢ **Page Title**

At the top of the UI, we have the page title area which defines a sort of title bar for the application. Users can use this section to orient themselves and also access pertinent help documentation via the HELP link in the top right-hand corner of the screen. Prior to the SAP NetWeaver 7.03 release, this section of the OIF floorplan was referred to as the *identification region* (IDR).

➢ **Information Area**

The information area (formerly known as the *extended IDR*) is an optional content area that, when present, shows up underneath the page title. This content area is used to provide additional header-level data that may be pertinent to the user based upon the current application state. For example, in Figure 3.1, you can see how the information area is being used to display sales order status information.

Internally, the information area is divided horizontally into two separate elements: on the left-hand side we have the *ticket area* and on the right-hand side we have the optional *header area*. The ticket area is further sub-divided vertically into a top and bottom section, both of which contain free-form text. The header area is used to display additional header-level attributes which are organized into key-value pairs (e.g. the LAST CHANGED BY and LAST CHANGED AT attributes shown in Figure 3.1).

Overall, the layout of the information area is fairly fluid. For example, if the ticket area is not filled in, but the header area is, the header area content will be shifted over to the left-hand side of the information area.

➢ **Message Area**

The message area is a dynamic content area which shows up whenever there are one or more messages present in the message collection of the FPM message manager. We'll learn more about messaging in FPM applications in Chapter 9.

➢ **Page Toolbar**

The page toolbar contains all of the top-level toolbar elements which affect the FPM application as a whole (e.g. SAVE or EDIT). Notice how we use the term "elements" here since the page toolbar can also contain navigation links, button menus, and so forth.

➢ **Content Area**

At the bottom of the OIF floorplan layout, we have the main content area. The layout of this content area is controlled by a specialized WDA UI element called the `HorizontalContextualPatternControl`. This UI element has a similar look-and-feel to the familiar `TabStrip` element in that it organizes the content area into a series of tabs. Collectively, the `HorizontalContextualPatternControl` and the view tabs it comprises make up what is known as the *Contextual Navigation Region* (CNR). We'll explore the makeup of the CNR in further detail in Section 3.1.2.

Additional Elements of the OIF Floorplan

In addition to the main page layout illustrated in Figure 3.1, the OIF floorplan also provides several other use case-specific page types including:

➢ **Initial Screen**

The initial screen of an OIF floorplan is an optional element that can be used to pre-select a particular business object instance for editing. Here, we might provide a selection form that allows users to lookup the target business object instance before they access the main editor area. This is preferable to cluttering up the main content area with selection form elements, for instance.

➢ **Confirmation Screen**

The confirmation screen is another optional element that is normally used in deletion scenarios. Here, if the user decides to delete a business object instance, it makes sense to route them to a confirmation screen rather than leaving them on an editor screen that no longer contains any data.

➢ **Dialog Boxes**

In some situations, we may want to solicit or display additional information that is not directly applicable to the business object in question. Here, rather than cluttering up the screen with unrelated data, we can provide dialog boxes so that users can access the auxiliary data in a separate popup window. We'll learn how to work with dialog boxes in Chapter 9.

Unlike the main content area which is split into a series of view tabs, the secondary content areas described above have a more straightforward layout. Here, UIBBs are normally stacked on top of one another to fill out the content area. Though we do have some more sophisticated layout options here, such refinement is rarely needed since these content areas should only contain a handful of UI elements in most circumstances.

3.1.2 Understanding the OIF Object Schema

From a technical perspective, the OIF floorplan is implemented using the
`FPM_OIF_COMPONENT` WDA component. As you can see in Figure 3.2, this component
defines a static usage relationship to another standard component provided by the FPM
framework: the `FPM_IDR_COMPONENT` WDA component. The `FPM_IDR_COMPONENT`
provides the content for the page title and information area of the floorplan layout.
Collectively, these two standard components take care of rendering the first four content
areas highlighted in Figure 3.1.

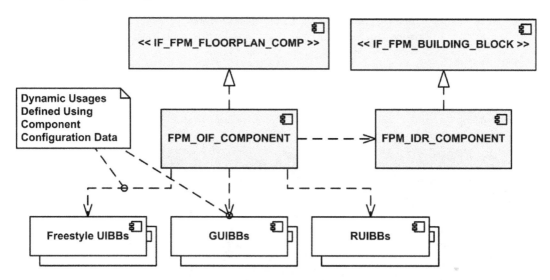

Figure 3.2: Component Diagram for OIF Floorplan

The main content area of the OIF floorplan is filled in by custom UIBBs which are
designed to assist users in editing a business object instance. Here, the component
usages are dynamically generated at runtime using declaratively-defined usage metadata
from the component configuration of the `FPM_OIF_COMPONENT`. To understand how this
works, we need to take a closer look at the aforementioned *Contextual Navigation
Region* (CNR).

As we mentioned previously, the CNR organizes the main content area into a series of
view tabs. These view tabs are part of a modeling schema defined within the
`FPM_OIF_COMPONENT` component. If you look closely at the component controller context
of this component, you can see how these schema elements are organized internally. At
runtime, the `FPM_OIF_COMPONENT` component uses this view tab metadata to dynamically
build the CNR. Luckily, such complexities are abstracted away deep within the

`FPM_OIF_COMPONENT` component itself; all we have to do is model the view tabs and the `FPM_OIF_COMPONENT` will take care of the rest.

Figure 3.3 illustrates how the CNR is configured within the FPM Configuration Editor tool. Though we haven't yet had much opportunity to become acquainted with this tool, we can still get some sense of how the CNR is laid out by following the annotated lines which show the relationships between schema elements and the corresponding visual elements that show up in the PREVIEW panel.

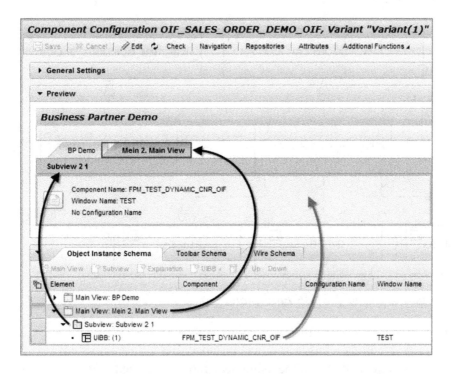

Figure 3.3: Object Schema for the OIF Floorplan © Copyright 2013. SAP AG. All rights reserved

Looking at Figure 3.3, we can see how view tabs within an OIF floorplan are hierarchically organized into three distinct element types:

➢ **Main Views**

Each main view represents a separate view tab within the main content area of the OIF floorplan at runtime. In the sample screenshot shown in Figure 3.3, there are two main views which represent the BP DEMO and MEIN 2. MAIN VIEW tabs on the screen, respectively.

From a configuration perspective, a main view is simply a logical construct used to organize the CNR. Their definition consists of an ID and a name attribute, the latter of which defines the label of the view tab at runtime. Though there are no hard restrictions on how many main views we can define within an OIF floorplan, a general rule of thumb would be to keep the number at a manageable size of 10 or fewer so that users don't have to scroll around to find what they're looking for.

It's also worth mentioning that a lone main view will not be rendered in a tabstrip control in situations where it only contains a single subview. In this case, only the embedded UIBB content will show up on the screen and the main view will act like a `TransparentContainer` element from a rendering perspective.

➢ **Subviews**

Subviews allow us to sub-divide main views into additional view tab pages. By default, each main view contains at least one subview, though we can define several more if needed. In situations where more than one subview is defined, the subview tab pages will be rendered in a viewswitch control which allows users to navigate between the pages by clicking on sub-tabs. Otherwise, the viewswitch will be hidden and users will only see the embedded UIBB content contained within the lone subview definition.

➢ **UIBBs**

Nested underneath the subviews are the UIBBs that provide the application content. Within a given subview, we can stack multiple UIBBs on top of one another to define the desired tab page layout. As you can see in Figure 3.2, we can choose between freestyle UIBBs, GUIBBs, and RUIBBs here.

Collectively, these three schema elements provide us with tremendous flexibility when it comes to laying out the main content area of an OIF floorplan. Here, we can define the view tab schema in all kinds of different ways. For example, if we don't want to organize the UI around a tabstrip control, we can simply define a single main view and subview and use the UIBBs to organize the content. We'll explore some of these different alternatives whenever we look more closely at UIBB development in Chapters 5 and 6.

3.1.3 When to Apply the OIF Floorplan

Given its singular focus, it should be pretty obvious by now that the OIF floorplan should be used in cases where you're building transactions to edit business objects. Such business objects could include entity objects such as products or business partners or transactional objects such as sales orders and purchase orders. In either case, the goal is to provide users with a unified look-and-feel so that the learning curve for new business object transactions is limited to coming up to speed with the business objects themselves as opposed to having to hunt down the SAVE button, etc.

> **Note**
>
> According to the online help documentation for the SAP NetWeaver 7.31 release, the OIF floorplan has been superseded by the *Overview Page Floorplan* (OVP) in the latest set of UI guidelines. However, since the OIF floorplan has been used extensively in the past, it's very likely that it will die a slow death in the coming years. We'll introduce the OVP floorplan in Section 3.4.

3.2 Quick Activity Floorplan (QAF)

As the name suggests, the *Quick Activity Floorplan* (QAF) floorplan type is used in situations where users need to quickly perform a particular activity on a business object. For example, we might use the QAF floorplan to make it easy for users to record goods receipts (GR) or create the shell of a purchase order (PO). In these scenarios, the use of a full-blown OIF floorplan is overkill since the user only needs access to a fraction of the fields available on the business object(s) in question.

3.2.1 Structure of the QAF Floorplan

Figure 3.4 illustrates what a QAF floorplan looks like at runtime. As you can see, there are a lot of similarities between the QAF floorplan layout and the OIF floorplan layout. This is not an accident since both floorplans are based on the same underlying `FPM_OIF_COMPONENT` WDA component.

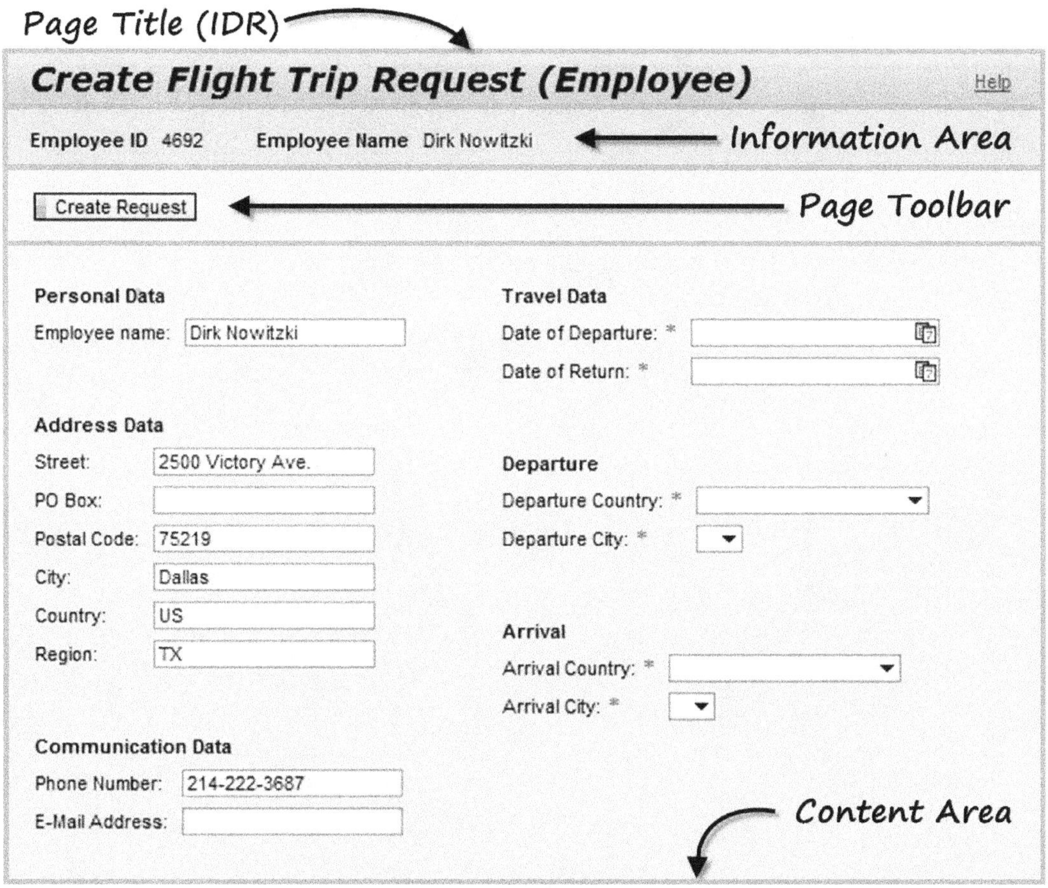

Page Title (IDR)

Create Flight Trip Request (Employee)   Help

Employee ID 4692   Employee Name Dirk Nowitzki   ◄──── Information Area

[Create Request] ◄────────────────────────── Page Toolbar

Personal Data

Employee name: [Dirk Nowitzki]

Travel Data

Date of Departure: * [   ]
Date of Return: * [   ]

Address Data

Street: [2500 Victory Ave.]

PO Box: [   ]

Postal Code: [75219]

City: [Dallas]

Country: [US]

Region: [TX]

Departure

Departure Country: * [▼]
Departure City: * [▼]

Arrival

Arrival Country: * [▼]
Arrival City: * [▼]

Communication Data

Phone Number: [214-222-3687]

E-Mail Address: [   ]

Content Area

Figure 3.4: Anatomy of a QAF Floorplan © Copyright 2013. SAP AG. All rights reserved

So what's the difference between applications based on the QAF floorplan vs. applications built using the OIF floorplan? Well, from a technical perspective, absolutely nothing. Both floorplan types have access to all of the supported features and page types of the FPM_OIF_COMPONENT. To see the differences, we must look at the two floorplan types from a functional point of view. Since FPM applications based on the QAF floorplan type are intended to support quick little one-off activities, they do not require complex UI layouts with multiple tab pages and multifaceted toolbar functions. Instead, as you can see in Figure 3.4, QAF floorplans are stripped down to just the essentials, allowing users to jump right in and get the job done quickly. We'll take a closer look at the mechanics of this in the next section.

3.2.2 Understanding the QAF Object Schema

Since both the OIF and QAF floorplans share the same underlying WDA component, you'll find the configuration process for both floorplan types to be quite similar. As you would expect, QAF floorplan configurations have the same cast of characters as OIF floorplans. The primary difference is that QAF floorplans are only intended to contain a single main view and subview as per SAP UI guidelines. Within this lone subview, we can embed multiple UIBBs, but again, the intent is to keep things simple (see Figure 3.5).

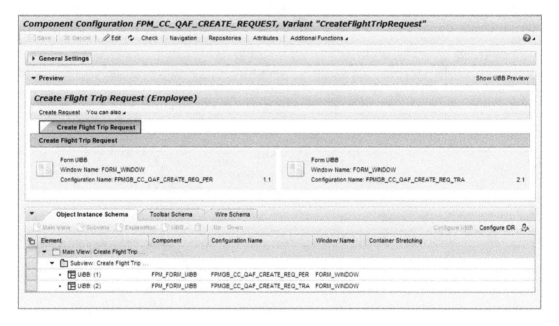

Figure 3.5: Object Schema for the QAF Floorplan © Copyright 2013. SAP AG. All rights reserved

Besides the single main view/subview requirement, the UI guidelines for the QAF floorplan type are pretty flexible. For instance, it's acceptable to make use of initial screens and/or confirmation screens as well as dialog boxes where they are needed. We can also provide additional functions within the page toolbar if it makes sense to do so. Ultimately, as is the case with all guidelines, there is some room for interpretation. Here, it's best to remember the spirit of the recommendation rather than getting bogged down in semantics.

3.2.3 When to Apply the QAF Floorplan

Before applying the QAF floorplan, there are several basic questions that you need to ask yourself:

1. First of all, you should ask yourself whether or not the activity in question can be performed quickly and with little setup. If the activity doesn't pass this basic litmus test, then the QAF floorplan type is not a good fit for your application requirements.

2. Is the activity complex enough that it could be split into multiple steps? If so, then the GAF floorplan type covered in Section 3.3 might be more appropriate.

3. Approximately how many data fields must the user populate in order to perform the activity? If the number of fields is substantial enough to fill up more than one screen, then you should look elsewhere at other floorplan types.

Again, the basic intent of the QAF floorplan is to provide a simple UI that allows users to step right in and get the job done quickly. Trying to force a more complex process into this mold will only cause confusion and frustration for users.

3.3 Guided Activity Floorplan (GAF)

So far, the floorplan types that we've looked at have had a very narrow focus (e.g. editing a business object instance or performing a quick little one-off activity). Surprisingly enough, this concentrated approach probably satisfies up to 75% of typical UI development requirements since the activities of well-designed business objects usually map very closely to related business processes. However, there are times whenever we need to model a more complex business process which spans multiple steps and/or touches several related business objects. In these circumstances, we can turn to the *Guided Activity Floorplan* (GAF).

3.3.1 Structure of the GAF Floorplan

Since we've already seen a live example of the GAF floorplan in Chapter 2, the basic layout of the GAF floorplan should feel pretty familiar by now. As you can see in Figure 3.6, the GAF floorplan layout is split into 6 distinct sections:

➢ **Page Title**

At the top of the UI, we have the page title area which defines the application title bar. The layout of this area is identical to that of the OIF floorplan type.

➢ **Information Area**

The information area (formerly known as the *extended IDR*) is an optional content area that, when present, shows up underneath the page title. This content area is used to provide additional header-level data that may be pertinent to the user based upon the current application state. Once again, the layout of this area is identical to that of the OIF floorplan type.

➢ **Message Area**

Though not depicted in Figure 3.6, the message area is a dynamic content area which shows up underneath the information area whenever there are one or more messages present in the message collection of the FPM message manager.

➢ **Roadmap**

This content area helps users orient themselves within the process flow. For instance, in the GAF example application shown in Figure 3.6, you can see how the flight booking process is being split up into a series of discrete steps: e.g. select an outbound flight, select a return flight, provide account information, and so on. At any point in the process flow, the user can look up at the roadmap element and determine where they are in the process.

➢ **Page Toolbar**

The page toolbar contains all of the top-level toolbar elements which affect the FPM application as a whole. Of particular interest are the PREVIOUS and NEXT buttons which are used to navigate back and forth between steps in the roadmap. Unlike the OIF floorplan whose toolbar elements are fairly static, the page toolbar for the GAF floorplan is fluid, changing in conjunction with the users progress within the roadmap. For example, at the beginning of the roadmap, there is no need to render the PREVIOUS button since the user cannot navigate backwards. The same sort of logic applies whenever the user reaches the end of the process.

➢ **Content Area**

Finally, at the bottom of the GAF layout, we have the main content area. This freeform content area contains the custom UIBBs that are needed to build the various steps within the process flow. Here, we once again have the choice of integrating freeform UIBBs, GUIBBs, and RUIBBs as per our requirements.

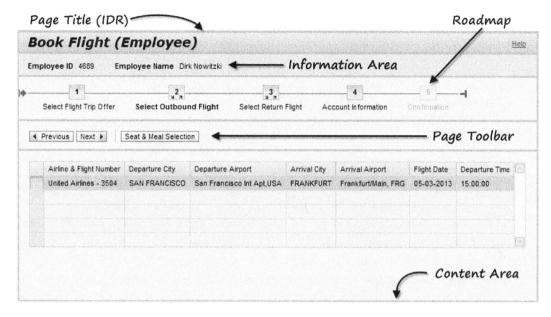

Figure 3.6: Anatomy of a GAF Floorplan © Copyright 2013. SAP AG. All rights reserved

Additional Elements of the GAF Floorplan

Much like the OIF floorplan, the GAF floorplan also provides several other use case-specific page types including:

➢ **Initial Screen**

The initial screen of a GAF floorplan is an optional element that can be used to seed the process before it's kicked off in earnest. Here, if we're performing an activity for a particular business object instance, we might want to provide a selection screen to allow the user to pre-select this instance before initiating the process.

➢ **Confirmation Screen**

The confirmation screen is another optional element that is normally used to display status information at the end of the process.

➢ **Dialog Boxes**

In some situations, we may want to solicit or display additional information that is not directly applicable to the process in question. Here, rather than cluttering up the screen with unrelated data, we can provide dialog boxes so that users can access the auxiliary data in a separate popup window. We'll learn how to work with dialog boxes in Chapter 9.

➢ **Substeps**

Besides the optional elements outlined above, GAF floorplans also allow us to sub-divide steps within the roadmap into a series of *substeps*. For example, in Figure 3.7, you can see how step two in the roadmap (i.e. the SELECT OUTBOUND FLIGHT step) contains two optional sub-steps: SELECT SEAT and SELECT MEAL. Here, users can specify additional details related to their outbound flight selection. Once the data is filled in, the user can return to the main roadmap step and continue on within the process flow as per usual.

Sticking with the roadmap metaphor, it's appropriate to think of sub-steps as being like a sort of detour that the application might take you on depending on various inputs. For instance, in the example application shown in Figure 3.7, it could be that the sub-steps are only made available if the user has selected a first class ticket on the outbound flight. Though we could conceivably retrieve these selections via a dialog box, substeps provide a more intuitive solution since users can track their progress directly within the roadmap element.

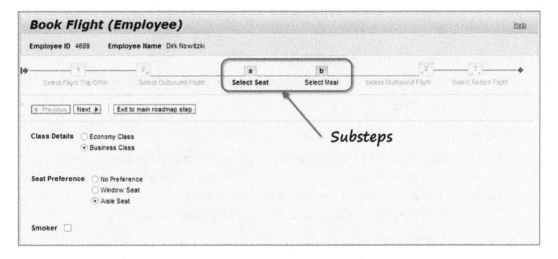

Figure 3.7: Substeps in a GAF Floorplan © Copyright 2013. SAP AG. All rights reserved

3.3.2 Understanding the GAF Object Schema

Comparatively speaking, the object schema for the GAF floorplan bears a number of similarities to that of the OIF floorplan. For instance, as you can see in Figure 3.8, the component architecture for the GAF floorplan is almost identical to that of the OIF floorplan (refer back to Figure 3.2). Here, the only real difference is the use of the

FPM_GAF_COMPONENT as opposed to the FPM_OIF_COMPONENT used in OIF and QAF floorplans.

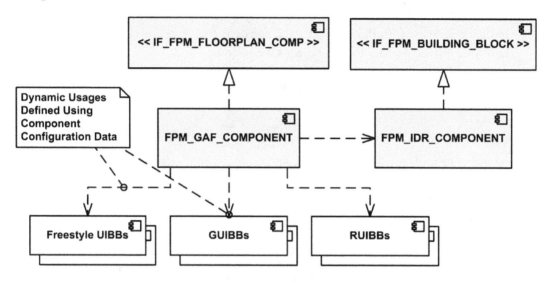

Figure 3.8: Component Diagram for GAF Floorplan

From a modeling perspective, the GAF floorplan has a hierarchical object schema that is organized into the following element types (see Figure 3.9):

➢ **Main Steps**

Each main step in the object hierarchy corresponds with a RoadMapStep element contained within the RoadMap element that controls the GAF process flow. Main step definitions consist of an identifier and a name attribute which defines the label text displayed underneath the roadmap step in the RoadMap control.

➢ **Substeps**

As we learned in the previous section, substeps are optional step definitions which can appear between two main steps. Looking at Figure 3.9, you can see that substeps are defined as subordinate elements of a main step definition. Like main steps, substep definitions consist of an identifier and a name attribute which defines the label text displayed underneath the substep in the RoadMap control.

> **UIBBs**

The content area for main steps and substeps is defined by embedding one or more UIBBs. Here, we can choose between freestyle UIBBs, GUIBBs, and RUIBBs to fill in the content area. Both main steps and substeps (when present) must embed at least one UIBB in order for the object schema to be valid.

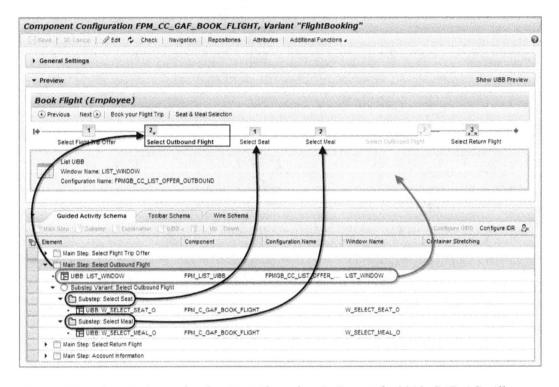

Figure 3.9: Object Schema for the GAF Floorplan © Copyright 2013. SAP AG. All rights reserved

3.3.3 When to Apply the GAF Floorplan

The GAF floorplan should be used whenever you need to control the *taskflow*[6] of some complex business process. We would emphasize the term "complex" here since simple one-step processes should be modeled using the QAF floorplan type described in Section 3.2. In general, GAF floorplans are applicable whenever:

> The business process can (and should) be split into multiple discrete steps.
> The process requires the coordination of multiple business objects.

---

[6] The term "taskflow" is borrowed from *Enterprise JavaBeans™ 3.0, 5th Edition* (O'Reilly, 2006).

➢ The process in question is not carried out on a regular basis by normal users.

If you're still unsure after reading through the checklist above, we would encourage you to re-read through the requirements and look at the language used to express the concepts you're trying to model your UI after. Here, if the concepts are expressed using mostly verbs, then you're probably on the right track. Otherwise, if the concepts are expressed as nouns, then it might be worth taking another look at the OIF or OVP floorplan types since it's likely that there are missing requirements for representing persistent business objects.

3.4   Overview Page Floorplan (OVP)

The *Overview Page* (OVP) floorplan was first introduced with the SAP NetWeaver 7.02 release, though it didn't really come to prominence until later with the SAP NetWeaver 7.03/7.31 releases. Around this same time, we learned from the latest set of UI guidelines that the OVP floorplan was positioned as a replacement for the OIF floorplan long term. From this, we can surmise that the OVP floorplan is intended to be used to edit business object instances.

As we'll see in the upcoming sections, the OVP floorplan offers quite a bit more flexibility compared to its predecessor. Naturally, such flexibility brings with it a certain amount of complexity that steepens the learning curve a bit early on. As you get more comfortable with the OVP floorplan though, we think that you'll find that the tradeoffs in flexibility make this added complexity well worth the trouble.

3.4.1 Structure of the OVP Floorplan

Conceptually speaking, the OVP floorplan is based upon the familiar page metaphor used in traditional web designs. This means that an OVP application design consists of a series of pages which are linked together via customizable navigation events. Here, there is little restriction regarding the content and layout of the OVP pages; we're basically free to design the pages however we like. Compared to the OIF and GAF floorplans seen already, most developers find this new approach to be quite liberating since we're no longer forced to organize the UI into a series of tab pages or roadmap steps.

Figure 3.10 illustrates the basic structure of an OVP floorplan page. Here, we can see that OVP page layouts are organized as follows:

➢ **Page Header**

At the top of the page, there is a fixed page header which contains the page title bar and toolbar. This content area is analogous to the page title/information area (formerly IDR) and page toolbar content areas from the OIF and GAF floorplan types.

➢ **Main Content Area**

Underneath the fixed page header is the main content area where we can layout our application-specific UIBBs. As you can see in Figure 3.10, this freeform content area allows us to arrange UIBBs in all kinds of different patterns.

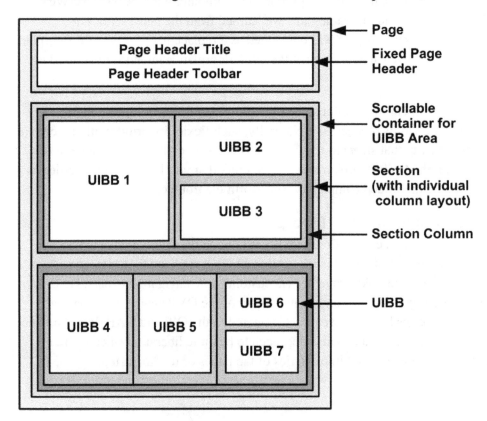

Figure 3.10: Structure of an OVP Floorplan Page

Even though the layout of the main content area of an OVP page is generally freeform, if we look more closely at Figure 3.10, we can see that there are some structural elements at play within an OVP page design. In particular, we can see that the main content area is split up into one or more *section* elements. Each section element can have its own layout, making it possible to compose UIBBs in all kinds of different configurations[7]. Sections are further sub-divided into *section columns*, which are like cells in the virtual grid that a section element defines. The UIBBs themselves are nested within section columns, yielding the hierarchical structure depicted in Figure 3.11.

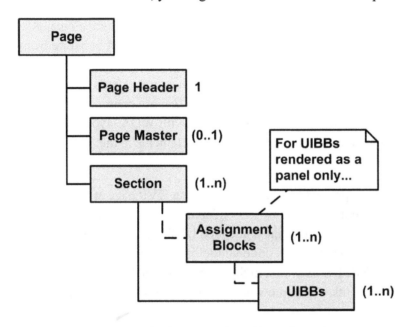

Figure 3.11: Structural Elements of an OVP Floorplan Page

UIBB Stacking in Section Columns

The structure diagram for an OVP page contained in Figure 3.10 illustrates how UIBBs are arrayed in a two-dimensional grid-like structure. Though this is the default layout option for OVP pages, the OVP floorplan does provide support for more sophisticated arrangements at runtime. In particular, it enables users to customize the layout by dragging-and-dropping UIBBs on top of one another to build *view stacks* (which are basically like tabstrips).

This functionality can be enabled within a section at design time by configuring the COLUMN STACK attribute of individual section columns. Whenever this attribute is configured, users can rearrange the UIBBs within the corresponding section columns at runtime by dragging-and-dropping them on top of one another. So, for example, if users

---

[7] See the sidebar entitled *UIBB Stacking in Section Columns* for additional options here.

wanted to maximize the vertical space within the second column of the first section depicted in Figure 3.10, they could do so by dragging UIBB 3 on top of UIBB 2. That way, both UIBBs would be displayed in a tabstrip-like control which filled in the entire section column.

Looking at the structure diagram contained in Figure 3.11, we can see that the relationship between OVP page sections and UIBBs is sometimes bisected by another organizational element: *assignment blocks*. Compared to the other structural elements that we've considered thus far, assignment blocks are very much abstract in nature from a design perspective. Indeed, if you look at the page schema of an OVP page in the FPM configuration editor tool, you won't find any references to this term. That's because assignment blocks are nothing more than embedded UIBBs that are configured to be rendered with a surrounding panel. If you've worked much with WDA layout elements, then you can think of these panels as being similar to `Tray` elements in that they are both collapsible.

Figure 3.12 illustrates what assignment blocks look like on an OVP page at runtime. Here, we can see that assignment block panels are rendered with a collapsible title bar which helps users understand the nature of the embedded UIBB content. Furthermore, assignment block panels can also contain an optional toolbar which contains functions specific to the embedded UIBB. For example, in the SECTIONS panel shown in Figure 3.12, you can see toolbar elements which allow users to add, edit, or remove items from the embedded list UIBB.

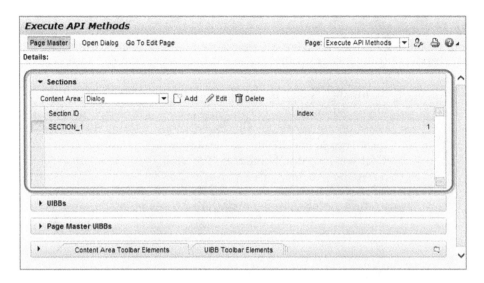

Figure 3.12: Assignment Blocks within an OVP Page © Copyright 2013. SAP AG. All rights reserved

OVP Page Type Overview

As we storyboard an application design using the OVP floorplan, we have several different page types to choose from. Table 3.1 describes each of these page types in detail.

Page Type	Description
Initial Page	This optional page type is used in situations where we need to route the user to a selection screen before the user accesses the main overview page(s). Here, we might include a search UIBB to allow users to lookup particular object instances, etc.
Main Overview Page	As the name suggests, this page type is the focal point of an OVP application. Conceptually speaking, Main Overview Pages are like landing/home pages in that they provide users with an overview of a given business object instance. From here, users can drill into the data and navigate to other pages as needed. Technically, it's possible to have more than one Main Overview Page within an OVP application. In these situations, one of the main pages will be marked with a DEFAULT attribute which causes it to be displayed by default in cases where an Initial Page doesn't exist or is bypassed at runtime.

Page Type	Description
Sub-Overview Page	If the business object type represented by an OVP floorplan is particularly complex, Sub-Overview Pages can be used to divide the UI content into smaller chunks that are easier to digest for the users. For example, if the business object in question contains sub-objects, we might use the Sub-Overview Page type to encapsulate content related to these sub-objects. That way, we don't clutter up the Main Overview Page with too many low-level details.
Edit Page	Historically, one of the major challenges in building applications to edit business object instances is figuring out how to support various *application modes*. Here, not only do we have to differentiate between "edit mode" vs. "display mode", we also sometimes have to account for different kinds of role-based access in which certain user types can only edit specific elements within a business object instance. These are the types of problems that Edit Pages are designed to solve.
	Conceptually speaking, Edit Pages allow us to define dedicated pages to handle mode and/or role-specific access requirements. Oftentimes, this simple designation can greatly simplify the design since we can avoid having to build in all kinds of custom mode handling logic at the UIBB layer.
Confirmation Page	The Confirmation Page type is normally only used in deletion scenarios. Here, it makes sense to route a user to a Confirmation Page after a business object instance is deleted since there's no longer any data to display on an editor screen.
Dialog Box	Dialog boxes are used for brief interactions with users that are oftentimes secondary to the task at hand. For example, in a sales order application, we might use a dialog box to display details about the sold-to customer, etc.

Table 3.1: OVP Page Types

Page Masters

In some application scenarios, it can be useful for users to be able to toggle back and forth between a series of related business object instances in an OVP application. For example, a user in the accounts payable (AP) department of a company might spend the better part of their day processing invoices in an invoice application. Here, rather than having to get out of the application in order to process another invoice, it's much more productive if the user can just select the next invoice and keep right on working.

Though we could certainly accommodate such requirements in a variety of different ways, the OVP floorplan provides a standard mechanism for implementing this kind of behavior. Here, we can supplement Main Overview Pages or Sub-Overview Pages with an optional page element called a *Page Master*.

From a functional perspective, the Page Master element is positioned like the sidebar elements we're accustomed to working with in common desktop applications (e.g. web browsers, word processors, and so on). Users can access this area to perform object selections. For instance, in our invoice application example above, we might use a Page Master to display a list of outstanding invoices. AP users can then use this list to toggle back-and-forth between open invoices as they are processing payments.

Within an OVP application, a Page Master can be positioned along the top or left-hand side of the main content area (see Figure 3.13). Unlike the sections that make up the main content area, we're somewhat restricted to the kinds of UIBBs that can be embedded in a Page Master. Here, we're restricted to the use of list or hierarchical tree UIBB types. This restriction makes sense when you think about it since the intent of the Page Header area is to provide users with an object selection list.

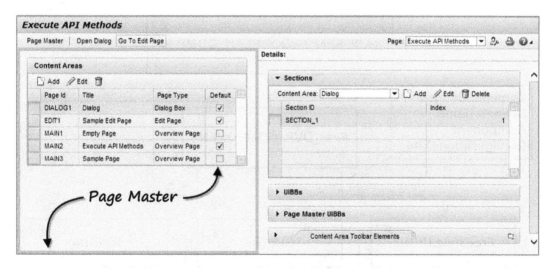

Figure 3.13: Page Masters in an OVP Application © Copyright 2013. SAP AG. All rights reserved

Whenever Page Masters are using in an OVP application design, we must take care to ensure that each of the UIBBs contained within the page layout are listening for selection changes. For instance, if a user selects a different object within the Page Master sidebar, the corresponding UIBBs on the Main Overview or Sub-Overview pages should refresh accordingly. Oftentimes, this sort of behavior can be achieved automatically whenever the wire model is used in the FPM application design. We'll learn more about the wire model in Chapter 7.

Design Tip

Normally, Page Masters are supplemented with a toggle button in the main application toolbar which allows users to hide the content area when it's not being used (i.e. the PAGE MASTER button shown in Figure 3.13). This is an optional, but useful, design touch that helps users maximize their UI space.

3.4.2 Understanding the OVP Object Schema

From a technical perspective, the OVP floorplan is based on the FPM_OVP_COMPONENT component. As you can see in Figure 3.14, the FPM_OVP_COMPONENT is a standalone component which assumes responsibility for all aspects of the floorplan layout. The basic idea here is to reduce the amount of static content in the floorplan so that developers have more control over the UI layout.

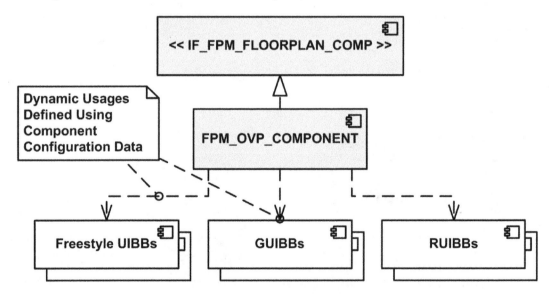

Figure 3.14: Component Diagram for the OVP Floorplan

Figure 3.15 shows what the object schema for the OVP floorplan looks like within the FPM Configuration Editor tool. As you can see on the left-hand NAVIGATION pane, the floorplan is divided into a series of page elements. For each page definition, we can organize the page schema using sections and UIBBs as described in Section 3.4.1. Here, we have quite a bit of flexibility to define different page layouts to match specific requirements, etc.

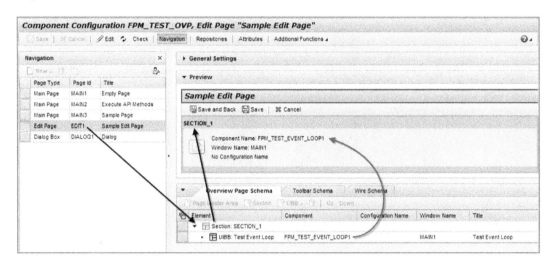

Figure 3.15: Object Schema for the OVP Floorplan © Copyright 2013. SAP AG. All rights reserved

3.4.3 When to Apply the OVP Floorplan

As we've mentioned at a couple of points within this chapter, the long-term goal for the OVP floorplan is to replace the OIF floorplan (and by extension, the QAF floorplan). In the meantime though, knowing when to apply the OVP floorplan can be a bit of a challenge for developers working in older SAP NetWeaver systems since the object schema/terminology of the OVP floorplan has evolved somewhat from its initial deployment in the SAP NetWeaver 7.02 release. Plus, there's also a question of what to do with existing OIF/QAF applications that may have been developed in house.

From our perspective, a good rule of thumb would be to start using the OVP floorplan for new applications being built in SAP NetWeaver 7.03/7.3x systems (or beyond). For existing applications, it's perfectly acceptable to stick with the status quo since the FPM_OIF_COMPONENT component is not going away anytime soon.

3.5   Summary

In this chapter, we became acquainted with each of the supported floorplan types provided with the FPM framework. Collectively, these floorplan types provide a basic template for satisfying the majority of UI application scenarios. With just a little bit of time and practice, we think that you'll begin to see most UI applications emerge through these pattern-based lenses.

In the next chapter, we'll shift gears a bit and take a closer look at the tools used to build and maintain FPM applications. Once you know your way around these tools, you'll be ready to hit the ground running with some of the more advanced FPM development concepts in Part II of this book.

Chapter 4

Working with the FPM Development Tools

Throughout the course of this book, we've seen how the FPM programming model leans heavily on declarative programming techniques. One of the obvious benefits of the declarative approach is that it speeds up the development process by allowing developers to *assemble* applications instead of building them from scratch. We emphasize the term "assemble" here since FPM applications are primarily constructed by stacking a series of UI building blocks (UIBBs) on top of one another.

A prerequisite for building applications using a declarative approach like this is having good visual editor tools to work with. Recognizing this, SAP has been working tirelessly over the past several years to provide FPM developers with intuitive and efficient tools for building and configuring FPM applications. In this chapter, we will introduce these tools and see how they are used to create, maintain, and enhance FPM applications.

4.1 Evolution of the FPM Toolset

As we have observed, FPM applications are defined as configurations of one of the three standard floorplan components: `FPM_OIF_FLOORPLAN`, `FPM_GAF_FLOORPLAN`, or `FPM_OVP_FLOORPLAN`. Here, we take an abstract floorplan component and use its component-defined object schema to integrate a series of UIBB components that provide the application specific content. Collectively, this yields an application model like the one shown in Figure 4.1.

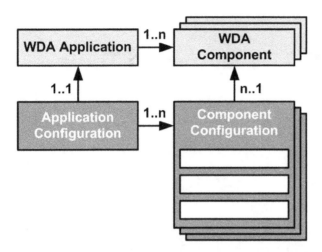

Figure 4.1: Composition of FPM Applications

In order to support an application model like the one shown in Figure 4.1, we need two different kinds of tools:

➤ **ABAP Workbench**

For all of the regular ABAP/WDA-based application content, we will use the ABAP Workbench as per usual. This includes the creation of the FPM application, freestyle UIBB components, feeder classes for GUIBBs, and so forth.

➤ **WDA Application and Component Configuration Editors**

These tools are used to configure the components created in the ABAP Workbench and then integrate them to create FPM applications.

Though used extensively in FPM application design, WDA application and component configuration objects are technically part of the overall *WDA Configuration Framework*, and are thus more generic in nature. From a tools development perspective, SAP's challenge has been to figure out how to customize these tools for FPM application development without compromising all of the built-in functionality of the WDA Configuration Framework.

To strike this balance, SAP has applied a series of enhancements to the WDA configuration editor tools as well as selected FPM-framework specific WDA components which are used to define FPM application layouts (e.g. GUIBB components). Collectively, these enhancements lead to a very different user experience when it comes to the development of FPM applications. This is evidenced by the differences seen in the screenshots captured in Figure 4.2 and Figure 4.3. Here, notice how different the WDA component configuration editor screen looks when editing a regular WDA component in Figure 4.2 as opposed to a floorplan component in Figure 4.3. In the latter case, we can see that FPM-specific panels are provided so that we can edit the general settings of the FPM application, see a preview of the application layout, review the floorplan object schema definition, and so on. Overall, this yields a development experience that is similar to modern WYSIWYG editor tools such as Microsoft's Visual Studio® or Adobe's Flash® Studio.

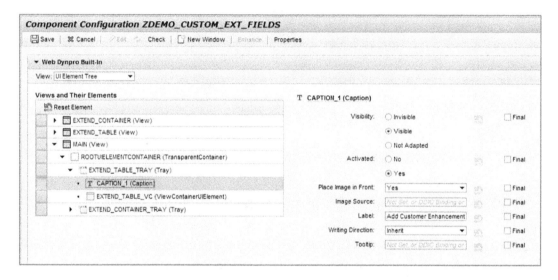

Figure 4.2: Configuration Editor Screen for a Normal WDA Component © Copyright 2013. SAP AG. All rights reserved

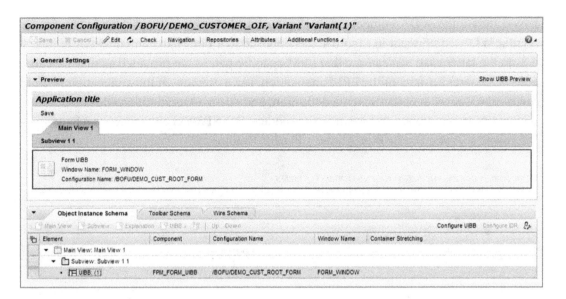

Figure 4.3: Configuration Editor Screen for a Floorplan Component © Copyright 2013. SAP AG. All rights reserved

If you've ever worked with modular IDEs such as Eclipse, then it's appropriate to think of these FPM-specific customizations as being part of something like a *perspective* or *screen variant* of the built-in WDA configuration tools. Over time, the terminology and look of the editor tools will continue to evolve, but the basic underlying concepts will remain the same.

4.2   FLUID (Flexible UI Designer)

Beginning with Enhancement Pack 3 of SAP NetWeaver 7.0, the editor(s) for FPM application configurations have been re-organized into a single tool offering: the *Flexible UI Designer* (or FLUID). Within the online help documentation for this release, SAP notes that FLUID replaces all the legacy configuration editors used to develop FPM applications prior to Enhancement Pack 3. Of course, as we learned in Section 4.1, it's perhaps more appropriate to think of FLUID as a re-imagining of the same tools used in these prior versions of SAP NetWeaver.

Terminology differences aside, it's not hyperbole to say that FLUID really changes the way that we develop FPM applications. From a developer's perspective, it offers a much more streamlined and productive development experience since everything is right there at our fingertips[8]. In the upcoming sections, we'll explore these features up close.

4.2.1 FLUID Layout

Before we begin looking at how FLUID is used to build and configure FPM applications, let's first take a look at the basic layout of the main editor screen. This layout is depicted in Figure 4.4.

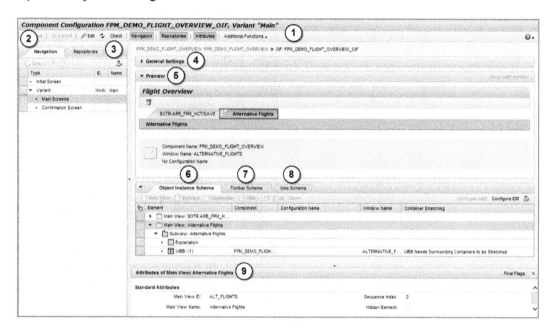

Figure 4.4: Basic Structure of the FLUID Editor Screen © Copyright 2013. SAP AG. All rights reserved

To make it easier to understand the layout of FLUID, we have annotated the screenshot contained in Figure 4.4 with callout numbers which highlight some of the more prominent content areas within the editor screen. These content areas are described in Table 4.1.

---

[8] This particular point will become clearer as we compare FLUID with legacy configuration editor tools in Section 4.3.

Content Area	Name	Description
1	Identification Region	At the top of the editor page, we have the Identification Region which groups together several header-level elements including:

❖ Page Title Bar
This top-level element provides information about the current configuration object.

❖ Page Toolbar
The page toolbar provides familiar editor buttons such as SAVE, EDIT, and CANCEL as well as toggle buttons which control the visibility of side bars and panels within the editor screen.

Additional functions of interest can be found in the correspondingly named ADDITIONAL FUNCTIONS button choice element on the right-hand side of the toolbar. Here, we can find menu options to load another instance of FLUID in a separate window, copy or enhance the selected configuration object, and so on.

❖ Message Area
The message area, when visible, shows up directly underneath the page toolbar. This content area is used to display system messages (e.g. validation errors, etc.).

❖ Bread Crumb
The bread crumb region, when visible, is used to navigate between various configuration objects accessed during the course of development. For example, we might use the bread crumb to navigate back and forth between an application configuration, its floorplan component configuration, and UIBB component configurations.

Content Area	Name	Description
2	Navigation Panel	If the NAVIGATION toggle button is enabled/pressed in the page toolbar, then the NAVIGATION panel will be displayed in a sidebar on the left-hand side of the editor screen. This panel is used to navigate between different page types in floorplan configurations (or tabbed UIBB configurations).
3	Repositories Panel	If the REPOSITORIES toggle button is pressed in the page toolbar, then the REPOSITORIES panel will be displayed in a sidebar on the left-hand side of the editor screen. This panel allows us to search for elements to add to the selected component's layout. In some respects, it's appropriate to think of the REPOSITORIES panel as being analogous to the UI element palette used to define view layouts in the WDA View Designer tool. For example, if we're editing a floorplan component, we can use the REPOSITORIES panel to search for UIBBs to be added to the floorplan layout. Once we find the target UIBB instance, we can use drag-and-drop to add the UIBB to the floorplan object schema.
4	General Settings Panel	As the name suggests, the GENERAL SETTINGS panel allows us to apply basic settings which affect the selected WDA component as a whole. Such settings include the specification of an application controller for floorplan configurations[9], layout of the message area, and so on.
5	Preview Panel	The PREVIEW panel provides us with a WYSIWYG view of a floorplan application or UIBB as it's being constructed.

---

[9] We'll cover application controllers in Chapter 8.

Content Area	Name	Description
6	Object Schema Panel	Underneath the PREVIEW panel, we have the main work area which provides us with editor panels to fill in the application-specific content of the selected floorplan or UIBB component. In order to maximize space within this work area, the various editor panels are arranged within a tabstrip control as shown in Figure 4.4. Here, the first tab page contains an OBJECT SCHEMA PANEL which allows us to edit the object schema for the selected floorplan or UIBB component. For example, in Figure 4.4, you can see how this panel is being used to layout an OIF floorplan. In this instance, the tab page label is adjusted to match the selected OIF floorplan component (i.e. the OBJECT INSTANCE SCHEMA label).
7	Toolbar Schema Panel	When editing floorplan components, the TOOLBAR SCHEMA tab page allows us to create/edit elements in the floorplan's application toolbar.
8	Wire Schema Panel	When editing floorplan components, the WIRE SCHEMA tab page allows us to define the wiring between the different UIBB components. We'll learn more about wires and the wire model in Chapter 7.
9	Attributes Panel	If the ATTRIBUTES toggle button is pressed in the application toolbar, then the ATTRIBUTES panel will be displayed at the bottom of the editor page. As you would expect, the contents of the ATTRIBUTES panel vary based upon the selected element on the editor page. Here, we can configure element-specific attributes by filling in attribute values in checkboxes, input fields, and so on.

Table 4.1: Content Areas of the FLUID Editor Screen

Looking at the screenshot contained in Figure 4.4, we can see that the FLUID editor screen layout is, well, *fluid*. With collapsible panels and sidebars that can be expanded and collapsed, we have many options for tweaking the UI to maximize screen space or drill into a particular configuration item as needed. Plus, since FLUID is implemented as a WDA application, we can use the personalization features of the WDA Configuration Framework to further customize the editor screen to match our preferences.

Note

FLUID is an evolving tool, and its feature set will likely expand and change over time. Therefore, we highly recommend that you browse through the SAP online help documentation from time to time to see what the latest innovations are with this tool. Here, a simple keyword search on the term "FLUID" will get you where you need to go.

4.2.2 Launching FLUID

Now that we have a general feel for what FLUID looks like, let's shift gears a bit and take a look at when and how it's accessed. Here, since there are so many different access points to choose from, we thought it made sense to consider these access points from a use case perspective. That way, we can get a sense of how FLUID is utilized during normal day-to-day development activities.

Editing Configuration Objects in the ABAP Workbench

The first use case we'll consider involves editing of configuration objects at design time. This scenario applies whenever we're editing custom-defined application/component configurations or displaying SAP-delivered configuration objects directly from within the ABAP Workbench. Here, we can launch FLUID in two different ways:

1. If we want to create a new application/component configuration, we can do so within the Web Dynpro Explorer perspective by right-clicking on the target WDA application/component and selecting the CREATE/CHANGE CONFIGURATION menu option as shown in Figure 4.5. This action will cause the FLUID tool to be launched in a separate browser window/tab. From here, we can proceed with the creation of the new configuration object as per usual.

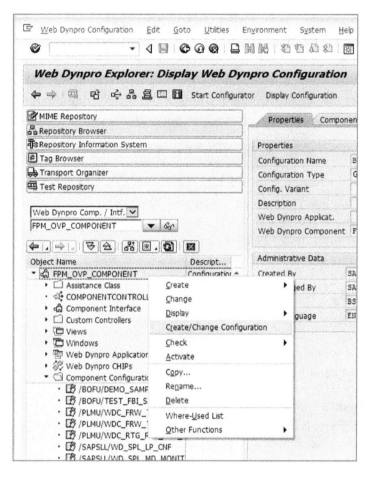

Figure 4.5: Launching FLUID from Within the ABAP Workbench – Part 1 © Copyright 2013. SAP AG. All rights reserved

2. If we want to edit/display an existing configuration object, we can do so by opening the object in the ABAP Workbench and choosing the START CONFIGURATOR or DISPLAY CONFIGURATION buttons located in the application toolbar (see Figure 4.6). The only difference between these two functions is that DISPLAY CONFIGURATION takes you directly into FLUID in display mode while START CONFIGURATOR opens up FLUID to the initial selection screen.

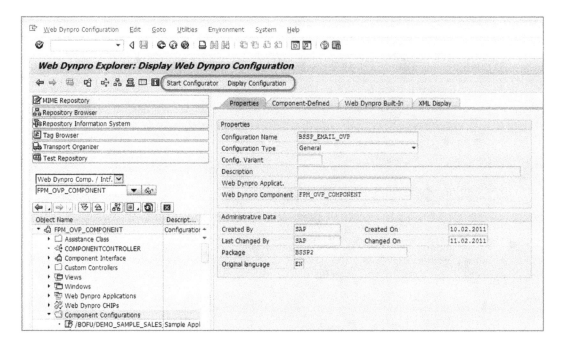

Figure 4.6: Launching FLUID from Within the ABAP Workbench – Part 2 © Copyright 2013. SAP AG. All rights reserved

Launching FLUID from Within a Running FPM Application

In the previous section, we observed how FLUID could be launched from within the ABAP Workbench. Here, a basic requirement is that we need to know the name of the configuration object(s) that we want to edit. Or, we at least need to know enough about the objects to locate them via a search in the ABAP Repository. Sometimes though, we may not even have this much information to go on. This is particularly the case whenever we're tasked with editing/adapting configuration objects created by other developers. In these situations, about the only thing we may have to go on is the FPM application itself.

Recognizing this relatively common occurrence, SAP has provided with a couple of options for locating and accessing configuration objects within a running FPM application:

1. The first option is to use the built-in technical help feature of the WDA runtime environment to obtain technical details about a particular screen element. Here, we can simply move the mouse cursor over the area of the screen that we need to edit, right-click, and choose the TECHNICAL HELP… menu option. This will open up the TECHNICAL HELP dialog box shown in Figure 4.7. As you can see, this

dialog box provides us with an overview of component usages, etc. Also of note are the hyperlinks which are attached to specific component configurations. We can click on these links to open the selected component configuration in FLUID.

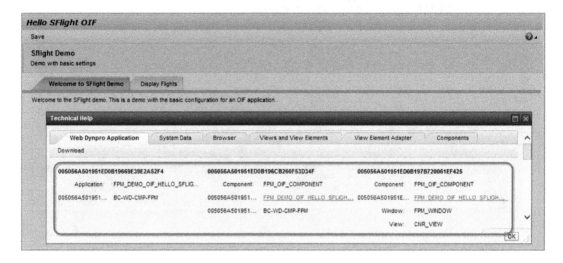

Figure 4.7: Using the Technical Help to Locate an FPM Component/Configuration

2. The second option is to launch the target application in *expert mode*. This mode can be accessed by configuring the FPM_CONFIG_EXPERT parameter in your user profile. Figure 4.8 shows how this is achieved using Transaction SU3.

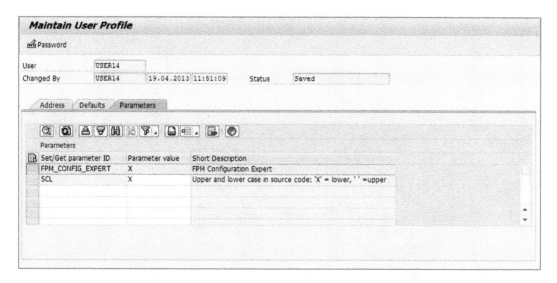

Figure 4.8: Setting the FPM_CONFIG_EXPERT Parameter © Copyright 2013. SAP AG. All rights reserved

Once the `FPM_CONFIG_EXPERT` parameter is set, the page toolbar of any FPM application that we launch will be enhanced to include three additional buttons on the far right-hand side of the toolbar:

❖ **Configure Page**

The CONFIGURE PAGE button provides us with a link to open up the FPM application's floorplan configuration in FLUID. Here, the FLUID editor will be opened up in a separate browser window/tab so that we can toggle back and forth between the running FPM application and the corresponding floorplan configuration.

❖ **Show Configurable Areas**

As you can see in Figure 4.9, the SHOW CONFIGURABLE AREAS button highlights configurable content areas within the current application screen. From here, we can then drill into the configurations of specific UIBBs by clicking on the blue wrench icon located in the top right-hand corner of a given content area (see Figure 4.9).

❖ **Application Hierarchy**

The last button in the enhanced toolbar provides us with a link to a useful WDA application called the *Application Hierarchy Browser*. We'll have a chance to look at this tool in Section 4.5.

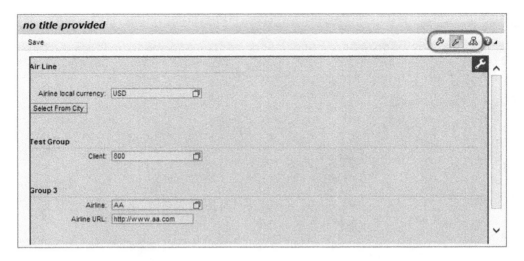

Figure 4.9: Launching FLUID in Expert Mode © Copyright 2013. SAP AG. All rights reserved

Either of the above approaches makes it very easy to locate the right configuration objects and jump right into FLUID to make the necessary changes. In Chapter 10, we'll see how these features also help us whenever we need to make enhancements to pre-delivered configuration objects (e.g. via FPM applications delivered by SAP).

Adapting Standard-Delivered Configuration Objects

In the previous two sections, we've observed some of the different ways that FLUID is used to edit configuration objects. Here, our focus has been on making changes to custom-defined configuration objects[10]. From the perspective of the WDA Configuration Framework, these changes are applied at the *configuration layer*. As you can see in Figure 4.10, this implies that we're making changes to objects within the ABAP Repository. In the parlance of the *Change and Transport System* (CTS), such changes would go into a *Workbench Request*.

---

[10] Technically speaking, it's also possible to use FLUID in this capacity to modify SAP-delivered objects, but we would urge you to avoid this path at all costs.

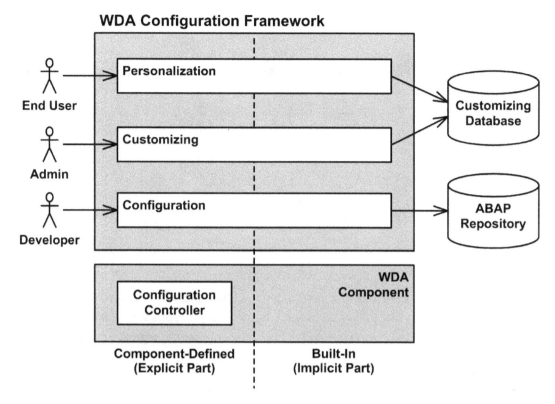

Figure 4.10: Layers of the WDA Configuration Framework

So what if we want to customize FPM applications delivered by SAP (or a 3rd party/partner)? As it turns out, we can use FLUID for these tasks as well. However, in order to access this customizing layer of the WDA Configuration Framework, we must launch FLUID in *administrator mode*. This specialized mode can be accessed in one of two ways:

➤ By launching the FPM application from the ABAP Workbench using the menu option WEB DYNPRO APPLICATION → TEST → IN BROWSER – ADMIN MODE (see Figure 4.11).

Figure 4.11: Launching FLUID in Administrator Mode © Copyright 2013. SAP AG. All rights reserved

➤ By opening up the FPM application using the URL query string parameter `sap-config-mode`. Here, the fully qualified URL would look something like *http://nwdev:8000/sap/bc/webdynpro/sap/zwda_test?**sap-config-mode=X***.

Regardless of which path we take, we'll end up with the FPM application loaded in a window which looks like Figure 4.12. Right off the bat, we can see that the FPM application layout has been enhanced to include an orange and yellow banner with the title *Customizing Mode*. This banner can be a useful reminder in cases where we may have multiple instances of an FPM application running in different browser windows.

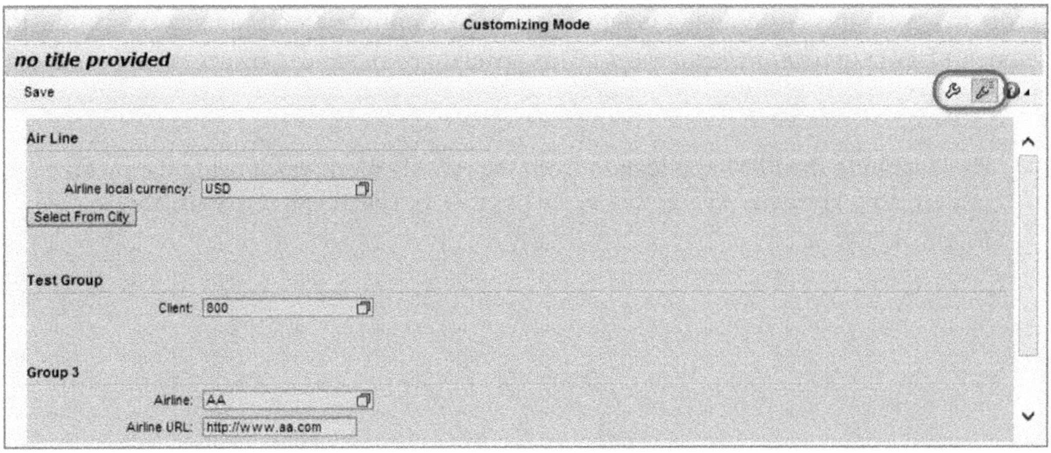

Figure 4.12: Working with FLUID in Administrator Mode © Copyright 2013. SAP AG. All rights reserved

In addition to the *Customizing Mode* banner, we can see that the page toolbar has also been enhanced with a couple of additional toolbar buttons:

> **Customize Page**

This button allows us to open up the FPM application's floorplan configuration in *customizing mode*. If a customizing record for the configuration doesn't exist already, we will be prompted to create one on the screen shown in Figure 4.13. Here, we can simply click on the NEW button to create the customizing record. From here, it's pretty much business as usual since FLUID's editor screen for customizing is virtually identical to the one used to create/edit component configurations from scratch (refer back to Figure 4.4). We'll explore such customizations in more detail in Chapter 10.

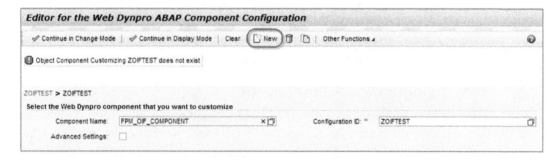

Figure 4.13: Creating a Customizing Record for a Configuration Object in FLUID

> **Show Customizable Areas**

The functionality behind this button mirrors that of the SHOW CONFIGURABLE AREAS button introduced whenever we looked at FLUID's expert mode. As you can see in Figure 4.12, whenever this button is pressed, customizable content areas will be highlighted by dark blue boxes. We can click on the wrench icon in the top right-hand corner of the content area to open up the UIBB in FLUID for customization.

Looking back at Figure 4.10, we can see that changes applied to the customizing layer of the WDA Configuration Framework are stored within the configuration database. Therefore, whenever we edit configuration objects in FLUID in administrator mode, we will be prompted to provide a CTS Configuration Request. At runtime, the customizing changes will be dynamically applied to the FPM application components using a functionality of the WDA Configuration Framework called *delta handling*.

Since this section is focused on working with FLUID, we'll table a further discussion of enhancement/customization techniques until Chapter 10. For now, our purpose was to illustrate the different modes of FLUID so that you'll be aware of the differences.

4.3   Configuration Editors Prior to FLUID

In Section 4.2, we mentioned that the FLUID tool was introduced in the SAP NetWeaver 7.03 release. So, if you're a developer working on system(s) based on the SAP NetWeaver 7.02 release (or older), you might be wondering about the level of tool support for FPM application development in these systems.

As it turns out, the tool support in these legacy SAP NetWeaver releases isn't all that different from what we have today. Here, FPM applications are developed using a specialized editor tool known as the *FPM Configuration Editor*. Like the FLUID tool which follows it, it's appropriate to think of the FPM Configuration Editor as being like a perspective or screen variant of the built-in WDA configuration editor tools. With that in mind, let's take a closer look at the FPM Configuration Editor.

4.3.1   FPM Configuration Editor Layout

Figure 4.14 illustrates the basic layout of the FPM Configuration Editor tool. As you can see, the layout is very different from that of the FLUID tool. Nevertheless, once we take inventory of all the different screen elements, we can see that most everything's there – it's just located in a different spot.

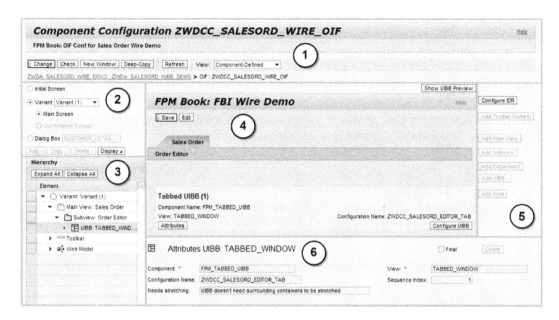

Figure 4.14: Basic Structure of the FPM Configuration Editor Screen © Copyright 2013. SAP AG. All rights reserved

As highlighted in Figure 4.14, the FPM Configuration Editor screen can be broken up into six basic sections:

1. **Header Area**

   The header area comprises the top-level Identification Region (IDR), page toolbar, and navigation path (bread crumb). Collectively, these elements provide us with all of the header-level functions needed during the editing process. When present, the message area element will also be displayed within the top-level header area.

2. **Control Area**

   As you can see in Figure 4.14, the control area provides us with the tools we need to navigate between floorplan pages, etc. From a functional perspective, it corresponds with the Navigation Area in the FLUID editor layout.

3. **Hierarchy Panel**

   The hierarchy panel allows us to view the object schema elements for the selected FPM component type. For example, in Figure 4.14, you can see how the hierarchy panel organizes schema elements for an OIF floorplan.

4. **Preview Panel**

    In the center of the editor page, we have the preview panel which provides an approximation of what the FPM application will look like at runtime.

5. **Action Area**

    The action area is kind of like a context-sensitive toolbar which provides functions for editing the selected FPM component/element.

6. **Attributes Panel**

    The attributes panel provides a form-based editor for configuring selected object schema elements. For example, in Figure 4.14, you can see how the attributes panel is set up to configure the tabbed UIBB component selected in the left-hand hierarchy panel. Naturally, the contents of the attributes panel will change as we make alternate selections within the hierarchy panel.

Since this book is primarily based on the more recent SAP NetWeaver releases, we won't be spending much more time looking at the layout of the FPM Configuration Editor tool. If you have questions about these features, we would encourage you to consult the SAP online help documentation. You can also find a hands-on demonstration of this tool back in Chapter 2.

4.3.2 Launching the FPM Configuration Editor

For the most part, the access points for the FPM Configuration Editor tool are similar to the ones we considered for FLUID in Section 4.2.2. In the upcoming sections, we'll see how the FPM Configuration Editor is utilized for common FPM development tasks.

Editing Configuration Objects in the ABAP Workbench

Within the ABAP Workbench, we can launch the FPM Configuration Editor in one of two ways:

1. If we want to create a new application/component configuration, we can do so within the Web Dynpro Explorer perspective by right-clicking on the target WDA application/component and selecting the CREATE/CHANGE CONFIGURATION menu option. This action will cause the FPM Configuration Editor tool to be launched in a separate browser window/tab. From here, we can proceed with the creation of the new configuration object as per usual.

2. If we want to edit/display an existing configuration object, we can do so by opening the object in the ABAP Workbench and clicking on the START CONFIGURATOR button (see Figure 4.15). This will cause the FPM Configuration

Editor to be opened up in a browser window/tab as shown in Figure 4.16. From here, we can use the provided toolbar buttons to open up the configuration object in whatever mode we prefer (e.g. CHANGE vs. DISPLAY).

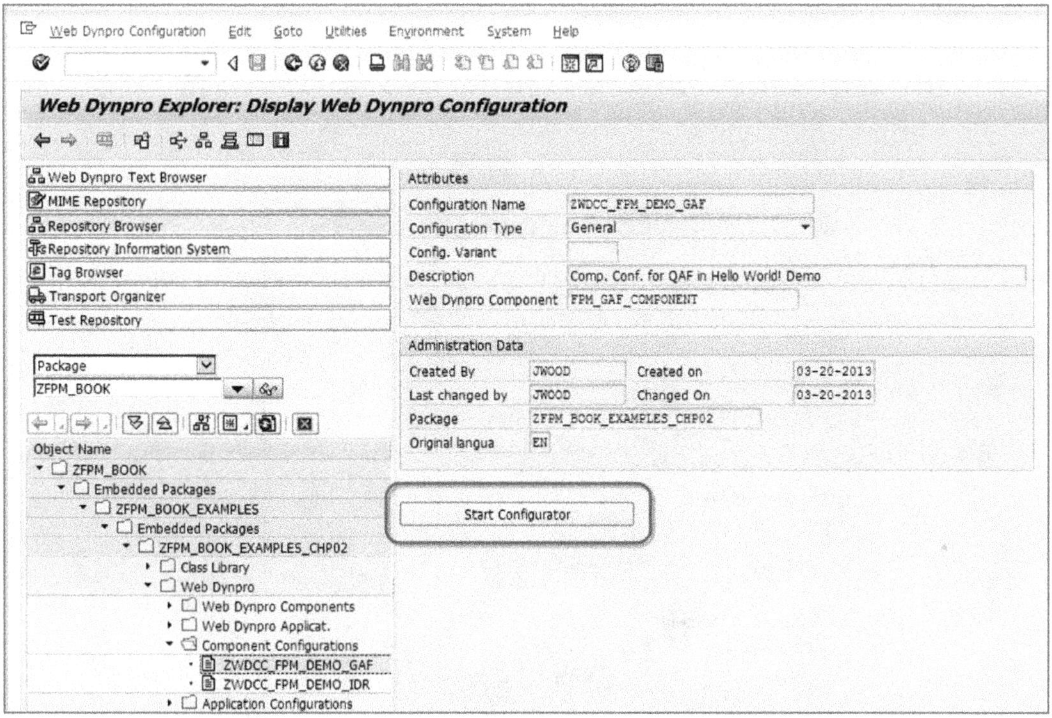

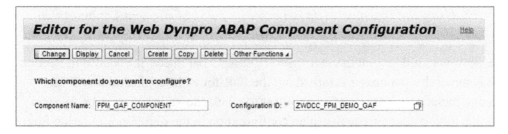

Figure 4.15: Launching the FPM Configuration Editor from the ABAP Workbench –
Part 1 © Copyright 2013. SAP AG. All rights reserved

Figure 4.16: Launching the FPM Configuration Editor from the ABAP Workbench –
Part 2 © Copyright 2013. SAP AG. All rights reserved

Launching the Editor from Within a Running FPM Application

Compared to the FLUID-based options considered in Section 4.2.2, our options for accessing the FPM Configuration Editor from within a running FPM application are rather limited. For example, as you can see in Figure 4.17, the technical help in the legacy SAP NetWeaver releases does not provide convenient links to component configurations. Instead, we must copy the configuration IDs and pull the configuration objects up in another session (e.g. via the ABAP Workbench).

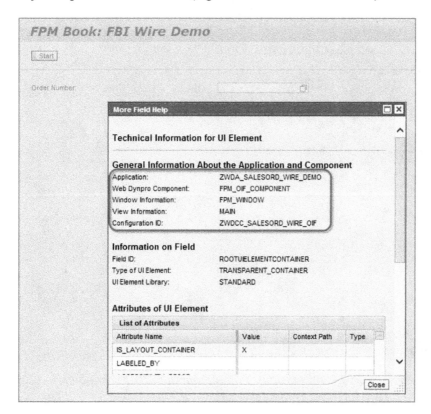

Figure 4.17: Using the Technical Help to Locate an FPM Component/Configuration

We can, however, still rely on the FPM_CONFIG_EXPERT parameter introduced in Section 4.2.2. Whenever this parameter is turned on, the IDR for FPM applications will be enhanced to include the CHANGE CONFIGURATION link shown in Figure 4.18. We can click on this link to open up the floorplan configuration in the FPM Configuration Editor tool. Unfortunately, there are not options for drilling right into the configurations of individual UIBBs. Instead, we must navigate to these UIBB configurations from within the floorplan configuration(s).

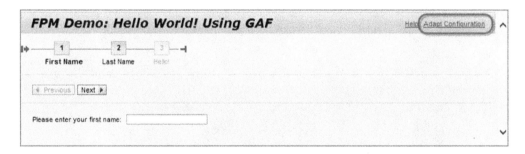

Figure 4.18: Launching the FPM Configuration Editor from within an FPM Application

Adapting Standard-Delivered Configuration Objects

If we want to customize FPM applications using the FPM Configuration Editor, we have two options:

1. By launching the FPM application from the ABAP Workbench using the menu option WEB DYNPRO APPLICATION → TEST → IN BROWSER – ADMIN MODE.

2. By opening up the FPM application using the URL query string parameter `sap-config-mode`. Here, the fully qualified URL would look something like
    *http://nwdev:8000/sap/bc/webdynpro/sap/zwda_test?**sap-config-mode=X**.*

In either case, we'll see the FPM application open up with an ADAPT CONFIGURATION link on the right-hand side of the IDR (see Figure 4.19). We can then click on this link to open up the FPM Configuration Editor in administrator mode. From here, we can apply our customizations as per usual.

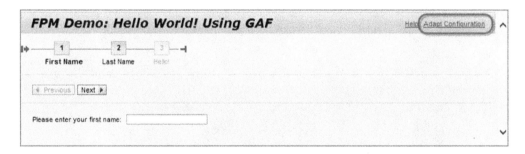

Figure 4.19: Adapting FPM Applications Using the FPM Configuration Editor Tool

4.4   Creating FPM Applications Using ACT

So far, we've seen that one of the major pain points of FPM application development is keeping up with all of the various artifacts created during the development process. This complication is particularly noticeable at the front end of the development process when we're assembling all of the main pieces: the WDA application and its corresponding application configuration, the floorplan component configuration, and so on. Once these objects are in place, we can use FLUID to manage most of the complexity from that point forward[11].

In an effort to reduce some of these upfront complexities, SAP has provided a specialized rapid development tool called the *FPM Application Creation Tool* (or ACT). As the name suggests, this tool allows us to quickly create the shell of an FPM application using a wizard-like approach. From here, we can dive right into the FLUID tool and proceed with development as per usual.

4.4.1 Launching ACT

From a technical perspective, ACT is implemented as a WDA application called `FPM_CFG_BO_MODEL_ACT`. Therefore, we can launch it just like any other WDA application (e.g. via the ABAP Workbench, directly via a URL, etc.). For convenience, we recommend that you add ACT as a favorite in your SAP GUI. This can be achieved as follows:

1. From the SAP EASY ACCESS screen of the SAP GUI, right-click on the FAVORITES folder and select the ADD OTHER OBJECTS menu option. Then, double-click on the Web Dynpro Application option as shown in Figure 4.20.

---

[11] It also helps to organize the development objects into an intuitive package structure based on the SAP Package Concept.

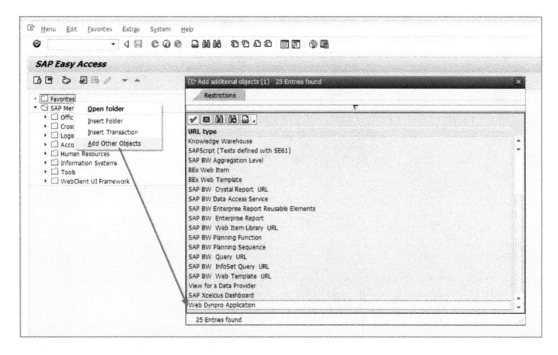

Figure 4.20: Adding ACT as a Favorite in the SAP GUI - Part 1 © Copyright 2013. SAP AG. All rights reserved

2. Then, in the resultant WEB DYNPRO APPLICATION dialog box, plug in the WDA application name in the correspondingly named field and hit the CONTINUE button (see Figure 4.21).

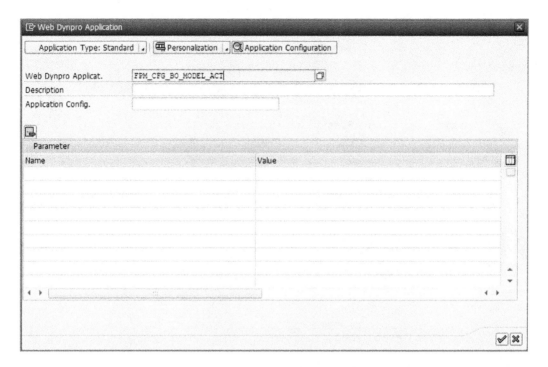

Figure 4.21: Adding ACT as a Favorite in the SAP GUI - Part 2 © Copyright 2013. SAP AG. All rights reserved

4.4.2 Using ACT to Create an FPM Application

Figure 4.22 shows what the initial screen of ACT looks like. As you can see, the ACT tool is based on the GAF floorplan, which implies that it uses a wizard-like approach to guide you through the application creation process. This process consists of two roadmap steps:

➢ **Enter Floorplan Objects**

At the first step, we provide names and optional descriptions for the main FPM application elements. For example, in Figure 4.22, you can see how we're defining an FPM application called ZACTTEST based on the GAF floorplan type. In addition, we've also specified names for the application configuration, floorplan configuration, and header (IDR) configuration. With these configuration names in place, we can click on the NEXT button in the page toolbar.

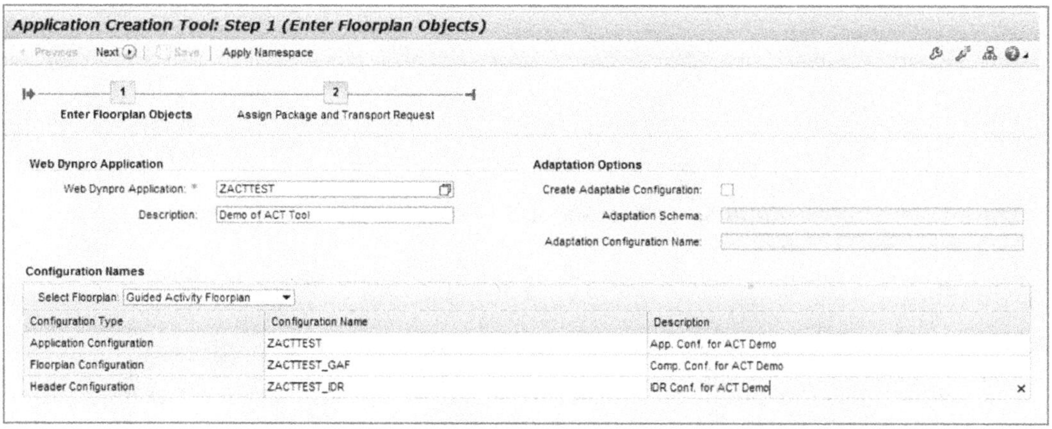

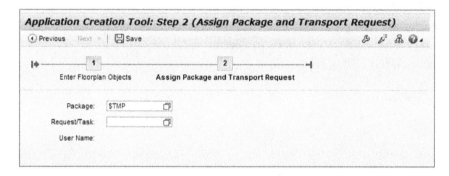

Figure 4.22: Creating an FPM Application Using ACT - Part 1 © Copyright 2013. SAP AG. All rights reserved

> **Assign Package and Transport Request**

At step two, we're prompted to select a package and a CTS transport request to track the changes (see Figure 4.23). Once these items are in place, we can hit the SAVE button to initiate the FPM application creation process.

Figure 4.23: Creating an FPM Application Using ACT - Part 2 © Copyright 2013. SAP AG. All rights reserved

After the FPM application is created, we will be routed to a confirmation screen like the one shown in Figure 4.24. From here, we can click on the LAUNCH CONFIGURATION EDITOR link to open up the floorplan configuration in FLUID.

Figure 4.24: Confirmation Screen for the ACT Tool © Copyright 2013. SAP AG. All rights reserved

4.5   Working with the Application Hierarchy Browser

Another useful FPM development tool is the *Application Hierarchy Browser*. As the name implies, this tool provides us with a view into an FPM application's configuration hierarchy - from the application configuration all the way down to the UIBB configurations. Though we could certainly compile such a list using FLUID, it's oftentimes quite convenient to have everything there at a glance.

4.5.1 Launching the Application Hierarchy Browser

Technically speaking, the Application Hierarchy Browser is implemented as a WDA application called `FPM_CFG_HIERARCHY_BROWSER`. This implies that we can access the tool just as we would any other WDA application. However, more often than not, the preferred method of accessing this tool is directly within running FPM applications. This can be achieved in expert mode by clicking on the APPLICATION HIERARCHY button in the page toolbar (see Figure 4.25). Refer back to Section 4.2.2 for information about how to enable expert mode in FPM applications (i.e. using the `FPM_CONFIG_EXPERT` user parameter).

Figure 4.25: Launching the Application Hierarchy Browser in an FPM Application © Copyright 2013. SAP AG. All rights reserved

4.5.2 Practical Uses of the Browser Tool

From a functional perspective, the FPM Application Browser Hierarchy tool operates in two different modes: *browser mode* and *deep-copy mode*. These modes are controlled by the correspondingly named toggle buttons in the page toolbar as demonstrated in Figure 4.26.

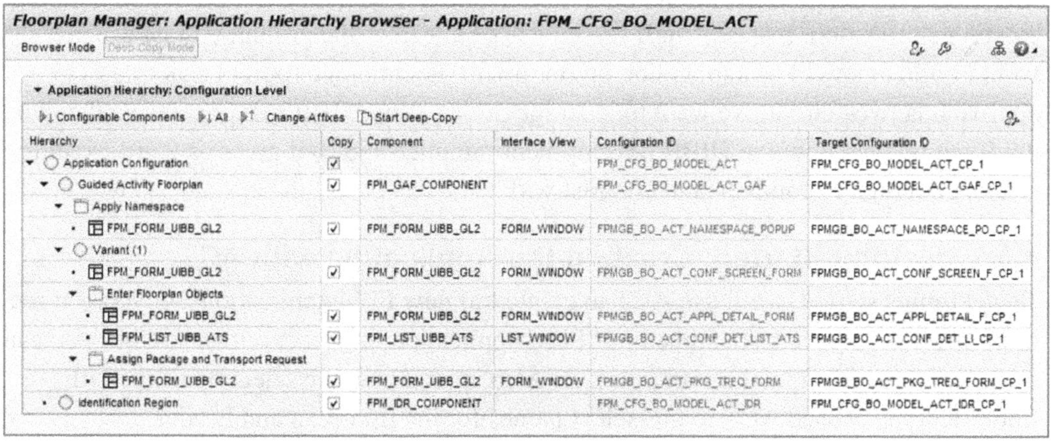

Figure 4.26: Working with the Application Hierarchy Browser Tool © Copyright 2013. SAP AG. All rights reserved

In browser mode, the hierarchy browser tool allows us to browse through each of the configuration elements that make up an FPM application: the application configuration, the floorplan configuration, UIBB configurations, and so on. Here, we can view metadata for each component configuration such as the target component, interface view, and configuration ID. Plus, with the configuration ID field, we're provided with a link which allows us to open up the configuration object in FLUID.

As the name suggests, deep copy mode allows us to make a deep copy of a given FPM application. Here, we can be selective about the elements we wish to copy using the COPY column shown in Figure 4.26. We can also apply our own personal naming conventions to the configuration objects to be generated using the TARGET CONFIGURATION ID column (which will provide a default configuration ID to begin with) and CHANGE AFFIXES toolbar button, respectively. Once we have the target configuration IDs set, we can click on the START DEEP-COPY to create a copy of the selected FPM applications. Naturally, this works a whole lot better than if we were to try and copy each object manually.

4.6 Case Study: Putting it all Together

Throughout the course of this chapter, we've looked at various FPM configuration tools in isolation. Now, with this knowledge in tow, let's take a look at how these tools are used in concert to build FPM applications. As the basis for this demonstration, we'll be recreating one of the demo applications delivered by SAP in the APB_FPM_DEMO package: FPM_DEMO_PLAYER. For the purposes of this contrived example, we won't be copying the existing application. Instead, we'll see how it's built from the ground up just like we would build a new FPM application on our own. The rationale for this example approach is two-fold: a) we want to leverage pre-existing UIBB components so that we don't get bogged down in UIBB development minutiae and b) it gives us a pre-existing reference model to compare and contrast with.

4.6.1 Getting Started: Creating the Application with ACT

To get things started, we'll use ACT to create our new FPM application. As you can see in Figure 4.27, we've have named our FPM application ZFPM_DEMO_PLAYER, but you can name your application whatever you like. Also, notice how the selection of the OIF floorplan type caused ACT to pre-select names for the floorplan and header configurations. With just a few keystrokes and a couple of clicks, we're up and running with a new FPM application (refer back to Section 4.4.2 for details on how to use ACT).

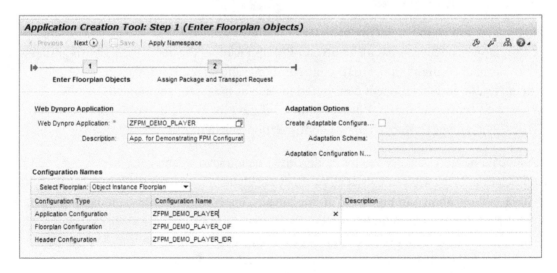

Figure 4.27: Creating the Demo Application in ACT © Copyright 2013. SAP AG. All rights reserved

4.6.2 Filling in Application Details in FLUID

From the confirmation page in ACT, we can navigate directly into FLUID to edit the floorplan configuration. From here, our next step is to fill in the OIF object schema with main views, subviews, and UIBBs. This can be achieved using the toolbar buttons provided on the OBJECT INSTANCE SCHEMA tab page as shown in Figure 4.28. For details here, refer to the standard-delivered component configuration `FPM_PLAYER_DEMO_OIF`.

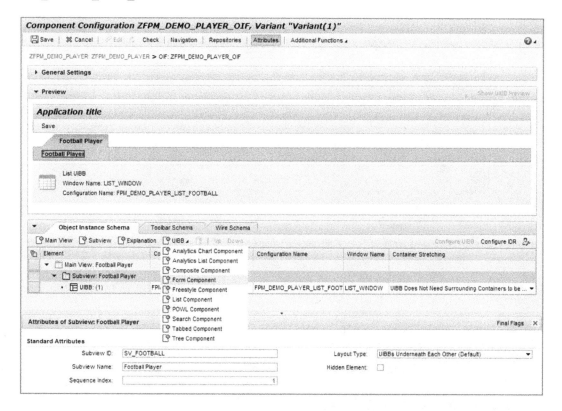

Figure 4.28: Filling in the OIF Object Schema © Copyright 2013. SAP AG. All rights reserved

Once the object schema is filled in, we can trace our progress using the ADDITIONAL FUNCTIONS → TEST menu option in FLUID as shown in Figure 4.29. It's a good idea to use this function periodically to make sure that we're on the right track.

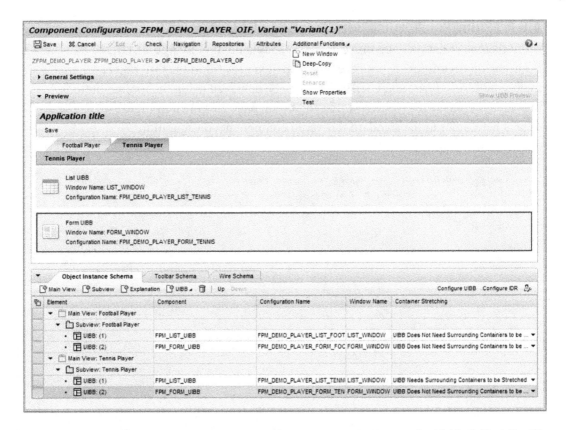

Figure 4.29: Testing the FPM Application from FLUID © Copyright 2013. SAP AG. All rights reserved

After the OIF tab pages are in place, we can move on to configure the page toolbar on the TOOLBAR SCHEMA tab. Here, we can add buttons to the toolbar using the ADD TOOLBAR ELEMENT button as shown in Figure 4.30.

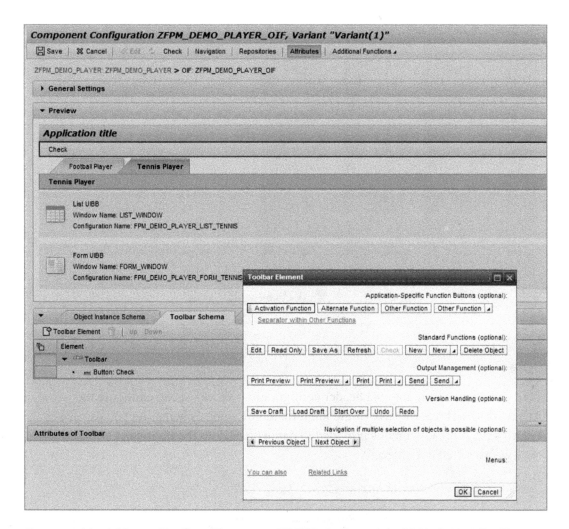

Figure 4.30: Adding a Toolbar Element in FLUID © Copyright 2013. SAP AG. All rights reserved

Lastly, we need to configure the page title (IDR) for the OIF floorplan. For this task, we can use the CONFIGURE IDR button on the right-hand side of the toolbar on the OBJECT INSTANCE SCHEMA tab page as shown in Figure 4.31.

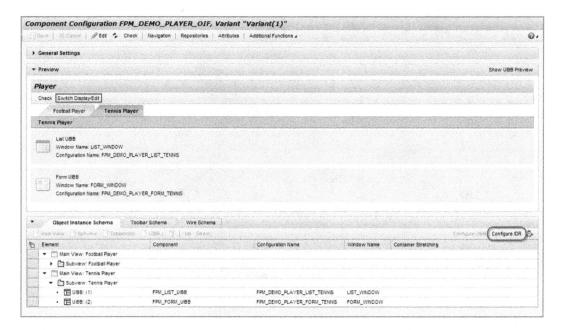

Figure 4.31: Configuring the IDR Component - Part 1 © Copyright 2013. SAP AG. All rights reserved

This will take us right into the header configuration where we can configure the APPLICATION TITLE property of the Identification Region Schema. As you can see in Figure 4.32, a bread crumb is provided to navigate back to the floorplan configuration once we've saved our changes.

Figure 4.32: Configuring the IDR Component - Part 2 © Copyright 2013. SAP AG. All rights reserved

4.6.3 Viewing the Finished Product in the Hierarchy Browser Tool

With our demo application now complete, we can view the finished product in the Application Hierarchy Browser tool as shown in Figure 4.33. This can be achieved by opening up the browser tool directly or via the correspondingly named toolbar button provided in expert mode. From here, we can see an overview of the used components and their configurations.

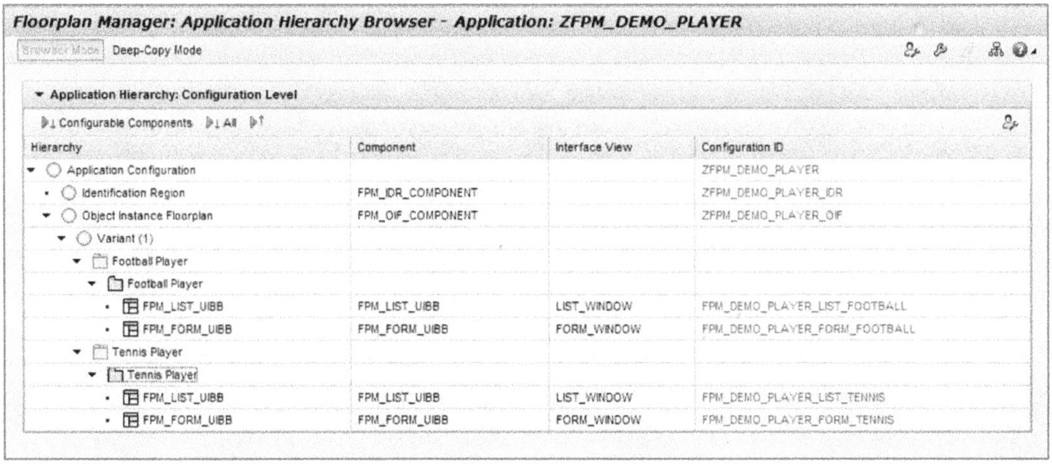

Figure 4.33: Viewing the FPM Demo Application in the Application Hierarchy Browser

4.7 Summary

In this chapter, we introduced you to the primary development tools used to build and maintain FPM applications. Collectively, these tools work in tandem to provide a comprehensive toolset for developing FPM applications. This was evidenced in Section 4.6, when we observed how the tools are used in practical development scenarios. Of course, in many respects, that demo only scratched the surface of what these tools can do. Therefore, we would encourage you to spend some time with these tools and play around with the different functions.

This chapter concludes the introductory portion of this book. At this point, all of the foundational elements are in place for us to begin exploring more advanced development topics. So, in Chapter 5, we'll do just that as we look at freestyle UIBB development concepts.

Chapter 5

Freestyle UIBBs and the FPM Event Loop

In the first part of this book, our focus was necessarily on high-level concepts within the FPM framework such as FPM application architecture, floorplans, and so on. During the course of this discussion, we certainly hit on the UIBB concept at different points, but only tangentially. Now that we have a better grasp on the essentials of FPM application development though, we're ready to narrow our focus and learn how to develop UIBBs to fill in the main content area.

In this chapter (and the one to follow), we'll take an up-close look at UIBBs and their place within the FPM application hierarchy. In particular, we'll consider how UIBBs are designed at the component level. We'll also see how UIBBs fit within the FPM phase model which governs the behavior of FPM applications.

5.1   User Interface Building Blocks (UIBBs)

As we learned in Chapter 3, floorplans within the FPM are positioned as templates for creating various types of applications. Here, the basic idea is that the floorplan component defines the overall structure of the UI and the core application logic is provided by a series of custom UIBB components. It's at this intersection that FPM applications come together.

In order for this plug-and-play development approach to work, the UIBB components themselves must have a consistent *interface*. In other words, each UIBB component must contain certain elements which provide embedding floorplan components with predictable points of interaction. As long as UIBBs fulfill these obligations, embedding floorplan components should have no problem integrating them into the application hierarchy.

Which brings us to the topic du jour for this section: what is the make-up of a UIBB and how do they fit into the overall FPM application hierarchy? In this section, we'll attempt to answer these questions both from a conceptual and technical point-of-view.

5.1.1 Understanding WDA Component Usages

To get things started, let's first take a brief moment to understand how component usages work within the Web Dynpro framework. Having a firm grasp on these concepts is crucial if you want to understand the touch points between the FPM framework, floorplan components, and individual UIBBs.

From a conceptual point-of-view, the internal makeup of a WDA component (FPM-based or otherwise) is hidden from the outside world. However, if we choose to do so, we can promote certain of these internal elements to become part of the WDA component's *component interface*. As you can see in Figure 5.1, a WDA component interface consists of two parts:

➢ **Interface Controller**

The interface controller defines the *programmatic portion* of the component interface. It consists of selected elements from the component's component controller (e.g. methods, events, and context nodes).

➢ **Interface Views**

Interface views define the *visual portion* of the component interface, packaging the view layout contained within a window into a reusable, view-like container. Because interface views are cast in the image of views, using components can embed the interface views of used components in places where internal views would normally be embedded.

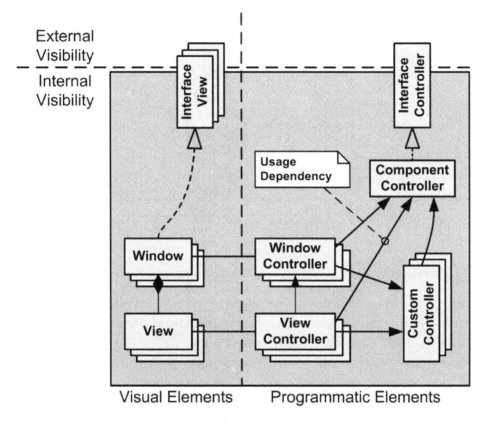

Figure 5.1: Web Dynpro Component Interface Architecture

Collectively, the elements of a WDA component's component interface provide leveraging components with the integration points they need to incorporate selected functionality from used components. For example, Figure 5.2 shows how a floorplan component integrates an interface view from a leveraged UIBB component into the UI element hierarchy of an FPM application.

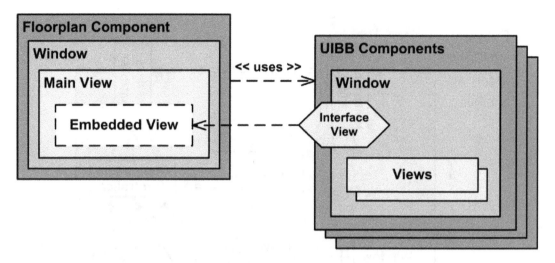

Figure 5.2: Understanding How UIBB Content is integrated into Floorplan Applications

Normally, component usages like the one depicted in Figure 5.2 are established *statically* at design time within the Web Dynpro Explorer tool as shown in Figure 5.3. However, in the case of generic floorplan components such as FPM_OIF_COMPONENT, such component usages must be established *dynamically* at runtime. This is where the object schema metadata collected in floorplan configurations comes into play.

Web Dynpro Explorer: Change Component

⬅ ➡ 🖉 🔏 🖼 ◎ 🔍 ┊ ⬛ 🔗 🖥 ⬜ 🔲 Component Documentation

Web Dynpro Component	ZWDC_REPORT_COMP		Inactive/revised
Description	Report Comp		
Assistance Class			
Created By	USER14	Created On	25.04.2013
Last Changed By	USER14	Changed On	25.04.2013
Original Lang.	EN	Package	$TMP

☑ Accessibility Checks Active

Used Components	Implemented interfaces

🔲 🔲

Used Web Dynpro Components

Component Use	Component	Description of Component
ALV_TABLE	SALV_WD_TABLE	ALV Component

Figure 5.3: Statically Defining a Component Usage at Design Time © Copyright 2013.
SAP AG. All rights reserved

As you can see in Figure 5.4, UIBB configuration elements in a floorplan configuration provide the floorplan component with everything it needs to dynamically embed the UIBB content at runtime: the target WDA component name, its interface view, and an optional component configuration. Behind the scenes, the floorplan components use this metadata as the basis for creating dynamic usage relationships to UIBB components and embedding UIBB content in the UI.

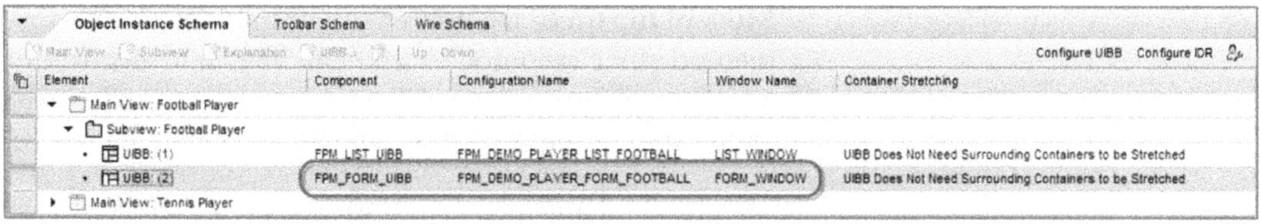

Figure 5.4: Defining Component Usage Metadata in Floorplan Configurations

In some respects, embedding the visual content of a UIBB is the easy part in all this. After all, embedding components really don't care all that much about how interface views are implemented internally. On the other hand, they do care a great deal about how UIBB's implement the programmatic portion of their component interface. Here, there is a hard requirement for UIBBs to implement a standard component interface so that floorplan components (and the overarching FPM framework) can tap into UIBB functionality using a common API. This component interface is the topic of our next section.

5.1.2 Interface IF_FPM_UI_BUILDING_BLOCK

From a technical perspective, UIBBs are nothing more than regular WDA components which happen to implement the IF_FPM_UI_BUILDING_BLOCK WDA component interface. Besides this minimum requirement, the FPM framework doesn't have much to say about the internal makeup of UIBB components. In this respect, it's appropriate to think of the IF_FPM_UI_BUILDING_BLOCK interface as being like a contract that UIBB components must fulfill in order to be recognized by the FPM framework.

If we look at the IF_FPM_UI_BUILDING_BLOCK interface in the ABAP Workbench, we can see that its definition is rather sparse, consisting of an interface controller which defines 5 controller methods. From a framework perspective, these controller methods are *callback methods*. In other words, the framework will invoke them at particular points within the application lifecycle. Table 5.1 describes the circumstances in which these methods are invoked and what they're used for.

Method Name	Description
flush()	This method is the first method called within the application lifecycle. As the name suggests, the FLUSH() method provides us with a hook for *flushing* modified data within the UIBB component so that other interested UIBBs have visibility to it. Most of the time, we don't need to implement this method since common shared data mechanisms usually take care of syncing up shared data automatically. We'll see evidence of this in Chapter 7 and Chapter 8.

needs_confirmation()	This method allows a UIBB to request a halt on the event processing loop so that it can display a confirmation dialog box. Based on a user's action in the dialog box, event processing can either resume or be cancelled altogether.
	
	Normally, this callback method is used to trigger data loss dialog boxes. For instance, if a navigation event is triggered, a UIBB might use this method to prompt the user if they want to save their changes before navigating away from the screen.
	
	The contents of the dialog box are defined via an instance of class CL_FPM_CONFIRMATION_REQUEST (or a subclass thereof). The source code excerpt below shows you how the confirmation request is issued from a programmatic perspective.
	
	``
	METHOD needs_confirmation.
	  CASE io_event->mv_event_id.
	    WHEN cl_fpm_event=>gc_event_cancel.
	      eo_confirmation_request =
	        cl_fpm_confirmation_request=>
	          go_data_loss.
	  ENDCASE.
	ENDMETHOD.
	``

`process_event()`

This callback method allows the UIBB to respond to various events triggered within the FPM application. These events could be coming from the core FPM framework, another UIBB, or the UIBB component itself. Regardless of the source, the `PROCESS_EVENT()` method provides the UIBB component with a hook to listen for and respond to pertinent events.

Information about the current event in the processing loop is encapsulated in an object reference parameter called `IO_EVENT` (which is of type `CL_FPM_EVENT`). This object reference provides us with several publicly defined instance attributes that can be used to process the event:

❖ `MV_EVENT_ID`
This string attribute contains the FPM event's ID value. It is normally used as the basis for developing a `CASE` statement to sift through various event types.

❖ `MO_EVENT_DATA`
This object reference attribute (of type `IF_FPM_PARAMETER`) provides us with access to any parameters included with the event whenever it was dispatched.

❖ `MS_SOURCE_UIBB`
This structure attribute provides us with information about the UIBB that triggered the event.

Based on the nature of the event being processed, we might use the body of the `PROCESS_EVENT()` method to perform local consistency checks (e.g. making sure that the data is valid) or implement logic to handle a particular user request (e.g. saving an object instance).

In any case, we can relay the results of the processing back to the FPM framework using the `EV_RESULT` exporting parameter. Here, we can use the `GC_EVENT_RESULT` constants provided via the `IF_FPM_CONSTANTS` interface to specify whether or not the event processing was successful.

`after_failed_event()`	This callback method is invoked whenever event processing fails in one of the FPM application's UIBB components (i.e. the `PROCESS_EVENT()` method on a UIBB component returns the failure code in its `EV_RESULT` parameter). In these situations, we sometimes need to respond to the failure by backing out changes that were made during the event processing loop.
`process_before_output()`	This callback method is the last method called on a UIBB before the FPM/WDA frameworks enter into the UI rendering phase. It is here that we should perform any sync-ups with the backend data model so that the UI data is up-to-date and accurate.

Table 5.1: Methods of the IF_FPM_UI_BUILDING_BLOCK Component Interface

5.1.3 Creating Freestyle UIBBs

Now that we have a better grasp on what the `IF_FPM_UI_BUILDING_BLOCK` interface is all about, let's see how it's used to build freestyle UIBBs. As it turns out, this process is pretty straightforward:

1. To begin, we simply create a new WDA component and define the `IF_FPM_UI_BUILDING_BLOCK` interface as an implemented interface on the IMPLEMENTED INTERFACES tab page of the WDA component editor screen as shown in Figure 5.5. Here, we must press the REIMPLEMENT button to retrofit the WDA component's component controller with the interface methods.

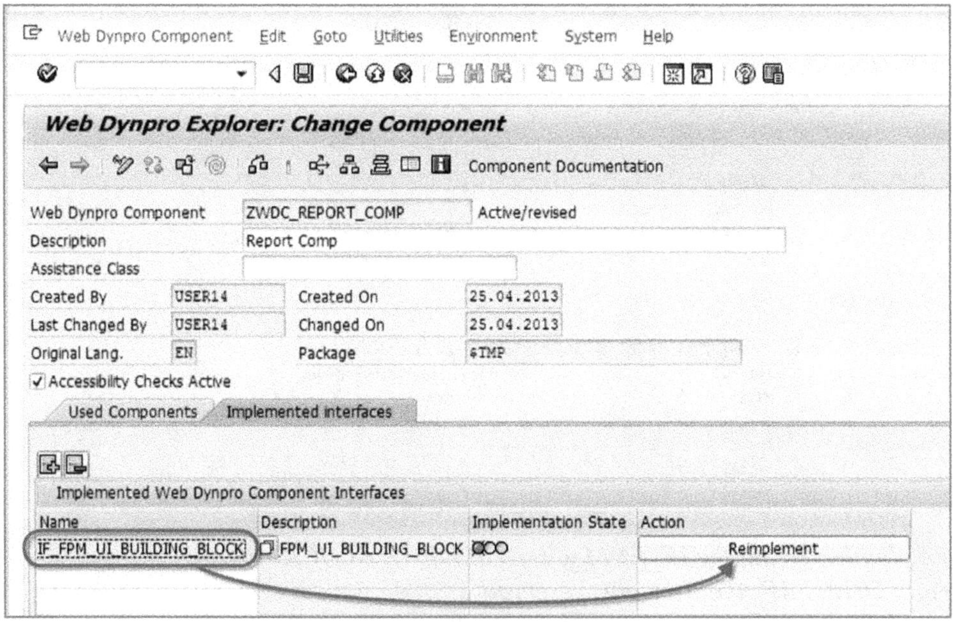

Figure 5.5: Implementing the IF_FPM_UI_BUILDING_BLOCK Interface – Part 1
© Copyright 2013. SAP AG. All rights reserved

2. Once the component interface is implemented and we've activated the changes, we can see that the UIBB callback methods have been added to the component controller (see Figure 5.6). From here, we can go about implementing these methods as needed to define application-specific logic and behaviors.

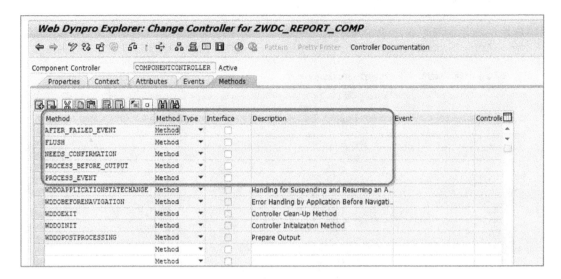

Figure 5.6: Implementing the IF_FPM_UI_BUILDING_BLOCK Interface – Part 2

3. The final step in the freestyle UIBB development process involves the creation of the UI content that will be added to the floorplan layouts. Here, it's pretty much WDA development as per usual: we create a window and then embed one or more views inside that window to define the UIBB content area. Within this UI element hierarchy, we can employ the use of any of the UI elements provided with the WDA framework including form elements such as the `InputField` and `DropDownListByKey` elements and complex elements such as the `Tree` and `Table` elements.

> **Design Tip**
>
> Though there are not any hard and fast rules regarding how a freestyle UIBB's layout is established, a basic rule of thumb would be to avoid the creation of deeply-nested UI element hierarchies and the like. In general, the layout of a UIBB shouldn't require the user to have to scroll around to find what they're looking for. Furthermore, UIBBs shouldn't contain redundant layout elements which exist in the embedding floorplan layout (e.g. `TabStrip` elements in an OIF floorplan). As UIBB designers, our goal is to fill in the pre-defined content areas of the floorplan, and not to reinvent the wheel.

5.2 Event Processing in the FPM Framework

From a conceptual point-of-view, UIBBs play a similar role to the one that views perform in traditional WDA application design: they "describe the layout and behavior of a rectangular area of a user interface.[12]" When approaching UIBB design, this basic definition is a good place to start. However, whenever we talk about defining a UIBB's *behavior*, we must be mindful of the fact that UIBBs do not exist in isolation. Rather, they are part of an overall FPM application hierarchy in which event processing must be coordinated across potentially many UIBB components.

In this section, we'll explore the ramifications of all this by taking a look at the FPM phase model. Here, we'll see how actions/events triggered in one UIBB are relayed to all of the other UIBBs in the FPM application in coordinated fashion. Then, once we understand how the phase model works, we'll see how custom UIBBs can raise application-specific events and participate in the event processing loop.

5.2.1 Understanding the FPM Event Loop

In the WDA programming model, user interactions are encapsulated in the form of *actions*. These actions are defined at the view level, with action handler methods defined within the corresponding view controller class. In the action handler methods, we must decide how we want to process the user interaction. Sometimes, we may be able to handle the interaction internally within the view controller. However, if the user interaction calls for a change to the backend data model, we need to pass the action up the ladder by handing it off to a top-level custom controller (e.g. the component controller). From here, the custom controller can work directly with the model layer to process the event.

When developing FPM applications, there are times whenever a particular user interaction may not only affect the source UIBB component, but other UIBB components in the FPM application as well. Whenever this happens, we need to dispatch the user interactions on to the FPM framework by triggering events which are then processed as part of the *FPM event loop*. This handoff is illustrated in Figure 5.7.

---

[12] This quote was taken from the SAP Help Library available online at *http://help.sap.com.* Here, you can find detailed information about the positioning of views by opening up the section entitled *Developing Web Dynpro ABAP Applications* and choosing the *Concepts of Web Dynpro ABAP* → *Architecture of Web Dynpro* → *Web Dynpro Component* → *View* menu path.

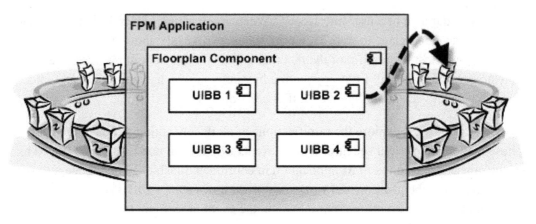

Figure 5.7: Visual Representation of the FPM Event Loop

As you can see in Figure 5.7, we used a conveyor belt as a metaphor for illustrating how the FPM event loop works. This visual imagery is appropriate since FPM events are literally processed in a loop which circumnavigates each of the UIBB components contained within an FPM application. This loop is orchestrated by a singleton instance of the FPM framework class CL_FPM as shown in Figure 5.8. Here, we can see how the FPM event loop is integrated into the overarching WDA phase model, allowing FPM application components to interject at the appropriate points within the process flow.

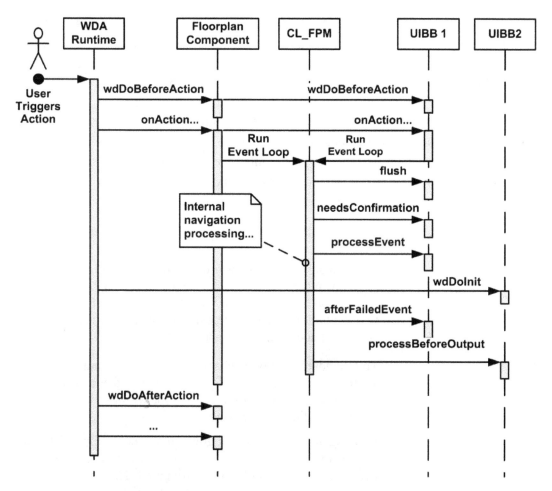

Figure 5.8: UML Sequence Diagram Depicting the Connections between the WDA & FPM Phase Models

In some ways, the two-dimensional nature of the sequence diagram contained in Figure 5.8 doesn't really do the FPM event loop justice. After all, in real world applications, it's not uncommon for the FPM framework to be juggling multiple events from different UIBBs simultaneously. In order to keep everything straight, all FPM events are funneled through a singleton instance of the aforementioned CL_FPM class. Here, events are serialized through a "first-in, first-out" (FIFO) queue maintained as an internal table attribute on the CL_FPM instance and dispatched via calls to the RUN_EVENT_LOOP() instance method.

In an effort to make the sequence diagram contained in Figure 5.8 more readable, we purposefully glossed over the inner workings of the RUN_EVENT_LOOP() method so that you could see how events are dispatched to individual UIBB components. Suffice it to say that there's quite a bit more going on under the hood here. For instance, there is quite a bit of logic which determines which UIBBs should be notified of an individual event. Fortunately, we as developers are mostly shielded from these underlying complexities. For our part, all we need to worry about is that we put our event handling code in the right place within the individual UIBB components. In particular, we need to pay careful attention to the implementation of the PROCESS_EVENT() method defined by the IF_FPM_UI_BUILDING_BLOCK component interface as this is the event handler method invoked by the CL_FPM singleton instance whenever it runs the event loop. Other freestyle UIBB methods of interest are outlined in Table 5.2.

Method	Usage Description
wddoinit()	This standard method is useful for initializing a UIBB component (and its views) before it is added to the FPM application hierarchy at runtime. It is unique in that it is the first method invoked on the component at runtime and also because it is only invoked once.
wddobeforeaction()	This standard method is invoked by the WDA runtime within a UIBB component. Therefore, it's an ideal place for inserting UIBB-specific validation logic (i.e. mandatory field checks) *before* an action is processed.
	Looking at the sequence diagram contained in Figure 5.8, you can see that the WDDOBEFOREACTION() method is executed before the FPM event loop gets triggered. Therefore, from a performance perspective, it makes a lot of sense to frontload UIBB validations in this method so that the user doesn't have to incur the overhead of the FPM event loop only to discover that an error occurred which prevented them from being able to perform the requested action.
onaction...()	These methods are the touch point between view-level actions in freestyle UIBBs and the FPM framework as a whole. Here, we can choose whether or not an event should be processed internally or broadcast to the entire FPM application hierarchy. We'll see how the latter is achieved in Section 5.2.2.

Table 5.2: Key Web Dynpro Methods Used for Event Processing

5.2.2 Triggering Events

In the previous section, we looked at how the FPM event loop works from a conceptual point-of-view. With these basic concepts in mind, let's now take a look at how UIBB components can participate with this event loop. This process begins with the triggering of an *FPM event*.

Within the FPM framework, events are encapsulated as instances of the standard CL_FPM_EVENT class. As you can see in the UML class diagram contained in Figure 5.9, the CL_FPM_EVENT class is positioned as a data carrier, containing attributes to capture event metadata such as the event's ID, a parameter list (defined by an IF_FPM_PARAMETER object reference), and so on. Other attributes of interest include the MS_SOURCE_UIBB structure attribute which contains information about the UIBB component which created the event and the various GC_EVENT_* constants which describe standard events[13] within the FPM framework (e.g. GC_EVENT_SAVE for the save event).

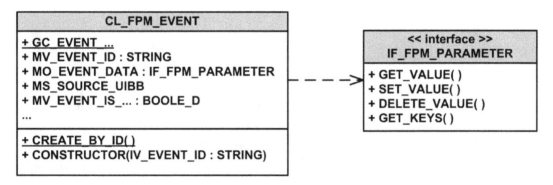

Figure 5.9: UML Class Diagram for Class CL_FPM_EVENT

As you can see in the class diagram shown in Figure 5.9, we have two options for creating event instances. If we just want to create a simple event, we can use the CREATE_BY_ID() factory method to build an event instance that contains an ID and nothing more. Otherwise, we can use the constructor method to build an event from scratch. In either case though, it's important to come up with a meaningful event ID so that interested UIBBs can detect the event in a consistent manner.

Once we have an event instance in hand, the FPM framework makes it very easy to trigger the event. All we have to do is obtain a reference to the FPM singleton instance

---

[13] Note that a similar list of constants can be found in the IF_FPM_CONSTANTS interface. Here, look at the GC_EVENT constant definition.

and invoke the RAISE_EVENT() method as demonstrated in Listing 5.1. Here, notice how we're using the CL_FPM_FACTORY class to obtain a reference to the FPM singleton instance. This factory class provides us with a convenient mechanism for obtaining a reference to the FPM framework whenever we need it.

```
METHOD action_handler.
  DATA lo_fpm   TYPE REF TO if_fpm.
  DATA lo_event TYPE REF TO cl_fpm_event.

  CREATE OBJECT lo_event
    EXPORTING
      iv_event_id = 'PARTNER_REMOVED'.

  lo_event->mo_event_data->set_value(
    iv_key   = 'PARTNER_ID'
    iv_value = mv_selected_partner ).

  lo_fpm = cl_fpm_factory=>get_instance( ).
  lo_fpm->raise_event( io_event = lo_event ).
ENDMETHOD.
```

Listing 5.1: Triggering Events in FPM – Part 1

Looking at the code excerpt contained in Listing 5.1, you can see that we used the MO_EVENT_DATA attribute of the CL_FPM_EVENT class to pass a parameter with the event: the so-called PARTNER_ID parameter. If you look at the definition of the IF_FPM_PARAMETER interface upon which the MO_EVENT_DATA attribute is defined, you can see that the signature of the SET_VALUE() and GET_VALUE() methods is generic enough that we could pass most any kind of parameter here. However, in practice, we recommend that you only pass small key-like values so that overhead is reduced within the FPM event loop.

Had we not wanted to pass a parameter in the code excerpt contained in Listing 5.1, we could have simply used the RAISE_EVENT_BY_ID() method to trigger the event as demonstrated in Listing 5.2. Behind the scenes, the FPM instance uses the ID parameter generate the CL_FPM_EVENT instance by invoking the aforementioned CREATE_BY_ID() factory method.

```
METHOD action_handler.
  DATA lo_fpm TYPE REF TO if_fpm.

  lo_fpm = cl_fpm_factory=>get_instance( ).
  lo_fpm->raise_event_by_id( 'PARTNER_REMOVED' ).
ENDMETHOD.
```

Listing 5.2: Triggering Events in FPM - Part 2

Before we wrap up our discussion on triggering events, one last thing we should mention is that the event triggering logic demonstrated in Listing 5.1 and Listing 5.2 applies equally to both custom-defined events and standard events. So, for example, if we wanted to trigger an application-wide refresh event, we could do so by raising the standard FPM_REFRESH event (using the GC_EVENT_REFRESH event ID constant from the CL_FPM_EVENT class). We'll see a demonstration of this in the next section.

5.2.3 Processing Events

As far as the FPM framework is concerned, all FPM events are created equal since they're all instances of the same CL_FPM_EVENT event class. Here, events are packaged up as CL_FPM_EVENT instances and forwarded through the FPM event loop indiscriminately. Such events could be custom-defined events or standard events which are triggered behind the scenes within the FPM framework. In either case, UIBB components are notified of event occurrences via the PROCESS_EVENT() callback method described in Section 5.1.2.

The generic nature of the FPM event loop implies that UIBB components get to react to any kind of event that occurs at runtime. So, for example, in a GAF application, UIBBs would be notified of requests to move between steps (via the FPM_NEXT_STEP and FPM_PREVIOUS_STEP events, respectively). Similarly, all UIBBs would be notified of major framework events such as a save request, refreshes, etc.

Within the PROCESS_EVENT() method, UIBBs can define logic to process particular event types using a CASE statement like the one shown in Listing 5.3. Here, notice how there's logic in place to process standard and custom-defined events. The basis of this logic is the IO_EVENT object reference parameter which, not surprisingly, is of type CL_FPM_EVENT. Looking back at the UML class diagram for this class contained in Figure 5.9, we can see that this parameter provides us with quite a bit of information about the event. In particular, we can see how the code excerpt contained in Listing 5.3 is using the MV_EVENT_ID and MO_EVENT_DATA instance attributes to determine which event was triggered and also to extract any parameters that might have been passed along with it.

```
METHOD process_event.
  DATA lv_partner_id TYPE bu_partner.

  CASE io_event->mv_event_id.
    WHEN cl_fpm_event=>gc_event_save.
      ...
    WHEN cl_fpm_event=>gc_event_undo.
      ...
    WHEN cl_fpm_event=>gc_event_redo.
      ...
    WHEN 'PARTNER_REMOVED'.
      CALL METHOD lo_event->mo_event_data->get_value
        EXPORTING
          iv_key   = 'PARTNER_ID'
        IMPORTING
          ev_value = lv_partner_id.

    "Handle the partner removed event...
  ENDCASE.
ENDMETHOD.
```

Listing 5.3: Reacting to FPM Events in the PROCESS_EVENT( ) Method

For the most part, we're free to implement the event handling logic in the PROCESS_EVENT() method however we like. With that said, it's important to be mindful of the fact that there are potentially many UIBBs waiting to process a given event, so we should be careful not to bog the FPM event loop down too much with long-running synchronous tasks. Instead, we should use asynchronous programming techniques to offload heavier tasks. Such techniques include the use of the update task, asynchronous RFC processing, SAP Business Workflow, and so forth.

5.3   Summary

In this chapter, we got a chance to become much more familiar with the components which drive an FPM application's functionality: UIBBs. Here, we learned about the IF_FPM_UI_BUILDING_BLOCK component interface which defines the integration points between UIBBs and floorplan components. We also got to see how these integration points fit in within the overall WDA/FPM phase model (colloquially known as the FPM event loop). Collectively, the knowledge obtained in this chapter should serve us well as we begin to look at how FPM applications come together in real life. In the next chapter, we'll move on from freestyle UIBBs and look at their more generic cousins: GUIBBs and RUIBBs.

Chapter 6
Generic and Reuse UIBBs

In the previous chapter, we saw how implementing the `IF_FPM_UI_BUILDING_BLOCK` interface transformed ordinary WDA components into full-fledged UIBBs which could be integrated into FPM applications. Armed with this knowledge, we technically have everything we need to create fully functional FPM applications. However, if we were to conclude our studies at this point in the journey, we would be missing out on arguably the most important element of the FPM framework: *Generic UIBBs* (GUIBBs).

In our estimation, the GUIBB concept is what sets the FPM framework apart from other web templating systems. Even though the floorplan concept is rather unique to SAP, there are many templating systems out there which make it easy for developers to define the overall structure/layout of web applications. However, defining the structure of a web application only gets us so far; we still have a lot of work to do in order to fill in the main content area. It's here that most templating systems turn things over to developers, giving them free reign to insert content however they like (e.g. via freestyle UIBBs, HTML fragments, and so on). With GUIBBs, it's a different story.

In this chapter, we'll see how GUIBBs make it easy to create UIBBs with a minimal amount of custom development. Besides the obvious benefits in terms of developer productivity, we'll also learn how the use of GUIBBs improves the configurability of FPM applications from a long-term maintenance perspective. We'll conclude our discussion by looking at a new breed of UIBB components introduced with SAP NetWeaver 7.03: *Reuse UIBBs* (RUIBBs).

6.1 Introducing GUIBBs

Up to now, our treatment of the GUIBB concept has been superficial at best. Alas, we've had more fundamental issues to wrestle with in earlier chapters. Now that we have a better understanding about what UIBBs are though, we're finally ready to tackle GUIBBs.

Because of their generic nature, it's difficult to come up with a succinct way of introducing GUIBBs. Indeed, to truly understand what GUIBBs are all about, we need to look at GUIBBs from several different angles. So, in the upcoming sections, we'll try to construct a panoramic view of GUIBBs so that you can not only see how they function internally, but also how they fit into the larger picture of FPM application development.

6.1.1 Conceptual Overview

In the field of software engineering, the term *generic* is often used to describe an elusive, yet desirable, characteristic of software components: *reusability*. Here, we're talking about a software component's suitability for use (and reuse) in a variety of different contexts. So, whenever we talk about GUIBBs, we're basically talking about *reusable UIBBs* that can be leveraged in many FPM application scenarios.

Based on this definition alone, there's no real difference between GUIBBs and freestyle UIBBs. Indeed, if we wanted to, we could put on our software architect's hat and create our own class of generic UIBBs. Of course, this is easier said than done; in reality, achieving widespread reuse in WDA components can be quite a challenge. So how did SAP accomplish it in their GUIBB designs? Well, just like the floorplans introduced in Chapter 3, SAP once again elected to abstract around pure UI patterns.

Each of the GUIBB components developed by SAP provides a basic template for laying out UI elements in familiar patterns. Within the FPM framework, we can find a form component that can be used to build input forms, a list component to display data in lists/tables, and so on. Internally, these components are based upon a particular UI abstraction (or schema) as opposed to any particular application model. This singular focus on a specific UI pattern is what makes GUIBBs so flexible.

Whenever we leverage a particular GUIBB component, we must adapt our application model to work within the confines of the GUIBB component model. For example, in Figure 6.1, you can see how we're using a list component to build a table to display flight information. To the list component, the table definition consists of nothing more than a series of generic `Column` elements; it's blissfully unaware of the intricacies of the flight data model or any other data model for that matter. These concerns are instead delegated to a standalone ABAP Objects class which is designed to fill in all of the custom application details – more on this in Section 6.1.2.

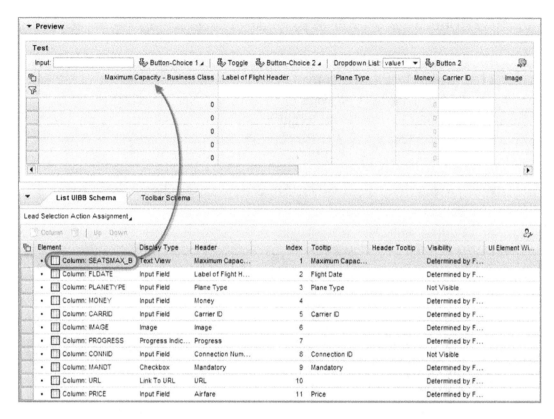

Figure 6.1: Configuring a List UIBB in FLUID © Copyright 2013. SAP AG. All rights reserved

When we look at GUIBBs in this light, we can begin to see the fundamental differences between GUIBBs and freestyle UIBBs. Most of the time, whenever we develop freestyle UIBBs, we combine UI logic and application logic together in a single component[14]. If we're careful, we might be able to structure a freestyle UIBB internally such that it can be reused in a handful of similar application contexts. However, for more widespread reuse, the component must be considerably more generic, drawing a clear line between UI and business logic concerns.

As we peel back additional layers of GUIBBs in the upcoming sections, we'll be able to develop an appreciation for why the GUIBB approach makes sense. In the meantime, we would ask that you keep an open mind to the possibilities. While some UI requirements might be just as easy (or easier) to develop using freestyle UIBBs, there are other

---

[14] Note that we're not necessarily suggesting that the lines between the controller and model layers have been blurred here. Rather, we're simply saying that most freestyle UIBBs contain a certain amount of built-in assumptions/application logic which limits their reusability.

benefits to GUIBB usage which might sway your decision once you see how everything plays out.

6.1.2 Technical Implementation

Having touched upon the basic concepts of GUIBBs in the previous section, in this section we'll turn our attention to the technical side of things. Specifically, we want to gain some understanding of how GUIBBs function underneath the hood.

Figure 6.2 contains a component diagram which highlights the basic architecture of GUIBB components. As you can see, GUIBB components implement the same IF_FPM_UI_BUILDING_BLOCK component interface that freestyle UIBBs implement. Thus, from an FPM framework perspective, GUIBBs are on an equal footing with freestyle UIBBs.

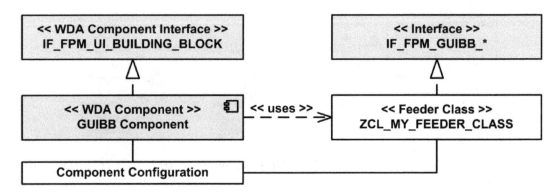

Figure 6.2: Component Diagram Illustrating GUIBB Architecture

Much like the floorplan components that we introduced in Chapter 3, it's appropriate to think of GUIBB components are being like *templates* for defining a particular UI pattern (e.g. a form or list). The implementation details for a particular GUIBB usage are provided via the component configuration definition shown at the bottom of Figure 6.2. Here, we can define and configure the GUIBB component's UI layout interactively using the FPM Configuration Editor tool. Internally, the GUIBB component stores this configuration metadata within a component-defined object schema that is used as the basis for dynamically rendering the UI layout at runtime.

Feeder Class Introduction

Another important aspect of the GUIBB component's configuration metadata is the *feeder class* assignment shown at the bottom of Figure 6.2. Feeder classes provide a link between the GUIBB component and the custom application layer. Within these classes, we can encode logic to query data from a backend data model, define custom event handling routines, and so forth.

The glue that binds a GUIBB component with its assigned feeder class is the GUIBB component-specific interface illustrated in top right-hand corner of Figure 6.2. These interfaces define a series of callback methods which allow GUIBB components to communicate with the feeder classes dynamically (or *polymorphically*) at runtime. In effect, this GUIBB-specific interface represents the boundary which separates the UI presentation layer of the GUIBB from the custom application layer[15]. These relationships are illustrated in the simplified UML sequence diagram contained in Figure 6.3.

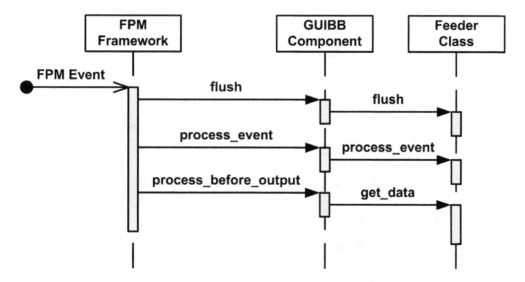

Figure 6.3: UML Sequence Diagram Depicting the Exchange between GUIBB Components and Feeder Classes

Each of the component-specific feeder class interfaces that we'll be looking at in Section 6.2 inherit from a base interface called IF_FPM_GUIBB. This interface defines two methods which are used to influence the initialization of a feeder class instance. Table 6.1 describes both of these methods in detail.

---

[15] In other web programming environments (most notably Microsoft's ASP.NET), this separation of UI and application logic is referred to as the "code-behind technique".

Method Name	Description
get_parameter_list()	This method is invoked by the FPM Configuration Editor at design time whenever we assign a feeder class in a GUIBB component configuration. Here, we can define a list of custom parameters which can be used to configure feeder class behavior at runtime.
initialize()	This method is invoked at runtime right after a feeder class instantiated. Here, we can apply any custom logic needed to initialize the feeder class. At runtime, any configured parameters (as defined by the GET_PARAMETER_LIST() method) will be passed in the IT_PARAMETER importing parameter. Application-level parameters are also passed in via the IO_APP_PARAMETER object reference.

Table 6.1: Methods of the IF_FPM_GUIBB Interface

Putting it all Together

Since we've covered a lot of ground in this section, let's summarize what we've learned here technically:

➢ Each GUIBB is realized in the form of an SAP-delivered WDA component which implements the familiar IF_FPM_UI_BUILDING_BLOCK component interface just like any other UIBB component.

➢ GUIBB components are like templates in that they don't provide any application functionality in and of themselves.

➢ In order to use a GUIBB component in an FPM application scenario, we must define a component configuration which fills in the application details. Such details include the relative positioning of elements within the UI layout, event binding, and so on.

➢ Internally, UI layout metadata specified in the FPM Configuration Editor tool is stored in an abstract object schema maintained within the GUIBB component. At runtime, the GUIBB component will use this metadata as the basis for rendering the UI. This rendering process is handled almost exclusively by the GUIBB component itself.

➢ The underlying application functionality for a particular GUIBB usage is provided via custom *feeder classes*. These feeder classes are regular ABAP Objects classes that implement a GUIBB component-specific interface. We'll have an opportunity to explore these interfaces as we look at specific GUIBB component types in

Section 6.2, but for now, suffice it to say that these interfaces bear a number of similarities to the `IF_FPM_UI_BUILDING_BLOCK` component interface in that they define callback methods which are used to respond to particular milestones in the FPM phase model.

➢ Feeder classes allow us to separate UI concerns from business logic concerns.

6.1.3 Advantages of Using GUIBBs over Freestyle UIBBs

So what are the advantages of going with generic UIBBs instead of freestyle UIBBs? As it turns out, there are quite a few:

➢ First of all, it's generally faster to develop UIs with GUIBBs than it is to develop a series of freestyle UIBBs from scratch. Here, we can delegate a good deal of the mundane UI-level concerns to the standard GUIBB components, adding our own tweaks here and there as needed – mostly through configuration. In Chapter 7, we'll learn how the FPM wire model can be used in conjunction with GUIBBs to achieve even more productivity on this front.

➢ The widespread use of standard GUIBB components leads to a more harmonized look-and-feel. For example, all forms based on the standard form component should look and behave similarly. This definitely shortens the learning curve for users since conforming FPM applications all pretty much work the same way.

➢ The GUIBB programming model promotes a clear separation of the UI and business logic. This separation of concerns allows SAP to continually add innovations into the UI layer without disturbing the underlying application layer.

➢ Finally, since GUIBBs are fully integrated into the FPM framework, they can be configured and enhanced using the same set of tools introduced in Chapter 4. In Chapter 10, we'll learn that GUIBBs are infinitely more customizable than their freestyle UIBB counterparts.

For these reasons, and others, we generally recommend that you attempt to use GUIBBs in lieu of freestyle UIBBs wherever possible. Of course, that's not to say that you should never use freestyle UIBBs. There are certainly valid cases for using freestyle UIBBs: whenever you have an existing WDA component that you want to reuse, complex UI requirements which exceed the capabilities of the standard GUIBB components, and so on. The point is to try and leverage as much of the FPM framework as we can. This has benefits not only in the short term, but also in the long term from a maintenance perspective. Plus, by leveraging standard-delivered components, we reduce the risk of letting our UI designs become dated since SAP continuously back ports UI innovation into the standard GUIBB components.

6.2   Working with GUIBBs

Now that we have a basic understanding for what GUIBBs are all about, let's take a closer look at the types of GUIBBs we have to work with within the FPM framework. At the time of this writing, there are 11 GUIBB components provided out-of-the-box with the SAP NetWeaver 7.03 release. However, since several of these components overlap with similar GUIBB components from earlier SAP NetWeaver releases, we elected to group related components together by function so that our focus is more on the UI patterns represented by the GUIBB components as opposed to the components themselves. Our hope is that this approach will make it easier to understand the role that each of the various GUIBB components play from a functional perspective.

6.2.1 Form Component

The first GUIBB component that we will be looking at is the *form component*. As you would expect, this component is used to build input forms like the one depicted in Figure 6.4. Here, you can see that we have most of the familiar WDA UI elements at our disposal: labels, input fields, drop-down lists, radio button groups, and so on. Collectively, the available elements allow us to build forms much like the ones we would create using freestyle UIBB components.

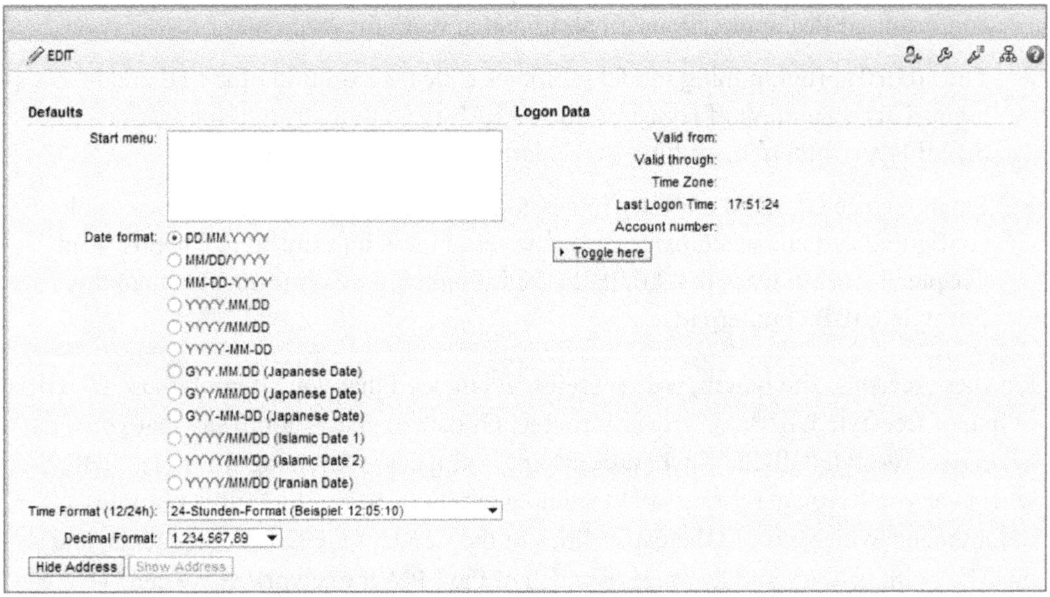

Figure 6.4: Working with the Form Component © Copyright 2013. SAP AG. All rights reserved

Evolution of the Form Component

These days, there are two different versions of the form component: the original form component provided with the initial release of the FPM framework and a new form component introduced in the SAP NetWeaver 7.03 release. So what's the difference between these two component types? From a functional perspective, not much. Both component types can be used to build forms like the one shown in Figure 6.4. With the new form component though, we have quite a bit more flexibility in the layout of the individual form elements. These flexibility enhancements were introduced in conjunction with version 2.0 of SAP's UI Guidelines (GL2).

For the most part, knowing which form component to choose from is pretty simple. If you're on an SAP NetWeaver system prior to the 7.03 release, then the legacy form component is the only game in town. On the other hand, if you're on a newer release, then you should prefer to use the GL2-based form component for any new developments. The only real exception to this rule is in cases where you need to enhance legacy form components in a newer SAP NetWeaver system. Here, keeping with the status quo is certainly acceptable since the original form component is not going away anytime soon.

Legacy Form Component

The legacy form component is implemented via a WDA component called `FPM_FORM_UIBB`. Internally, this GUIBB component models the form UI using a metamodel/object schema whose structure is depicted in Figure 6.5. The logical elements depicted here are described in further detail in Table 6.2.

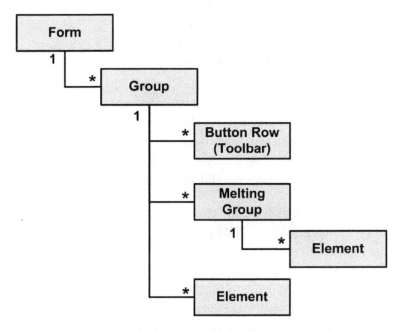

Figure 6.5: Metamodel for the Legacy Form Component

Element Name	Description
Group	As you can see in Figure 6.5, group elements constitute the basis of the form component's UI structure. If we think of the form component as being analogous to a view, then it's appropriate to think of group elements as being like `Group` UI elements in the Web Dynpro programming model. In other words, they're containers for embedding lower-level UI elements. In order to specify a form component's UI layout, we must have at least one group element defined. Each group element has an optional name/title attribute which can be used to specify the title in the top-level title bar of the group. Besides the name attribute, we must also choose a *layout type* for the group to determine how UI elements within the group are aligned. Here, we have three different layout types to choose from: ❖ Full screen width with one column ❖ Full screen width with two columns ❖ Half screen width with one column Within a given column, UI elements are arranged in line-by-line fashion from top to bottom. This is to say that only one element can be displayed per line within the column layout.
Button Row (Toolbar)	Each group element can optionally embed one or more *button rows*. These button rows are like group-level toolbars in which we can attach a series of buttons that point to specific FPM events. As a rule, a given group will not contain more than one button row assignment.

Element Name	Description
Element	Within the form component object schema, form-based UI elements are referred to simply as *elements*. For a given element definition, we can specify the following attributes (among others):

❖ Component Name

This attribute refers to a field defined in the field catalog of the form component's associated feeder class. We'll explore this field binding concept in further detail in the upcoming sections.

❖ Display Type

We can use this attribute to determine what kind of UI element we want to use to render the field. Here, we can choose between a number of familiar WDA UI element types such as the `InputField`, `TextView`, and `DropDownByKey` elements.

❖ Label

This attribute can be used to attach a label to a given UI element on the screen. The label text can be defined statically within the FPM Configuration Editor or dynamically via OTR text assignments.

❖ Action Assignment

Depending on the element type, we might want to use this attribute to assign an action to a given element. For example, if the selection of a line in a drop-down list should cause a screen refresh, we would want to assign an action to the element so that the FPM framework triggers an event whenever users make selections on the screen.

Element Name	Description
Melting Group	Melting groups are kind of like aggregate elements in the sense that they combine a handful of elements together in a single package. This grouping makes it possible for related elements to be displayed side-by-side within a group column (like they've been *melted* together). From the group element's perspective, a melting group is just like any other element, so melting groups and elements can be used interchangeably.
	In practice, melting groups are normally used in situations where it makes sense to combine certain fields which belong together logically (e.g. a date field, time field, and time zone field). They're also useful for aligning an input field holding a match code value with an adjacent text view which contains the match code value's descriptive text.

Table 6.2: Elements of the Form Metamodel

Once we develop a firm grasp on the object schema elements outlined in Table 6.2, defining forms using the legacy form component is pretty straightforward. Here, we simply organize the form fields into specific groups which are laid out in a grid as shown in Figure 6.6. Then, within each group, we can fill in the details by plugging in elements, melting groups (i.e. a group of elements), and so on. Finally, we can tweak the form elements themselves by specifying the various element-specific attributes.

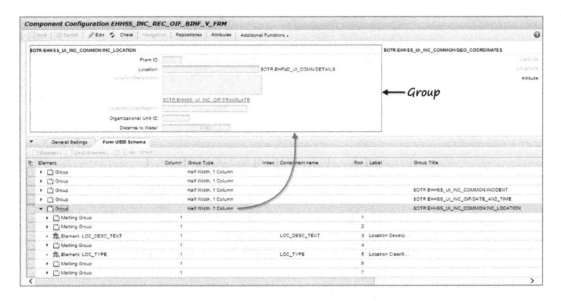

*Figure 6.6: Specifying the Object Schema for a Form UIBB © Copyright 2013. SAP AG.
All rights reserved*

Form GL2 Component

Though the legacy form component is suitable for defining basic form layouts, it's not
without its limitations. In particular, its generic UI structure doesn't allow us to be very
precise about where elements are placed in the screen layout. For this reason, and others,
SAP decided to redesign the form component so that its layout would be more flexible.
Since these efforts were coordinated in conjunction with the aforementioned GL2 UI
guidelines, the new form component goes by the name FPM_FORM_UIBB_GL2.

From a structural perspective, the GL2-based form component doesn't really change the
key model elements that make up a form component's object schema. However, if we
look under the hood at the FPM_FORM_UIBB_GL2 component, we can see that many of
these elements have been cast in different roles. For example, with the form GL2
component, elements have been promoted to first-class citizens that can exist
independently from a group assignment. Indeed, there is no longer a hard requirement to
even have a group element definition within a GL2-based form; though they're still
there if we need them.

Besides relaxing the rules around element organization, the form GL2 component also
introduces a brand new set of layout types. These layout types partition the UI into two-
dimensional grids of different sizes. Once these grid lines are established, we can place
individual elements in specific cells (e.g. cell A1) similar to spreadsheet programs such

as Microsoft Excel®. Such placement is illustrated in Figure 6.7. Here, positional attributes determine the boundaries of individual labels and input fields, etc.

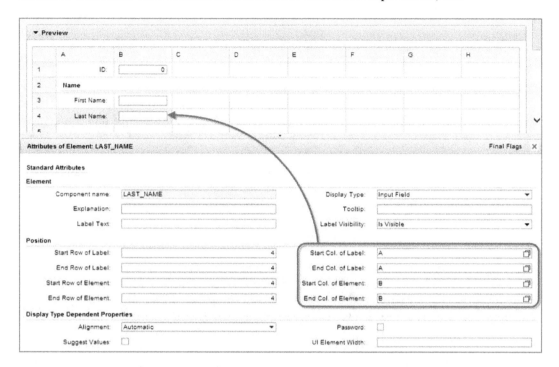

Figure 6.7: Specifying the Object Schema for a Form GL2 UIBB © Copyright 2013. SAP AG. All rights reserved

Feeder Class Overview

Regardless of which form component we choose to work with, the underlying feeder class implementation remains largely the same. Here, our feeder class must implement the IF_FPM_GUIBB_FORM interface designed for form components. As we noted in Section 6.1.2, this feeder class interface, like all of the feeder class interfaces that we'll cover in this chapter, inherits from a top-level GUIBB interface called IF_FPM_GUIBB. The IF_FPM_GUIBB interface defines methods that can be used to initialize GUIBB components at runtime.

Table 6.3 describes the main methods defined by the IF_FPM_GUIBB_FORM interface. For completeness, we've also included descriptions of the methods provided by the optional IF_FPM_GUIBB_FORM_EXT interface in Table 6.4. This optional interface allows a form component instance to participate more fully in the FPM event loop.

Method Name	Description
`get_definition()`	This method is used to provide metadata about a particular form component instance at startup. Such metadata includes the specification of a field catalog (similar to the ones created in the ALV programming model), custom action types, field groups, and so on.
	Conceptually speaking, the `GET_DEFINITION()` method is like a glue method in that it adapts an arbitrary application model to fit within the form component metamodel. Such application models could be implemented via business objects, plain ABAP Objects classes, function modules, and so on. From the perspective of the form component, we simply need to define a field catalog which abstractly defines the fields that will be included in the form definition.
	Though the `GET_DEFINITION()` method signature contains a number of exporting parameters, we usually only have to fill in the `EO_FIELD_CATALOG` parameter. This object reference parameter is of type `CL_ABAP_STRUCTDESCR`, a standard class from the ABAP RTTI API. In Section 6.3, we'll see how this RTTI class can build a form component's field catalog pretty easily based upon structure types from the ABAP Dictionary, etc.
	If we need to override or expand on the field metadata contained in the `EO_FIELD_CATALOG` parameter, then we can fill in the `ET_FIELD_DESCRIPTION` table parameter. Here, we create a separate record for the field(s) that we want to enhance and fill in the various details (e.g. field label/tooltip, assigned value help, and so on).
	One final note we should make about the `GET_DEFINITION()` method is that the field catalog we create defines a *superset* of available fields to include in a form definition. Component configurations based on a given feeder class may only use a subset of these fields for the actual implementation.

Method Name	Description
flush()	This method corresponds with the FLUSH() method defined in the IF_FPM_UI_BUILDING_BLOCK component interface. Like its counterpart, it can be used to sync up data between the frontend and the backend.
process_event()	This method corresponds with the PROCESS_EVENT() method defined in the IF_FPM_UI_BUILDING_BLOCK component interface. Like its counterpart, it is used to respond to FPM events. Here, we can use the familiar IO_EVENT parameter (which is of type CL_FPM_EVENT) to obtain details about the event that was triggered. In addition to the standard parameters forwarded from the UIBB interface, the PROCESS_EVENT() method also defines two further parameters which make it easier for form UIBBs to process events: ❖ IV_RAISED_BY_OWN_UI This Boolean flag can tell us whether or not the event was triggered by the form UIBB itself or some other UIBB. ❖ ET_MESSAGES We can use this table parameter to add a series of T100-style messages to the message area of the UI container housing the form UIBB. We'll learn more about messaging in Chapter 9.
get_data()	This method is called from within the PROCESS_BEFORE_OUTPUT() method of the form component. Here, as the method name suggests, we can perform data lookups for the form component. In order to optimize the data transfer process, the GET_DATA() method provides us with a number of parameters that can help us determine when and where to sync up the data. We'll see how this works in Section 6.3.

Method Name	Description
`get_default_config()`	This convenience method is used to provide a default configuration for form UIBBs that will be based on the feeder class. Such default configurations can be called upon within the FPM Configuration Editor tool to speed up the UIBB configuration process.

Over time, the signature of this method has changed to reflect changes to overarching form component. Therefore, depending on which form component you're using, you'll want to choose between the `IO_LAYOUT_CONFIG` and `IO_LAYOUT_CONFIG_GL2` parameters, respectively, when defining the default configuration. |
| `check_config()` | This method allows us to define design-time level checks of the form component's configuration whenever a user saves their changes in the FPM Configuration Editor. Here, we are provided with parameters to introspect the layout configuration data and determine if there are any inconsistencies. If there are, we can convey these errors back to the editor tool UI by populating messages in the `ET_MESSAGES` exporting parameter. |

Table 6.3: Methods of the IF_FPM_GUIBB_FORM Interface

Method Name	Description
`needs_confirmation()`	This method corresponds with the `NEEDS_CONFIRMATION()` method defined by the `IF_FPM_UI_BUILDING_BLOCK` component interface. This method allows the form component to issue a confirmation dialog box in the event that it needs some sort of confirmation in order to continue with its processing.
`after_failed_event()`	This method corresponds with the `AFTER_FAILED_EVENT()` method defined by the `IF_FPM_UI_BUILDING_BLOCK` component interface. This method allows the form component to respond to failed events which may be triggered by other UIBBs.

Method Name	Description
`before_dispatch_event()`	This callback method is invoked from deep within the form component as it reacts to actions triggered within the underlying WDA view component. Here, we can define any pre-event handling logic that might be required.

Table 6.4: Methods of the IF_FPM_GUIBB_FORM_EXT Interface

6.2.2 List Component

As its name implies, the *list component* provides a template for displaying data in *lists*. Visually, these lists are realized in the form of a table, having a very similar look-and-feel to the standard `Table` UI element provided by the WDA framework. Indeed, as you can see in Figure 6.8, list components provide us with all the same kinds of features we've come to expect in WDA tables (e.g. customizable cell editors, sorting and filtering, and so on). We'll learn how to tap into these different features in the upcoming sections.

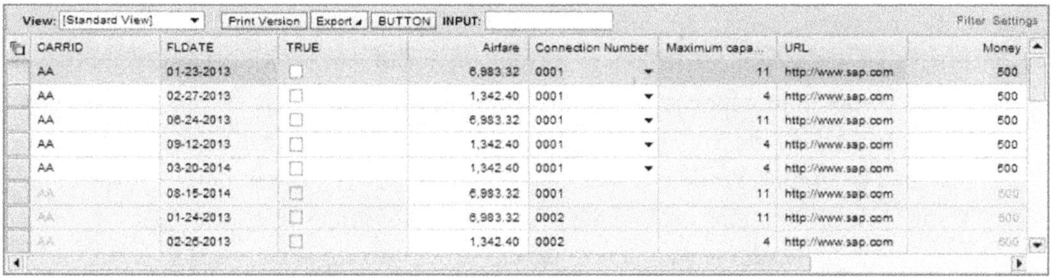

Figure 6.8: Example Usage of the List Component © Copyright 2013. SAP AG. All rights reserved

Evolution of the List Component

Much like the form component described in Section 6.2.1, the list component has also been subject to several enhancements since its initial release. For the most part, these enhancements have been focused on providing out-of-the-box solutions for addressing common user requirements such as sorting, filtering, drag-and-drop, and so on. The graph depicted in Figure 6.9 highlights how these expanded features evolved across SAP NetWeaver releases. Here, we can see that this evolutionary process has culminated in the creation of a new list component called the *list ATS component*.

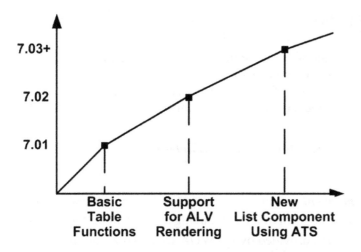

Figure 6.9: Innovations to the List Component across SAP NetWeaver Releases

So why did SAP decide to create a new list component? Well, in the time that passed since the initial list component was created, there were a couple of developments which made it difficult to proceed with the existing code base. First of all, the UI guidelines around list behavior changed in some rather incompatible ways with GL2. Secondly, SAP found that it was rather difficult to provide out-of-the-box innovations to the existing list component which were both robust and efficient. A classic example of this tradeoff occurred with the SAP NetWeaver 7.02 release whenever the list component was enhanced to support rendering using *SAP List Viewer* (ALV) technology. Here, the plethora of built-in functions provided by ALV was oftentimes overshadowed by the overhead associated with coupling these two technologies together.

Rather than continuing to try to overhaul the design of the initial list component, SAP elected to start over with a new design which incorporated a more flexible framework for delivering end user functionality: *ABAP Table Services* (ATS). We'll highlight some of the features of the ATS framework in the upcoming sections. For now though, suffice it to say that the newer ATS-based list component is designed to replace the basic list component available in earlier SAP NetWeaver releases. So, if you're on an SAP NetWeaver 7.03+ system, then the list ATS component is the way to go for any new development requirements which call for a list display.

Legacy List Component

The legacy list component is implemented using the `FPM_LIST_UIBB` WDA component. Internally, this component models the list output as a collection of *column* elements.

Whenever we go to configure the list component at design time, we can specify the details for each of these columns by filling in the following attributes:

➢ **Column Name**

Within the list component metamodel, this attribute serves dual purposes. Besides providing the column with a unique name/identifier, it also creates a binding to an abstract field defined within the field catalog created by the list component's associated feeder class. We'll explore this data binding in more detail whenever we take a closer look at the list component's feeder class interface.

➢ **Display Type**

This attribute defines the cell editor used to render a particular column at runtime. Here, we can choose between familiar UI elements such as text views, input fields, drop-down lists, and so on.

➢ **Header**

This attribute is used to specify the column header text.

➢ **Index**

This attribute determines the positioning of the column within the layout (e.g. first column, second column, and so forth).

Besides the basic attributes described above, other display type-specific attributes are provided to further customize the design/layout. We also have the option of configuring a toolbar to support list-specific actions (e.g. add/remove list items, etc.). Collectively, these attributes make it possible for us to construct a list/table based on most any kind of two-dimensional data model. Figure 6.10 illustrates how these model elements come together in the FPM Configuration Editor tool.

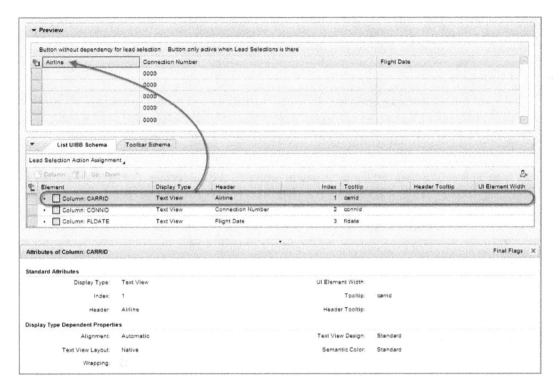

Figure 6.10: Configuring the List Component with FLUID © Copyright 2013. SAP AG. All rights reserved

Once we identify the various column elements within the list component object schema, all that's left from a UI configuration perspective is the configuration of the table's look-and-feel. Here, several attributes are provided which mirror those used to configure the WDA `Table` element. We can use these attributes to configure the table's title, visible row/column count, list width, rendering style, etc. Also, as we mentioned earlier, as of the SAP NetWeaver 7.02 release we also have the option of turning on ALV rendering with the list component. Whenever this setting is turned on, users can tap into expanded list functionality provided by the ALV component including sorting/filtering, exporting data to spreadsheets, and so on.

List ATS Component

As we mentioned earlier, SAP introduced a new list component with the SAP NetWeaver 7.03 release: the `FPM_LIST_UIBB_ATS` component. From a modeling perspective, this new list component is almost identical to the legacy `FPM_LIST_UIBB` component. This is to say that both components model their lists using column elements with (almost) identical attributes.

To see the differences between the new list ATS component and the legacy list component, we have to look at the two components from a *functional perspective*. Here, we can see that the list ATS component sets itself apart with its sophisticated personalization capabilities and built-in support for common features such as sorting, filtering, and grouping of records. These features are provided by the aforementioned *ABAP Table Services* (ATS).

The screenshot contained in Figure 6.11 demonstrates the list ATS component at work within a sample application. Here, you can see how users can access the sorting/filtering capabilities of the ATS by simply clicking on a target column's heading. This will cause a pull-down menu to open up, providing the user with various sorting and filtering options.

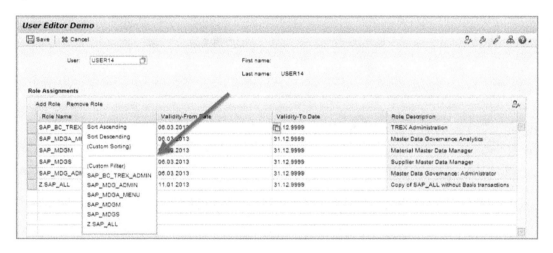

Figure 6.11: Working with ABAP Table Services (Part 1) © Copyright 2013. SAP AG. All rights reserved

Figure 6.12 provides us with a glimpse of the advanced personalization features available with the list ATS component. Here, we can adjust column ordering, display properties, and so on. These settings can be saved between sessions, making it easy for users to tailor screens to their own individual preferences. Of course, we can always revert back to the standard layout by selecting the RESET TO DEFAULT button.

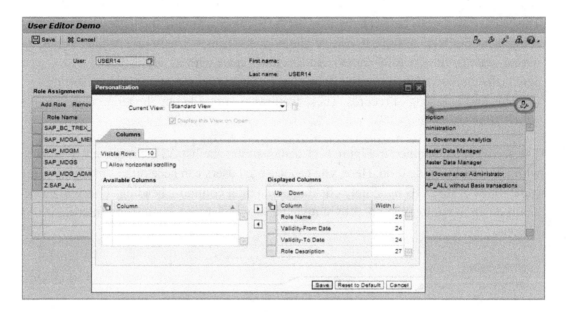

Figure 6.12: Working with ABAP Table Services (Part 2) © Copyright 2013. SAP AG. All rights reserved

Figure 6.13 demonstrates another useful feature of the list ATS component: *grouping*. Here, we can see how the table was grouped by the values in the VALIDITY-FROM DATE column. This feature can be useful in situations where we need to visualize splits within the list data. Whenever grouping is turned on, users can access this feature by clicking on a column's heading and choosing the GROUP menu option. The data can then be ungrouped by selecting the UNGROUP menu option which is made available whenever grouping is turned on.

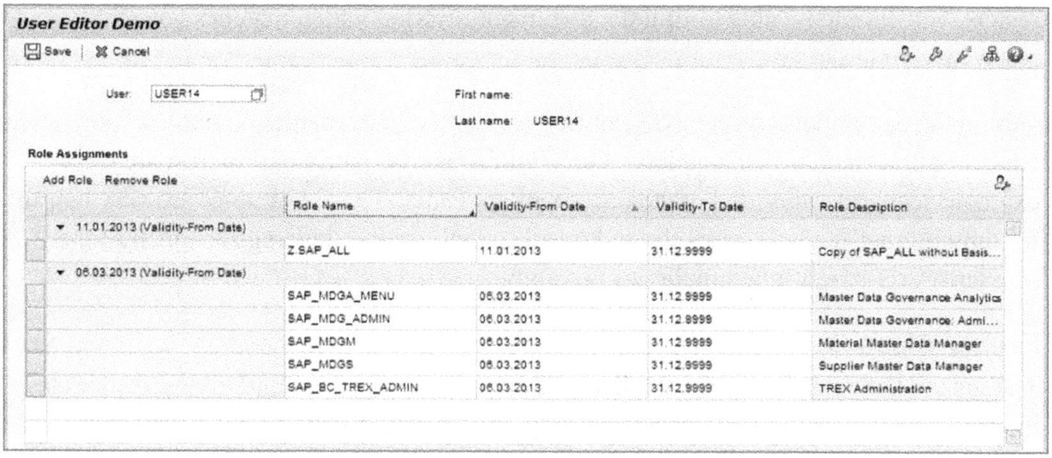

Figure 6.13: Working with ABAP Table Services (Part 3) © *Copyright 2013. SAP AG.*
All rights reserved

Generally speaking, there's not much we have to do as FPM developers to enable these features; we just configure the desired services at design time and the ATS component takes care of *most* of the dirty work behind the scenes at runtime. We emphasize the term "most" here since there is one basic development requirement that we have to take into account: we need to keep the ATS framework apprised of changes made to the source data within the feeder class.

At first glance, this may seem like a daunting task. However, in practice, SAP makes this process pretty easy by providing a series of built-in classes which can be used to record changes made within the GET_DATA() method of the list ATS component's assigned feeder class. Internally, these classes maintain a change log which the ATS framework uses to update the index-like structures that map rows from the source data table to filter list views, etc. This sync-up process allows the ATS to operate autonomously without requiring costly updates in memory. This in turn frees feeder classes from having to keep track of what's been filtered, what the current sort order is, and so on.

Where to Go Next

Before you get started with the list ATS component, we highly recommend that you read through the documentation provided in the *FPM Developer's Guide* provided by SAP on the SAP Developer Network (SDN). This document can be found by opening up the SDN main page at *http://scn.sap.com* and performing a search against the document title: *Floorplan Manager for Web Dynpro ABAP – Developer's Guide*. Within the list results, you should be able to find the document revision which matches your SAP NetWeaver release.

Within the developer's guide, you can find a wealth of information about list component editor modes, standard change log editors, and so on. Of particular interest are the example scenarios provided in the document appendix. These examples are very helpful in framing your feeder classes the right way so that you can leverage as much of the standard ATS-based functionality as possible.

Feeder Class Overview

The legacy list component and the list ATS both share the same underlying feeder class interface: IF_FPM_GUIBB_LIST. Structurally, this interface is quite similar to the IF_FPM_GUIBB_FORM interface introduced in Section 6.2.1. Consequently, both feeder class types are implemented in much the same way. Of course, there are certain list component-specific wrinkles to take into account.

Table 6.5 describes the methods provided by the IF_FPM_GUIBB_LIST interface. You can find more information about these methods in the aforementioned *FPM Developer's Guide*.

Method Name	Description
`get_definition()`	This method is used to provide metadata about a particular list component instance at startup. Such metadata includes the specification of a field catalog (similar to the ones created in the ALV programming model), custom action types, field groups, and so forth.

To define the set of possible columns supported by the feeder class, we must assign a value to the `EO_FIELD_CATALOG` exporting parameter. This object reference parameter is of type `CL_ABAP_TABLEDESCR`, a standard class from the ABAP RTTI API. We can use the methods of this class to build a model of the internal table that will be used to store the list data. Internally, the list component will use this metadata to construct field/column definitions dynamically.

In some cases, we may want to enhance/override some of the field attributes derived via the `EO_FIELD_CATALOG` parameter. In these situations, we can fill in the missing details using `ET_FIELD_DESCRIPTION` parameter. One example where we would want to do this is whenever we're working with the list ATS component. Here, we can use attributes such as `ALLOW_SORT` and `ALLOW_FILTER` to turn on sorting and filtering features, respectively. |
| `flush()` | This method corresponds with the `FLUSH()` method defined in the `IF_FPM_UI_BUILDING_BLOCK` component interface. Like its counterpart, it can be used to sync up any data which might be shared across multiple UIBBs. Or, in editing scenarios, we might want to use the provided `IT_CHANGE_LOG` parameter to track changes within a local cache. |

Method Name	Description
process_event()	This method corresponds with the PROCESS_EVENT() method defined in the IF_FPM_UI_BUILDING_BLOCK component interface. Like its counterpart, it is used to respond to FPM events. Here, we can use the familiar IO_EVENT parameter (which is of type CL_FPM_EVENT) to obtain details about the event that was triggered. In addition to the standard parameters forwarded from the UIBB interface, the PROCESS_EVENT() method also defines several other parameters which can be used to ascertain the selected row/column in which the event occurred, whether or not the event was raised within the current UIBB, etc.
get_data()	This method is called from within the PROCESS_BEFORE_OUTPUT() method of the list component. Here, is where we perform data lookups for the list component. To optimize this process, the GET_DATA() method provides us with a number of parameters that can help us determine when and where to sync up the data. We'll see how this works in Section 6.3. When designing a feeder class to work with the list ATS component, we may also need to add some tweaks to the GET_DATA() method in order to make sure that the ATS framework is notified of changes to the list data. These changes are recorded in the new EO_ITAB_CHANGE_LOG parameter added with the SAP NetWeaver 7.03 release. As we mentioned earlier, the *FPM Developer's Guide* provides a number of examples which demonstrate how to work with this change log parameter.
get_default_config()	This convenience method is used to provide a default configuration for list UIBBs that will be based on the feeder class.
check_config()	This method allows us to define design-time level checks of the list component's configuration whenever configurators save their changes in the FPM Configuration Editor.

Table 6.5: Methods of the IF_FPM_GUIBB_LIST Interface

Since both list component types introduced in this section utilize the same
`IF_FPM_GUIBB_LIST` interface, it's generally a pretty painless process to migrate the use
of a feeder class from the legacy list component over to the list ATS component. Of
course, in order to get the most out of the list ATS component, we may need to subclass
the original feeder class and override a feeder class method here and there. Also, when
adopting legacy feeder classes for use with the list ATS component, it's a good idea to
see if the feeder class happens to implement the `IF_FPM_GUIBB_LIST_PAGING`
interface[16]. Since this interface is not used by the list ATS component, it's probably
worth taking a look to see if any of the core feeder class functionality will be
compromised if the inherited methods are not invoked at runtime.

6.2.3 Form Repeater Component

With the SAP NetWeaver 7.03 release, SAP introduced an alternative to the list
component for displaying collections of data: the *form repeater component*. As the name
suggests, the form repeater component visualizes each record in the data collection using
a series of repeating forms. This hybrid approach can be quite useful in cases where we
want to allow users to browse through records one at a time. For example, we might use
a form repeater to build a product catalog similar to the one shown in Figure 6.14. Here,
pertinent details about each product are arranged in a form layout which is much easier
for users to read.

---

[16] This interface provided hooks to allow implementing feeder classes to implement *pagination*.
This was a useful feature in cases where the legacy list component was used to process large
amounts of data (e.g. more than 100 rows).

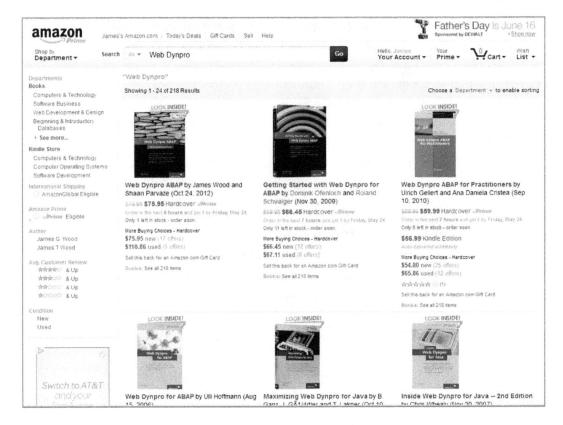

Figure 6.14: Browsing through a Product Catalog on Amazon.com

Structure and Design Concepts

The form repeater component is implemented technically using the
`FPM_FORM_REPEATER_UIBB` WDA component. Internally, this component maintains an
object schema that is almost identical to the one used by the `FPM_FORM_UIBB_GL2`
component introduced in Section 6.2.1. This is evidenced by the screenshot of the FPM
Configuration Editor tool shown in Figure 6.15.

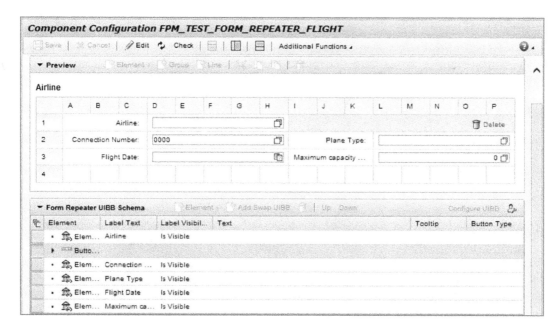

Figure 6.15: Configuring the Object Schema for a Form Repeater Component

When you think about it, these similarities make sense since the form repeater component renders its line items as forms. So, we basically layout the form elements for a single line item and then the FPM_FORM_REPEATER_UIBB component will repeatedly apply this layout for each bound line item at runtime. This is demonstrated by the sample FPM application FPM_TEST_FORM_REPEATER shown in Figure 6.16. Here, we can see how the FPM_FORM_REPEATER_UIBB component renders a form view for each of the flight records contained within a flight list.

Figure 6.16: Example Application Demonstrating the Form Repeater Component
© *Copyright 2013. SAP AG. All rights reserved*

One observation we can make by looking at the sample application contained in Figure 6.16 is that each of the individual forms within the repeater list are relatively small. From a design perspective, this approach makes a lot of sense. After all, if we're going to be displaying a large number of records, we don't want each individual form to take up half the screen. That would be a scrolling nightmare.

Of course, such an approach doesn't mean we can't provide users with a mechanism for displaying additional details concerning a selected record; we just need to display this information elsewhere so that we don't clutter up the screen with too many details. Here, there are a couple of standard approaches that make this task pretty straightforward:

➤ In Chapter 9, we'll learn how to provide links to dialog boxes that can display this information in a separate popup window. Here, for example, we might enhance the flight details form illustrated in Figure 6.16 to include a DISPLAY DETAILS link above the DELETE link. That way, if users wanted additional information about a flight connection, they could simply click this link and a dialog box would open up with the expanded details.

➤ Another alternative is to use a specialized schema element of the FPM_FORM_REPEATER_UIBB component: the so-called *swap UIBB*. Conceptually speaking, a swap UIBB represents an alternative (or expanded) view for a selected record. This view plays pretty much the same role as the dialog box described above. The only difference is that the swap UIBB is more tightly integrated with the FPM_FORM_REPEATER_UIBB component. Here, you can think of the relationship as being similar to the one between a Table and TablePopin UI element in the WDA programming context. You can find out more information about swap UIBBs in the online help documentation.

Feeder Class Overview

The FPM_FORM_REPEATER_UIBB component is designed to work with feeder classes that implement the IF_FPM_GUIBB_FORM_REPEATER interface. From an implementation perspective, feeder classes based on the IF_FPM_GUIBB_FORM_REPEATER interface are almost identical to feeder classes used with the list component (based on the IF_FPM_GUIBB_LIST interface). When you think about it, this is not all that surprising since we're basically just putting a different face on the same type of data.

Because of the similarities between these two different feeder class types, we won't repeat a method-by-method overview of this interface like we did in Section 6.2.2. However, if you have specific implementation questions, you can refer back to Section 6.2.2 or consult the *FPM Developer's Guide* for more details.

6.2.4 Search Component

To handle search scenarios, the FPM framework provides us with the generic *search component*. This component provides a design template for building query screens. In the upcoming sections, we'll see how this template is much easier to work with than if we were to attempt to build our own query screens from scratch (e.g. using the form and list components).

Structure and Design Concepts

The search component is implemented technically using the FPM_SEARCH_UIBB WDA component. Internally, this component uses metadata from its associated feeder class to construct a query model based on generic elements such as *search attributes*, *search operators*, and *result tables*. Collectively, these elements provide us with the flexibility we need to construct just about any selection screen imaginable.

To put these abstract search elements in perspective, consider the screenshot contained in Figure 6.17. Here, we have an example of a search UIBB used to allow users to search for flights based upon a flexible set of search attributes.

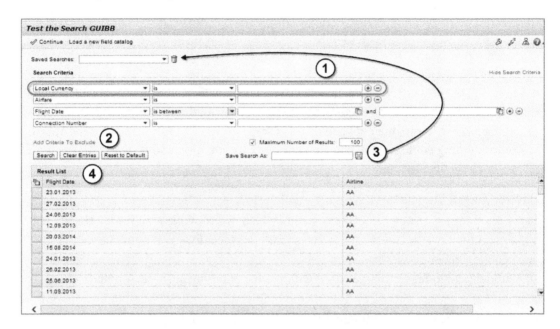

Figure 6.17: Anatomy of a Search UIBB © Copyright 2013. SAP AG. All rights reserved

Looking closely at the screenshot contained in Figure 6.17, we can see that search component instances are comprised of the following elements:

1. **Search Rows**

    At the top of the search component UI, we have a series of *search rows* such as the LOCAL CURRENCY row highlighted in Figure 6.17. Conceptually speaking, search rows are like conditions in an SQL WHERE clause in that they codify a logical expression which helps drive the selection process. Each search row is made up of the following elements:

    ❖ **Search Attributes**

        Search attributes are the operands which are used to refine the selection criteria. Within a given search row, search attributes are the first element in the expression (e.g. the LOCAL CURRENCY, AIRFARE, FLIGHT DATE, and CONNECTION NUMBER attributes in Figure 6.17). Whenever a search is executed, these search attributes will be used to narrow down the search result list along different dimensions. For example, in the flight query example shown

in Figure 6.17, we might use the FLIGHT DATE search attribute as the basis for
locating flights that occur within a given date range.

❖ **Search Operators**

Search operators are analogous to the Boolean operators used in SQL WHERE
clause expressions. With search operators, we can build logical expressions such
as `search attribute = search value`, `search attribute > search value`,
and so on.

❖ **Search Values**

The search value represents the right-hand operand within the search expression.
Its value set is naturally dependent upon the data type of the corresponding
search attribute.

2. **Search Functions**

Underneath the provided search rows are a handful of buttons which are used to
control the search component's behavior. We can use these buttons to execute a
search, reset the search form, and so on. Also of interest is the MAXIMUM
NUMBER OF RESULTS input field which can be used to control the number of
search results generated in a given query.

3. **Search Variant Selection**

Adjacent to the button row described in (2), we can observe a nice personalization
feature of the search component: *search variants*. This functionality allows end
users to save a particular query so that it can be reloaded at a later date using the
SAVED SEARCHES drop-down list shown at the bottom of the page. Of course, use
of this feature is strictly optional, but it's nice to know it's there if you need it.

4. **Results Table**

Finally, at the bottom of the page, we have the optional results table which looks
and behaves almost identically to the legacy list component described in Section
6.2.2.

In terms of configuration, the search component is pretty easy to set up. To add new
search rows to the UI layout, we simply click on the SEARCH CRITERIA button in the
toolbar above the SEARCH UIBB SCHEMA editor panel and choose the appropriate
search attributes from the field catalog defined by the associated feeder class (see Figure
6.18).

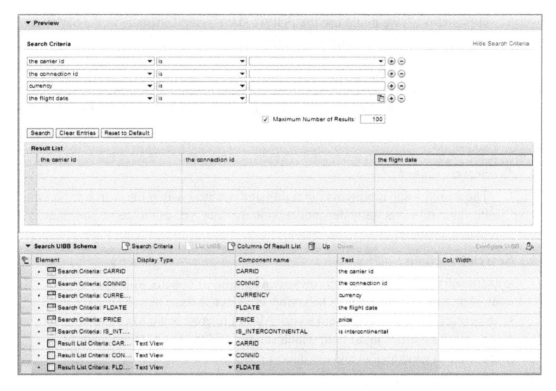

Figure 6.18: Configuring the Search Component © Copyright 2013. SAP AG. All rights reserved

Once the search rows are in place, we can proceed with the definition of the results table. As of the SAP NetWeaver 7.03 release, we have two options for defining the contents of this table:

➢ We can click on the COLUMNS OF RESULT LIST button in the toolbar above the SEARCH UIBB SCHEMA editor panel to build the result list table directly within the search UIBB (see Figure 6.18).

➢ Alternatively, we can click on the LIST UIBB button (grayed out in Figure 6.18) to substitute a separate FPM_LIST_UIBB_ATS configuration for the standard search result list. In this scenario, we have to come up with a mechanism for piping the search results into the external list ATS component. In some situations though, this extra effort is worth the trouble since the list ATS component provides users with so much more flexibility when it comes to analyzing the search results.

Finally, after the relevant search UIBB schema elements are in place, we can configure them as necessary using the ATTRIBUTES panel as shown in Figure 6.19. Here, we can (among other things):

➤ Specify the default search operator for a given search row.

➤ Define an exclusion list to filter out search operators that we don't want to provide for a given search row.

➤ Configure the look and feel of columns in the results table.

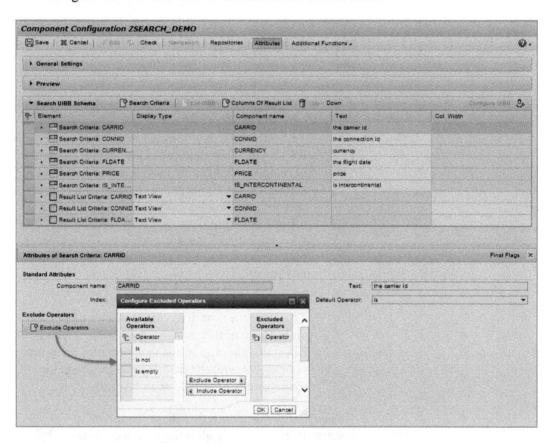

Figure 6.19: Configuring Search Rows in a Search UIBB © Copyright 2013. SAP AG. All rights reserved

Feeder Class Overview

Feeder classes for the search component are based on the IF_FPM_GUIBB_SEARCH interface. This interface provides us with the callback methods needed to initialize the search form, execute the search, and produce a search result set. Table 6.6 describes each of these methods in detail.

Method Name	Description
`get_definition()`	This method is used to provide metadata about a particular search component instance at startup. Such metadata includes the specification of a field catalog to define supported search attributes, a field catalog to define the search result set, custom action types, available search options, and so on. In typical scenarios, there are two main exporting parameters that we need to account for: ❖ `EO_FIELD_CATALOG_ATTR` This object reference parameter defines the search attribute field catalog using the `CL_ABAP_STRUCTDESCR` class from the ABAP RTTI API. This class provides us with a number of methods that can be used to compile the set of supported search attributes. Perhaps the easiest way to build this list is to define the attributes using a structure from the ABAP Dictionary. That way, we can use the static `DESCRIBE_BY_NAME()` factory method to build the field catalog in one fell swoop. ❖ `EO_FIELD_CATALOG_RESULT` To define the search results table, we must create an instance of the `CL_ABAP_TABLEDESCR` class. This table descriptor instance provides the search component with the details it needs to handle dynamically-generated search results. As usual, if we need to refine these dynamically-generated field catalogs after the fact, we can do so by specifying the `ET_FIELD_DESCRIPTION_ATTR` and `ET_FIELD_DESCRIPTION_RESULT` parameters, respectively.

Method Name	Description
flush()	This method corresponds with the FLUSH() method defined in the IF_FPM_UI_BUILDING_BLOCK component interface. Therefore, it's the first method invoked within the FPM event loop. If we look at the signature of this method, we can see that it has been enhanced to provide details about current selection criteria and/or selected results. These attributes can be cached internally so that they are visible to other callback methods invoked within the FPM event loop (notably the GET_DATA() method).
get_data()	As we have seen in other feeder classes observed throughout this chapter, this method is used to transport data from the feeder class over to the search UIBB. Typically, there are two milestone events that we need to watch out for in this method:

❖ FPM_EXECUTE_SEARCH

Whenever this event is triggered, we need to pass back the search results (if any) in the exporting ET_RESULT_LIST parameter. Normally, these search results are compiled in the preceding PROCESS_EVENT() method.

❖ FPM_RESET_SEARCH

This event is triggered whenever the user clicks on the RESET TO DEFAULT button on the search screen. The appropriate response here would be to refresh the result list so that the search screen is re-initialized.

Method Name	Description
process_event()	This method corresponds with the PROCESS_EVENT() method defined in the IF_FPM_UI_BUILDING_BLOCK component interface. Normally, this method is used to respond to search requests (based on FPM event ID IF_FPM_GUIBB_SEARCH=>FPM_EXECUTE_SEARCH). Here, we can use the following parameters as the basis for conducting our custom search scenarios:

❖ IT_FPM_SEARCH_CRITERIA
This table parameter contains all of the user's search criteria (encoded as a series of search rows). Because the search rows bear a striking resemblance to range tables, they can easily be incorporated into SELECT statements or query engines/frameworks.

❖ IV_MAX_NUM_RESULTS
This parameter corresponds with the MAXIMUM NUMBER OF RESULTS parameter on the search screen. Therefore, it should be included in the query logic to make sure that the number of search results brought back matches the user selection.

❖ IO_SEARCH_CONVERSION
This object reference provides a handful of utility methods which make it easy to convert search rows into ABAP range tables, etc.

If you look closely at the signature of the PROCESS_EVENT() method, you'll note that it does not provide an exporting table parameter to pass back the search results. This task falls to the GET_DATA() method which is invoked next in the FPM event loop. In the meantime, we need to cache the search results so that they can be picked up later on (e.g. by storing them in an instance attribute).

Method Name	Description
`get_default_config()`	This convenience method is used to provide a default configuration for search UIBBs that will be based on the feeder class. Such default configurations can be called upon within the FPM Configuration Editor tool to speed up the UIBB configuration process.
`check_config()`	This method can be used to apply custom validations against configuration settings made in the FPM Configuration Editor tool.

Table 6.6: Methods of the IF_FPM_GUIBB_SEARCH Interface

6.2.5 Hierarchical List Component

The *hierarchical list component* provides us with a template for displaying data that is of a hierarchical nature. For example, we might use the hierarchical list component to display an organizational model or the contents of a file system. In general, the hierarchical list component can be used in just about any scenario in which we need to visually portray parent-child relationships in a tree-like structure.

Structure and Design Concepts

In order to understand how the hierarchical list component is structured, let's take a look at an example. Figure 6.20 contains a screenshot of a sample FPM application used to display the contents of the SAP MIME Repository[17]. As you can see in Figure 6.20, the UI layout of the hierarchical list component combines characteristics of the `Tree` and `Table` UI elements from the WDA framework to produce a sort of "tree table" in which table rows are organized into outline (or indexed) form. This design approach provides us with tremendous flexibility, making it possible to simultaneously display a hierarchy of items along with a handful of associated attributes in one unified structure.

---

[17] Refer to the WDA application `ZWDA_TREE_UIBB_DEMO` in the book's code bundle for implementation details.

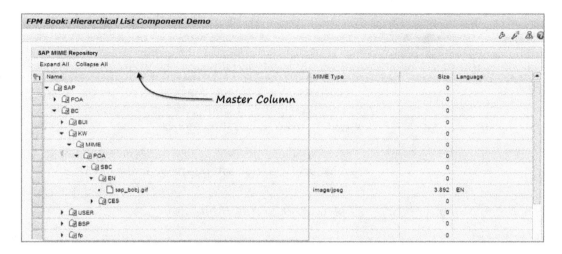

Figure 6.20: Displaying MIME Repository Data with the Hierarchical List Component

Looking at the example UIBB contained in Figure 6.20, we can see that the hierarchical list content is divided into two column types:

> **Master Column**

   The very first column in the hierarchical list display is the so-called *master column*. This fixed column controls the hierarchical list display, providing functions to expand/collapse tree nodes as we navigate through the data hierarchy. Functionally, a master column is similar to the `TreeByKeyTableColumn` UI element used to construct tree tables with the `Table` UI element of the WDA framework.

> **Non-Master Columns**

   To the right of the fixed master column, we have the option of defining a series of non-master columns which can be used to display additional information about a particular list record. For example, in the sample application depicted in Figure 6.20, you can see that we have included columns to display attributes of a selected element from the repository (e.g. MIME type, size, and so on).

The hierarchical list component is implemented technically using the `FPM_TREE_UIBB` WDA component. In order to be able to construct hierarchies like the one shown in Figure 6.20, this component requires two main pieces of information from its associated feeder class:

> The data itself must be flattened out into a two-dimensional internal table in which each record has a unique key field as well as a foreign key field which points to the

row's parent (provided that the row in question is not the root, in which case the parent key will be null).

➤ Within the field catalog definition, we must associate particular column fields with a *column type* as shown in Figure 6.21. This designation helps the FPM_TREE_UIBB component figure out how to interpret the data contained in its bound internal table (e.g. which field contains the row key, which field contains the text to display on individual nodes, and so on).

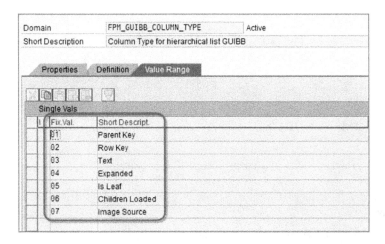

Figure 6.21: Column Types for the Hierarchical List Component © Copyright 2013. SAP AG. All rights reserved

Once we've modeled our data according to this format, configuring the FPM_TREE_UIBB component is pretty straightforward. As you can see in the screenshot contained in Figure 6.22, the object schema for the hierarchical list component is quite similar to that of the list component. The only real wrinkle in all this is that we have to configure a master column in addition to the normal columns used in the list display.

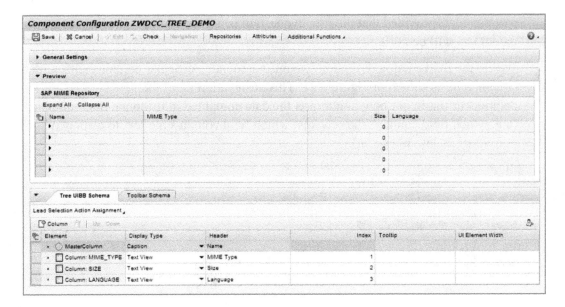

Figure 6.22: Configuring the Hierarchical List Component © Copyright 2013. SAP AG. All rights reserved

Feeder Class Overview

Feeder classes for the hierarchical list component are based on the `IF_FPM_GUIBB_TREE` interface. This interface provides us with the callback methods needed to initialize the list, respond to selection events, and so on. Table 6.7 describes selected methods of this interface in detail.

Method Name	Description
get_definition()	This method is used to provide metadata about a particular hierarchical list component instance at startup. Such metadata includes the specification of a field catalog to define list columns, custom action types, and so on.
	Much like the list component, we can build the field catalog (parameter EO_FIELD_CATALOG) using methods of the CL_ABAP_TABLEDESCR RTTI class. Here, we're basically free to define our source internal table however we like. However, there are a handful of fields that we need to provide within our table layout:
	❖ Row Key/Parent Key These fields help the FPM_TREE_UIBB component determine where a given row fits into the overall hierarchy.
	❖ Text The contents of this field are used to label a given node (master column) within the tree.
	❖ Expanded / Is Leaf / Children Loaded These Boolean attributes provide state information which makes it easier for the FPM_TREE_UIBB component to render the hierarchical list at runtime.
	❖ Image Source If desired, we can use this field to assign an image icon to a particular row.
	Once these fields are accounted for, we must identify them in the field description table contained in the ET_FIELD_DESCRIPTION parameter (within the aforementioned COLUMN_TYPE field).
flush()	This method corresponds with the FLUSH() method defined in the IF_FPM_UI_BUILDING_BLOCK component interface. It's typically used to synchronize user selections on the frontend with an internal instance attribute containing the hierarchical list data. Here, the IT_CHANGE_LOG parameter can be used to optimize selection updates.

Method Name	Description
`process_event()`	This method corresponds with the `PROCESS_EVENT()` method defined in the `IF_FPM_UI_BUILDING_BLOCK` component interface. It's normally used to respond to user selections on the frontend. For example, whenever a user expands a node within the tree, an FPM event with ID `ON_LOAD_CHILDREN` is triggered, allowing us to implement lazy loading of the selected data on demand. This method can also be used to respond to events triggered within individual table cells, etc.
`get_data()`	This method is used to transport data from the feeder class over to the hierarchical list UIBB. Here, data is normally synchronized at particular milestone events such as `FPM_START`, `ON_LOAD_CHILDREN`, and so forth.

Table 6.7: Methods of the IF_FPM_GUIBB_TREE Interface

6.2.6 Tabbed Component

The *tabbed component* is a composite component which can be used to layout UIBB components within a tabstrip control. In some respects, you can think of the tabbed component as being like a lightweight and embeddable OIF component. We would emphasize the term "embeddable" here since the tabbed component can be embedded anywhere that we would normally embed smaller discrete UIBB types. So, for example, we can plug in a tabbed component as a subview in an OIF floorplan, a main step in a QAF floorplan, and so on.

Functionally, the tabbed component is used to compose a series of related UIBBs into a single container so that we can simplify the UI design. This is preferable to creating a large monolithic UIBB which takes on too much responsibility.

Structure and Design Concepts

The tabbed component is implemented technically using the `FPM_TABBED_UIBB` WDA component. Internally, this component organizes the content area into two distinct sections as shown in Figure 6.23:

➤ **Master Area**

The master area is normally used to display any header level data which relates to subordinate data that will be displayed in the individual tab pages. Within the master area, we can stack one or more UIBBs on top of one another.

➤ **Tab Area**

The tab area contains the various tab pages to be displayed within the tabbed UIBB. As you can see in Figure 6.23, a given `Tab` element may embed multiple UIBBs which are stacked on top of one another. The name of the `Tab` element is determined by its `Tab Name` attribute.

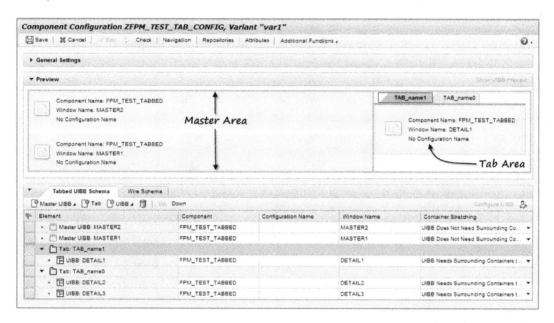

Figure 6.23: Layout of the Tabbed Component's Content Area © Copyright 2013. SAP AG. All rights reserved

As we lay out a tabbed component's content area, there are several global attributes that influence the overall look-and-feel of the tabbed component at runtime:

➤ **Layout Alignment**

This attribute determines the basic arrangement of the master area and the tab area within the overall content area. Here, we can choose to stack the elements vertically (e.g. with the master area on top and the tab area on bottom) or horizontally as shown in Figure 6.23.

➤ **Tabstrip Display**

This attribute determines how the tabstrip control will be rendered at runtime. Here, we can stick with the default tab-based approach or choose to organize the tab pages into a drop-down list.

> ➤ **Hide Tabstrip if Single Tab**
>
> This setting determines whether or not the tabstrip control is rendered in cases where there is only one tab.

Feeder Class Overview

Unlike the other GUIBB components reviewed throughout the course of this chapter, the tabbed component does not have an associated feeder class. When you think about it, this makes sense since all the tabbed component really does is arrange other UIBBs together into a composite layout.

Of course, there are times whenever we may want to influence the output of certain tab pages, etc. For these tasks, we can encode our logic inside the FPM application's application controller. We'll learn how this works in Chapter 8.

6.2.7 POWL Component

The POWL Component is a new component that was made available as part of the SAP NetWeaver 7.03 release. Its purpose is to provide seamless integration with applications based on SAP's *Personal Object Worklist* (POWL) framework[18].

Background Information

If you're not familiar with the POWL framework, then a brief description is in order. At a high level, it's appropriate to think of the POWL as a flexible reporting framework which makes it easy to build web-based lists without getting your hands dirty creating WDA components, etc. This is made possible through the framework elements highlighted in Figure 6.24.

---

[18] In some reference materials, the POWL acronym is described as being short for *Power List*. For the purposes of this book though, we'll stick with the terms used within the SAP Help Library documentation.

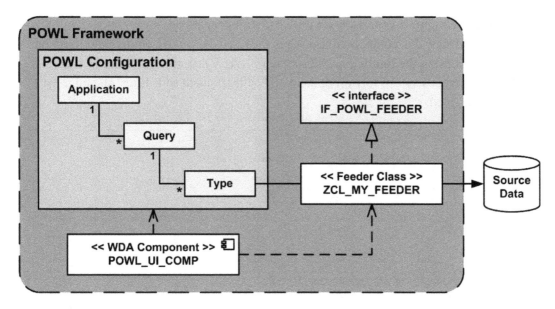

Figure 6.24: Understanding the POWL Framework

Looking at the framework diagram contained in Figure 6.24, we can observe certain similarities between POWL applications and GUIBBs in the FPM framework:

➢ The UI rendering is handled by a standard component provided by the framework (POWL_UI_COMP in this case).

➢ Custom application logic is encoded in a separate *feeder class* which implements a standard interface defined by the POWL framework. Looking at the makeup of the IF_POWL_FEEDER interface, we can see that it has a lot in common with the feeder class interfaces for GUIBB components reviewed in this chapter.

➢ The links that bind various framework components together are defined via *configuration*. This configuration is performed in the SAP GUI using Transaction POWL_COCKPIT.

At runtime, POWL applications are launched using a WDA application called POWL. This application is based on the POWL_UI_COMP component illustrated in Figure 6.24. Internally, the POWL_UI_COMP component is able to bootstrap itself using application parameters defined by the POWL application. These parameters are used as a key for querying the POWL configuration model. With this configuration metadata in hand, it's able to locate the target feeder class and invoke the callback methods defined by the IF_POWL_FEEDER interface to construct a field catalog for the list output, extract report data from the database, and so forth.

The actual list output is generated via a used component called POWL_TABLE_COMP. Behind the scenes, this component leverages the SALV_WD_TABLE component to render the list output using the familiar *SAP List Viewer* (ALV) control as shown in Figure 6.25. From here, users can rely on built-in ALV functions to sort, filter, and aggregate the data as needed.

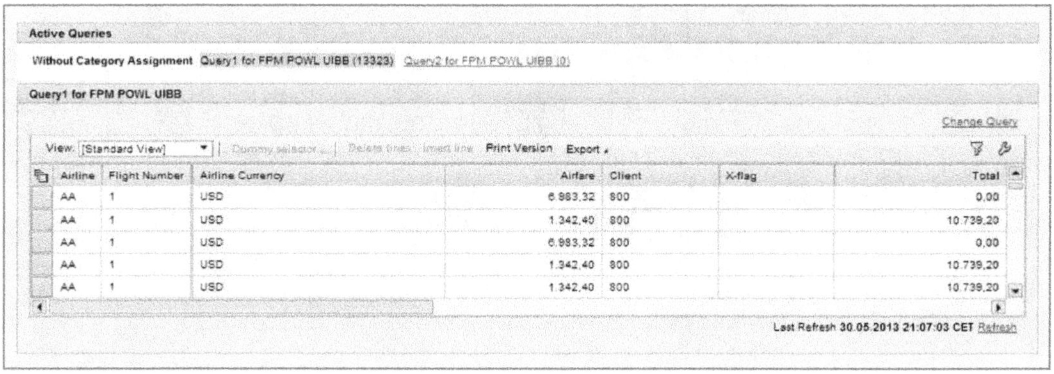

Figure 6.25: Working with the POWL © Copyright 2013. SAP AG. All rights reserved

If you're interested in learning more about the POWL, we would encourage you to browse through the POWL documentation provided in the SAP Help Library available online at *http://help.sap.com*. Within this documentation, you can find detailed information about POWL configuration topics, how to go about creating POWL feeder classes, and so on.

Structure and Design Concepts

For the most part, it's appropriate to think of the POWL component as a thin FPM-based adapter/wrapper around the POWL_UI_COMP component introduced in the previous section. In essence, it provides a mechanism for easily integrating reports/lists created using the POWL framework.

Underneath the hood, the POWL component is implemented technically using the FPM_POWL_UIBB WDA component. Since this component delegates almost all of the heavy lifting to the aforementioned POWL_UI_COMP component, there's not a whole lot for us to configure at design time on the FPM side of things. Basically, all we have to do is fill in attributes in the GENERAL SETTINGS section which correspond with application parameters normally provided with the standalone POWL WDA application described in the previous section (see Figure 6.26). With this information in hand, the

`FPM_POWL_UIBB` component has everything it needs to be able to integrate the POWL list into the UIBB content area.

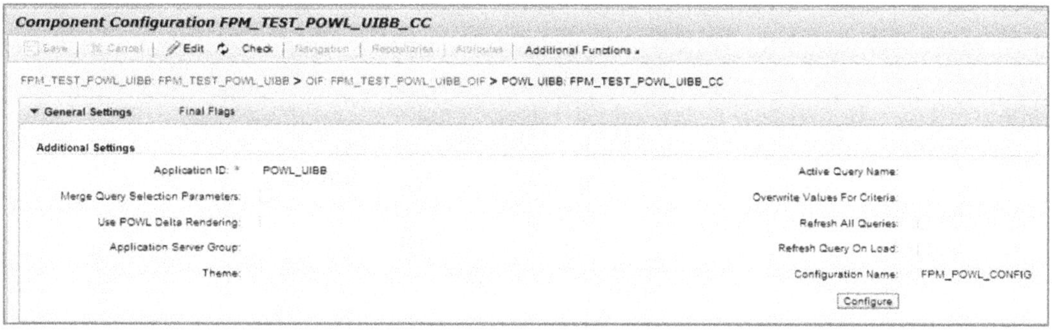

Figure 6.26: Configuring the POWL Component © Copyright 2013. SAP AG. All rights reserved

> **Note**
>
> At the time of this writing the `FPM_POWL_UIBB` component only supports integration with Standard POWL applications.

Feeder Class Overview

Given its role as a sort of pass-through to the POWL framework, the `FPM_POWL_UIBB` component does not rely on an FPM-based feeder class to control application behavior. Instead, all of the list processing functionality is delegated over the POWL framework (which defines its own feeder classes).

This begs the question: how do other UIBBs communicate with the POWL component? For example, what if we want to sync-up a form UIBB with a POWL UIBB such that the selection of a row in the POWL UIBB causes data to show up in the form UIBB? In these situations, we can rely on FPM events triggered within the `FPM_POWL_UIBB` component. Here, POWL events are basically recast as FPM events so that we can respond to lead selection events, query refreshes/switches, and so on. You can find detailed information about the supported events in the *FPM Developer's Guide*.

6.2.8 Launchpad Component

The launchpad component is useful in situations where we need to construct an overview (or landing) page from which users can branch out and navigate to a series of related applications/transactions. Here, instead of having to build something from scratch, we can tap into the SAP-standard *Launchpad* framework. In the upcoming sections, we'll see how this works.

Background Information

If you're not familiar with the launchpad concept, then a brief introduction is in order. According to the SAP online help documentation[19], a launchpad is defined as "a collection of navigation links that is stored as a separate technical object in the system". These navigation links can point to all kinds of different applications: WDA applications, external web pages, SAP BI queries/reports, SAP transactions, and so on.

From a development perspective, the launchpad framework reduces the burden of application integration by:

➤ Providing a mechanism for storing system and application connection parameters as customizing objects.

➤ Taking care of low-level connection details at runtime whenever specific links are accessed.

Indeed, most of the time, launchpads can be defined exclusively via customization without having to write a single line of code.

Besides handling the low-level communication details, the launchpad framework also includes a robust UI which can be customized to present application links in different ways. Figure 6.27 demonstrates what this UI looks like for a sample launchpad provided by SAP. Here, you can see how links can be organized into groups, annotated with descriptive text, and highlighted using visual icons. Collectively, these features are designed to make it easy for users to hit a landing page and quickly determine which applications are available to them.

---

[19] You can access this help documentation in the SAP Help Library available online at *http://help.sap.com*. Within the SAP NetWeaver library, you can find detailed information about the Launchpads framework under the section entitled *UI Technologies in ABAP*.

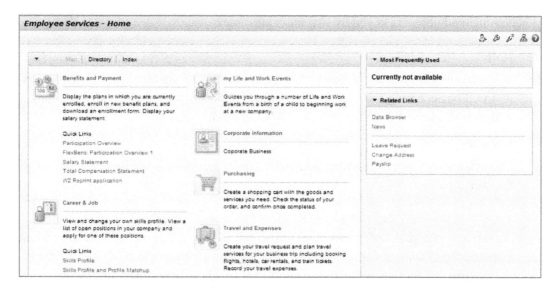

As we mentioned earlier, launchpads like the one depicted in Figure 6.27 are defined through *configuration*. This configuration takes place in Transaction LPD_CUST in the SAP GUI. Figure 6.28 shows what the initial screen of this transaction looks like. Here, we can create new launchpads or edit existing ones in the table below.

Overview of Launchpads

New Launchpad   New Repository

Role	Instance	Description	Re.	Embedded	FPM GUIBB	Ch.	Dis.	Del
GTS_SPL	TRADE_COMPLIANCE				X			
HAAPF	RELATED_LINKS	Related Links for Home and area page		X				
HAP	HAP_GENERIC_UI							
HAP	PMP							
HDLT2	HDLT2	For Role SAP_EP_HR_PA00						
HDLT3	HDLT3	For Role SAP_EP_HR_PA00						
HOME_AND	AREA_PAGE	Home and Area Page			X			
HRADM_NAV	OBN	OBN for HR Admin						
HRCA_NAV	OBN	LP entry for Course Admin OBN navigation						
HRECM	HRECM_LAUNCH_PLANNING	Revise Planning						
HRECM_NAV	OBN	Launchpad for ECM						
HRESS_BEN	CREDIT_PLANS	Credit Plans Additional Documents						
HRESS_BEN	EOI_FORM	EOI Form Link		X				
HRESS_BEN	FSA_PLANS	Flexible Spending Acco. Additional Doc.						
HRESS_BEN	HEALTH_PLANS	Health Plans Additional Documents						
HRESS_BEN	INELIGIBLE_PLAN	Ineligible plan information		X				

Each launchpad object is keyed by two main attributes:

> **Role**

  The role attribute is a text-based identifier which loosely identifies the kind of users that will be accessing the launchpad. It should not be confused with roles defined within SAP Identity Management (i.e. PFCG roles).

> **Instance**

  The instance attribute is another text-based identifier which specifies the purpose of the launchpad.

Once we have uniquely defined a launchpad using these arbitrarily-defined attributes, we can proceed with its configuration on the screen shown in Figure 6.29. Here, you can see that launchpad content is organized into folders (which can be nested). Within these folders, we can use buttons in the top-level toolbar to add new applications, create visual separators, and so on.

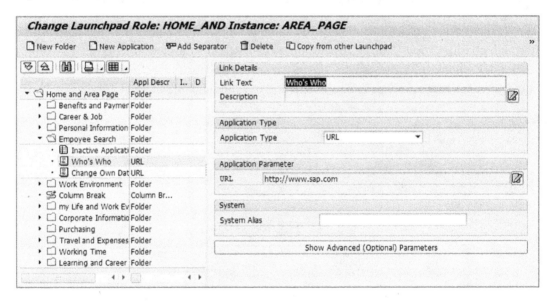

Figure 6.29: Configuring a Launchpad - Part 2 © Copyright 2013. SAP AG. All rights reserved

Looking closely at the right-hand side of Figure 6.29, you can see how application links are configured using various parameters. Naturally, these parameters vary between application types[20]. The point is that, within the configuration, we can specify everything the framework needs to connect to an application: the application URL, system aliases, and so forth.

After a launchpad is configured, it can be transported throughout the system landscape using CTS. With careful definition of system aliases, the promotion process can be more or less turn-key. Otherwise, some tweaks may have to be made in specific environments to handle certain connection requirements. Still, this is definitely preferable to hard-coding connection details in WDA components or putting them in the TVARV table.

Structure and Design Concepts

The launchpad component is implemented technically using the FPM_LAUNCHPAD_UIBB WDA component. Much like the FPM_POWL_UIBB component reviewed in the previous section, it does not maintain a complex object schema. Instead, it uses a handful of attributes defined in the GENERAL SETTINGS section of the FPM Configuration Editor to determine which launchpad(s) to load within its UI content areas (see Figure 6.30).

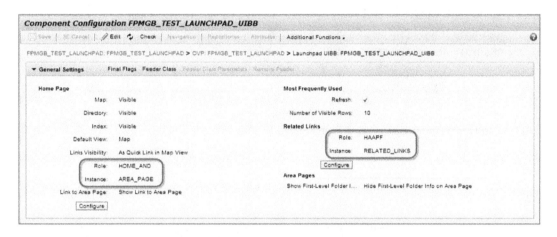

Figure 6.30: Configuring the FPM_LAUNCHPAD_UIBB Component © Copyright 2013. SAP AG. All rights reserved

---

[20] We would point you in the direction of the online help documentation for questions about specific application types/parameters.

As we go to configure the launchpad component layout, there are three different content areas that we can account for (refer to Figure 6.31):

➤ **Main View**

On the left-hand side of the UI, we have the *main view* content area which renders the launchpad selected in the HOME PAGE attributes panel shown in Figure 6.30. Here, the launchpad can be rendered in several different ways: as a map, a directory, or as an index. You can see these different visualization modes on display in the sample application FPMGB_TEST_LAUNCHPAD which is provided by default with SAP NetWeaver systems.

➤ **Most Frequently Used**

The top right-hand section of the UI contains the dynamic MOST FREQUENTLY USED content area. As the name suggests, this content area contains a list of frequently used application links for the current user.

➤ **Related Links**

On the bottom right-hand section of the UI, we have the option of plugging in a secondary launchpad which contains related links that supplement the application links provided in the main view.

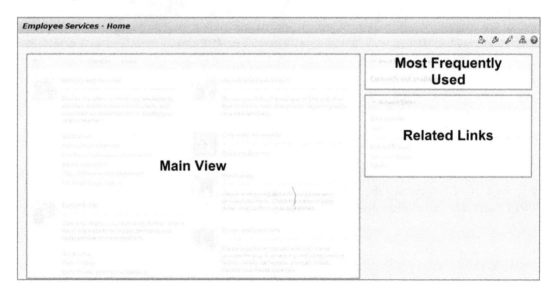

Figure 6.31: FPM_LAUNCHPAD_UIBB Component Layout © Copyright 2013. SAP AG. All rights reserved

Collectively, these content areas tend to take up quite a bit of space on the screen. As a result, the FPM_LAUNCHPAD_UIBB component is intended to be used exclusively with the OVP floorplan.

Feeder Class Overview

As we mentioned earlier, the launchpad component is designed to make it possible to rapidly build overview pages without having to write a lot of custom code. Therefore, unlike most of the other GUIBB components reviewed in this chapter, the assignment of a feeder class in launchpad component configurations is purely optional. Indeed, about the only time a feeder class is called for is in cases where we want to override the launchpad configuration at runtime. In these situations, we can employ methods of the IF_FPM_GUIBB_LAUNCHPAD interface to carry out these tasks. For more information about these methods, consult the *FPM Developer's Guide*.

6.2.9 Composite Component

As the name suggests, the composite component is a *composite* which groups together multiple related UIBBs into a single UIBB. As UI developers, we can use this component to build larger UIBB assemblies that are easier to work with. For example, we might group together a search UIBB, a list UIBB, and a form UIBB together into a sub-assembly that can be reused in several application instances.

Structure and Design Concepts

The composite component is implemented technically using the FPM_COMPOSITE_UIBB WDA component. As you can see in Figure 6.32, its configuration is pretty straightforward. Basically, we're provided with a grid in which we can embed several related UIBBs. The grid layout is defined by the LAYOUT TYPE attribute highlighted in Figure 6.32. Here, we can choose between a one or two-column layout as needed. Beyond this basic setup, there's not much else to the composite component; it's basically just a layout container.

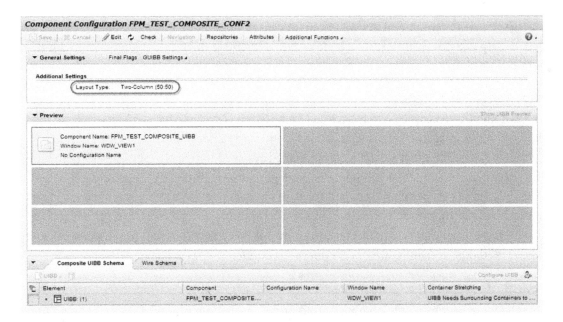

Figure 6.32: Configuring the FPM_COMPOSITE_UIBB Component © Copyright 2013.
SAP AG. All rights reserved

6.3   Case Study: Creating an FPM Application Using GUIBBs

Now that we've had an opportunity to survey the various GUIBB types provided with
the FPM framework, we thought it would be a useful exercise to apply what we've
learned towards the creation of a sample FPM application. Here, since we already
learned how to create FPM applications in Chapter 4, our focus will be on configuring
GUIBBs and integrating them into a finished product.

6.3.1 Design Approach

In order to keep things simple, we'll base our sample application off of a business object
that is available in any SAP NetWeaver system and well known by developers: the *user
master* business object. Here, we'll create a simple editor application that allows
administrators to adjust user role assignments. Figure 6.33 shows what the finished
product looks like.

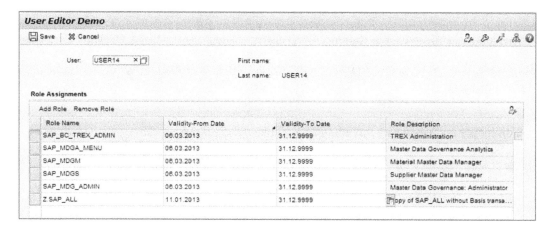

Figure 6.33: Sample FPM Application Used to Edit User Master Records © Copyright 2013. SAP AG. All rights reserved

Since this application focuses on a single business object instance, we'll base our user editor application off of the OVP floorplan, though we could have also used the OIF floorplan instead. To layout the main content area, we'll be using three GUIBB types:

➤ **Form GL2 Component**

We'll use this component to create the user selection form shown at the top of the page in Figure 6.33.

➤ **List ATS Component**

This component will be used to create the ROLE ASSIGNMENTS table shown at the bottom of Figure 6.33.

➤ **Tabbed Component**

This component will be used organize the form and list component content into a composite that can be embedded directly into our OVP floorplan. This is, of course, an optional step, but useful for demonstration purposes in this instance.

In the upcoming sections, we'll take a closer look at how these components are implemented from a technical perspective.

6.3.2 Defining the User Selection Form

To get things started, we'll first take a look at what it takes to build out the user selection form. The steps required here are as follows:

1. First, we need to define a feeder class that implements the IF_FPM_GUIBB_FORM interface as described in Section 6.2.1.

2. Next, we need to create a component configuration for the FPM_FORM_UIBB_GL2 component.

3. Finally, we need to configure the form GL2 component by laying out the form elements and assigning any custom actions, etc.

In the upcoming sections, we'll step through each of these tasks in turn.

Creating a Form Feeder Class

To create the form feeder class, we simply create a brand new ABAP Objects class (we called ours ZCL_USER_INFO_FORM) and have it implement the IF_FPM_GUIBB_FORM interface as shown in Figure 6.34. After the class is initially saved, it's a good idea to go into each of the inherited methods and activate them – even though there's no implementation yet. Otherwise, you may experience short dumps whenever the callback methods get invoked at runtime.

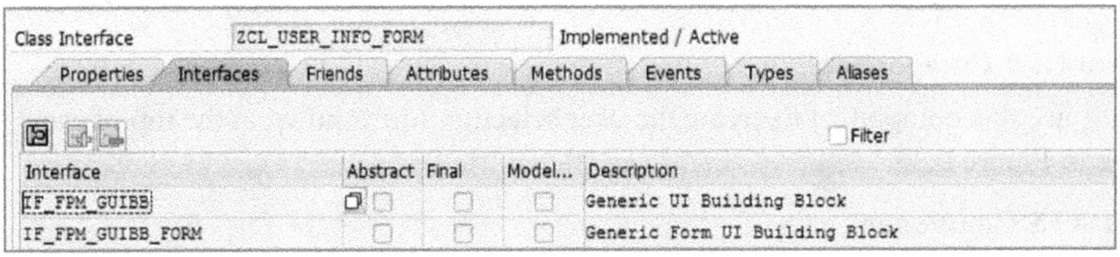

Class Interface	ZCL_USER_INFO_FORM			Implemented / Active			
Properties	Interfaces	Friends	Attributes	Methods	Events	Types	Aliases

Interface	Abstract	Final	Model...	Description
IF_FPM_GUIBB	☑☐	☐	☐	Generic UI Building Block
IF_FPM_GUIBB_FORM	☐	☐	☐	Generic Form UI Building Block

Figure 6.34: Implementing the IF_FPM_GUIBB_FORM Interface © Copyright 2013. SAP AG. All rights reserved

Once the feeder class is defined, the next step is to define a structure that will be used to encapsulate the data represented on the form. As you can see in Figure 6.35, we've defined an instance attribute called MS_USER_INFO for this purpose. This attribute is defined in terms of a local structure type which contains fields to represent the user's ID and first/last names.

Class Interface	ZCL_USER_INFO_FORM			Implemented / Active					
Properties	Interfaces	Friends	Attributes	Methods	Events	Types	Aliases		

Attribute	Level	Visibility	Read-Only	Typing	Associated Type		Description	Initial value
<IF_FPM_GUIBB>			☐					
MS_PARAMETER_RENDER	Instance .. Public		☐	Type	FPM_COMPONENT_KEY	⇨	Component key for pa...	
MS_USER_INFO	Instance .. Private		☐	Type	TY_USER_INFO	⇨		
CO_SELECT_USER_EVENT	Constant Public		☐	Type	FPM_EVENT_ID	⇨	ID of the FPM Event	'SELECT_USER'
CO_USER_SELECTED_EVENT	Constant Public		☐	Type	FPM_EVENT_ID	⇨	ID of the FPM Event	'USER_SELECTED'

Figure 6.35: Defining Instance Attributes for the Feeder Class © Copyright 2013. SAP AG. All rights reserved

With the basic infrastructure elements defined, we can proceed with the implementation of the GET_DEFINITION() method which is used to define the form UIBB's field catalog. Listing 6.1 provides a sample implementation for this method. Here, notice how we're using the DESCRIBE_BY_DATA() method of class CL_ABAP_STRUCTDESCR is being used to dynamically define the form UIBB's field catalog. Aside from that, the only other thing going on is the definition of a custom action which will be used to respond to user selection events on the user form.

```
method IF_FPM_GUIBB_FORM~GET_DEFINITION.
  FIELD-SYMBOLS <ls_field>  LIKE LINE OF et_field_description.
  FIELD-SYMBOLS <ls_action> LIKE LINE OF et_action_definition.

  "Build the field catalog for the user info form:
  eo_field_catalog ?=
    cl_abap_structdescr=>describe_by_data( me->ms_user_info ).

  "Customize the field descriptions:
  APPEND INITIAL LINE TO et_field_description
            ASSIGNING <ls_field>.
  <ls_field>-name       = 'USERNAME'.
  <ls_field>-ddic_shlp_name = 'USER_COMP'.

  "Define custom actions used within the form:
  APPEND INITIAL LINE TO et_action_definition
            ASSIGNING <ls_action>.
  <ls_action>-id      = co_select_user_event.
  <ls_action>-enabled = abap_true.
  <ls_action>-text    = 'Select User'.
endmethod.
```

Listing 6.1: Implementing the GET_DEFINITION() Method

Since this form is being used primarily as a selection form, we don't have to work too hard to load the data from the backend data model. As you can see in Listing 6.2, we're synchronizing data selection around a custom user selection event. Here, we're using BAPI_USER_GET_DETAIL to load the user data into context so that the first/last name for the selected user will show up on the screen.

```
method IF_FPM_GUIBB_FORM~GET_DATA.
  DATA ls_address TYPE bapiaddr3.
  DATA lt_return  TYPE STANDARD TABLE OF bapiret2.

  "Update the local form cache as needed:
  CASE io_event->mv_event_id.
    WHEN zcl_user_info_form=>co_select_user_event.
      "Cache the user information locally:
      me->ms_user_info = cs_data.

      CALL FUNCTION 'BAPI_USER_GET_DETAIL'
        EXPORTING
          username = me->ms_user_info-username
        IMPORTING
          address  = ls_address
        TABLES
          return   = lt_return.

      MOVE-CORRESPONDING ls_address TO me->ms_user_info.
      cs_data = me->ms_user_info.
      ev_data_changed = abap_true.

      "Broadcast the user selection event to other UIBBs:
      raise_user_selection( ).
    WHEN if_fpm_constants=>gc_event-cancel.
      CLEAR: cs_data, me->ms_user_info.
      ev_data_changed = abap_true.
  ENDCASE.
endmethod.
```

Listing 6.2: Implementing the GET_DATA() Method

The other major task taking place in the GET_DATA() method is the call to a helper method called RAISE_USER_SELECTION(). This method is being used to broadcast a user selection event to other interested UIBBs (i.e. the role maintenance list UIBB in this example). Listing 6.3 shows how this method is implemented. If you recall our discussion on event processing in Chapter 5, this should be pretty straightforward. Indeed, about the only thing special that we're doing is plugging in the selected user name as an event parameter so that it can be picked up by other UIBBs. This is a crude form of inter-UIBB communication; we'll look at ways of improving on this design in Chapters 7 and 8.

```
method RAISE_USER_SELECTION.
  DATA lo_fpm   TYPE REF TO if_fpm.
  DATA lo_event TYPE REF TO cl_fpm_event.

  "Raise an event so that subordinate UIBBs can be aware of the
  "user selection:
  CREATE OBJECT lo_event
    EXPORTING
      iv_event_id = co_user_selected_event.

  lo_event->mo_event_data->set_value(
    iv_key   = 'USER_ID'
    iv_value = me->ms_user_info-username ).

  lo_fpm = cl_fpm_factory=>get_instance( ).
  lo_fpm->raise_event( lo_event ).
endmethod.
```

Listing 6.3: Implementing the RAISE_USER_SELECTION() Method

With these three methods defined, we're ready to move on to the form component configuration step.

Configuring the Form GL2 Component

To configure the form GL2 component, we must create a new component configuration. During the creation process, we're prompted to plug in a feeder class as shown in Figure 6.36. Since we didn't define any custom parameters, we can simply click past the EDIT PARAMETERS button to get to the main configuration screen.

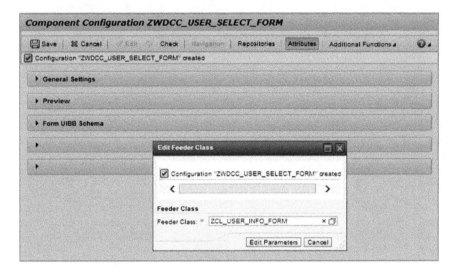

Figure 6.36: Configuring the Form GL2 Component © Copyright 2013. SAP AG. All rights reserved

On the main editor screen, we can configure the form layout as shown in Figure 6.37. Here, we can choose from the form fields defined in the field catalog returned by the GET_DEFINITION() method illustrated in Listing 6.1.

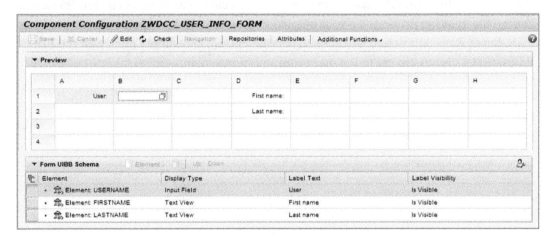

Figure 6.37: Laying out the Form Elements © Copyright 2013. SAP AG. All rights reserved

The last thing we need to do in the configuration process is assign an FPM event ID to the USER input field. As you can see in Figure 6.38, we're using the SELECT_USER event defined in the GET_DEFINITION() method of the feeder class (refer back to Listing 6.1).

At runtime, users can trigger this event by entering a user ID in the USER field and hitting the Enter key. With this step complete, we can save our changes and move on to the list component definition.

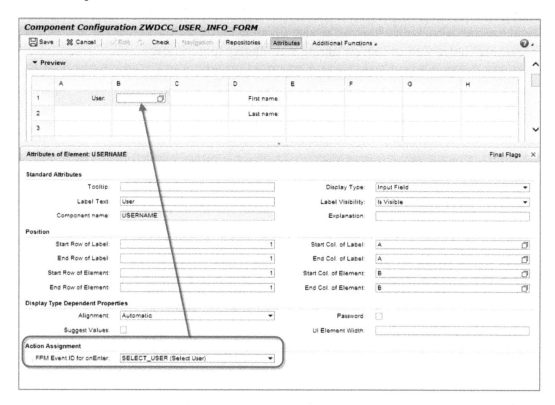

Figure 6.38: Assigning an Action to the User Input Field © Copyright 2013. SAP AG. All rights reserved

6.3.3 Defining the Role Maintenance List

To a large degree, the process for defining the role maintenance list is quite similar to the one used to define the user selection form. Basically, we define a new feeder class, create a component configuration for the FPM_LIST_UIBB_ATS component, and then fill in all the details.

Creating the List Feeder Class

To create the list feeder class, we simply create a new ABAP Objects class and implement the IF_FPM_GUIBB_LIST interface. Once again, we'll want to go in and activate all of the inherited methods so that we won't run into short dumps at runtime.

Implementation-wise, the list feeder class is slightly more complicated that the form feeder class demonstrated in Section 6.3.2. Listing 6.4 shows how we're implementing the GET_DEFINITION() method. As you can see, we're using the CL_ABAP_STRUCTDESCR and CL_ABAP_TABLEDESCR classes from the ABAP RTTI API to define the list UIBB's field catalog. Also, notice how we're also filling in the ET_FIELD_DESCRIPTION parameter so that we can turn on sorting and filtering (e.g. via the ALLOW_SORT and ALLOW_FILTER attributes, respectively). Finally, we're also adding in two custom events which will be used as the basis for building the ADD and REMOVE buttons on the list toolbar.

```
method IF_FPM_GUIBB_LIST~GET_DEFINITION.
  DATA lo_line_type_desc TYPE REF TO cl_abap_structdescr.
  DATA lt_components TYPE cl_abap_structdescr=>component_table.

  FIELD-SYMBOLS <ls_component> LIKE LINE OF lt_components.
  FIELD-SYMBOLS <ls_field>     LIKE LINE OF et_field_description.
  FIELD-SYMBOLS <ls_action>    LIKE LINE OF et_action_definition.

  "Use the ABAP RTTI API to construct the field catalog:
  lo_line_type_desc ?=
    cl_abap_structdescr=>describe_by_name( 'BAPIAGR' ).
  lt_components = lo_line_type_desc->get_components( ).

  eo_field_catalog =
    cl_abap_tabledescr=>create(
      p_line_type = lo_line_type_desc ).

  "Turn on sorting and filtering on the columns:
  LOOP AT lt_components ASSIGNING <ls_component>.
    APPEND INITIAL LINE TO et_field_description
                ASSIGNING <ls_field>.
    <ls_field>-name        = <ls_component>-name.
    <ls_field>-allow_sort  = abap_true.
    <ls_field>-allow_filter = abap_true.
  ENDLOOP.

  "Define the custom actions used for list maintenance:
  APPEND INITIAL LINE TO et_action_definition
              ASSIGNING <ls_action>.
  <ls_action>-id      = co_add_role_event.
  <ls_action>-enabled = abap_true.
  <ls_action>-text    = 'Add Role'.

  APPEND INITIAL LINE TO et_action_definition
              ASSIGNING <ls_action>.
  <ls_action>-id      = co_remove_role_event.
```

```
  <ls_action>-enabled = abap_true.
  <ls_action>-text    = 'Remove Role'.
endmethod.
```

Listing 6.4: Implementing the GET_DEFINITION() Method

Since the contents of the role list is determined by the user selected in the user selection form, we need to use the PROCESS_EVENT() method to synchronize the contents of the list UIBB at runtime. Listing 6.5 shows how we've implemented this method for our sample application. Here, we're using a CASE statement to handle the following event types:

➢ **User Selected Event**

Whenever this event is triggered, we retrieve the selected user from the FPM event parameters and call BAPI_USER_GET_DETAIL to load the user's role assignments. These role assignments are cached in an instance attribute called MT_USER_ROLES which is based on the BAPIAGR structure type.

➢ **Role Removal Event**

Whenever the user attempts to remove a role using the REMOVE ROLE button (see Figure 6.33), we need to perform a check to make sure that the selected index (provided via the IV_LEAD_INDEX parameter) is within a valid range.

➢ **Application Save Event**

This event is triggered whenever the user clicks on the SAVE button in the top-level toolbar of the OVP floorplan. Here, we take the cached role assignments table (MT_USER_ROLES) and pass it into BAPI_USER_ACTGROUPS_ASSIGN, which performs an overlay of user role assignments.

```
method IF_FPM_GUIBB_LIST~PROCESS_EVENT.
  DATA lt_return TYPE STANDARD TABLE OF bapiret2.
  FIELD-SYMBOLS <ls_message> LIKE LINE OF et_messages.

  "Process based upon the selected event type:
  CASE io_event->mv_event_id.
    WHEN zcl_user_info_form=>co_user_selected_event.
      "Retrieve the selected user ID:
      io_event->mo_event_data->get_value(
        EXPORTING iv_key   = 'USER_ID'
        IMPORTING ev_value = me->mv_user_id ).

      "Lookup the selected user's role assignments:
      REFRESH me->mt_user_roles.
```

```
          CALL FUNCTION 'BAPI_USER_GET_DETAIL'
            EXPORTING
              username      = me->mv_user_id
            TABLES
              activitygroups = me->mt_user_roles
              return        = lt_return.

          "Error handling...
        WHEN 'REMOVE_ROLE'.
          "Make sure the user has made a valid selection:
          IF iv_lead_index IS INITIAL OR
             iv_lead_index GT lines( me->mt_user_roles ).
            APPEND INITIAL LINE TO et_messages
                        ASSIGNING <ls_message>.
            <ls_message>-plaintext =
              `You must select a role record first!`.

            ev_result = if_fpm_constants=>gc_event_result-failed.
            RETURN.
          ENDIF.
        WHEN if_fpm_constants=>gc_event-save.
          "Save the changes to the user-role assignments.
          CALL FUNCTION 'BAPI_USER_ACTGROUPS_ASSIGN'
            EXPORTING
              username      = me->mv_user_id
            TABLES
              activitygroups = me->mt_user_roles
              return        = lt_return.

          "Error handling...
      ENDCASE.

    ev_result = if_fpm_constants=>gc_event_result-ok.
  endmethod.
```

Listing 6.5: Implementing the PROCESS_EVENT() Method

In Listing 6.5, you can see how we're using the PROCESS_EVENT() method to load role assignment data from the backend data model into an instance attribute. To then propagate that data over to the UI, we must provide an implementation for the GET_DATA() method. Listing 6.6 illustrates how we're implementing this method in our sample application. As you can see, we're once again using the selected FPM event ID to determine when and where to synchronize the data. For example, notice how we're initially loading the CT_DATA parameter whenever a user selection event occurs. Once this data is loaded, we must keep track of the changes made on the frontend. Here, users can add/remove role assignments and/or edit existing ones.

```
method IF_FPM_GUIBB_LIST~GET_DATA.
  DATA lr_data TYPE REF TO data.
  DATA ls_role LIKE LINE OF me->mt_user_roles.

  FIELD-SYMBOLS <lt_data>     TYPE table.
  FIELD-SYMBOLS <ls_data>     LIKE LINE OF me->mt_user_roles.
  FIELD-SYMBOLS <ls_role>     LIKE LINE OF me->mt_user_roles.
  FIELD-SYMBOLS <ls_field>    LIKE LINE OF ct_field_usage.
  FIELD-SYMBOLS <ls_action>   LIKE LINE OF ct_action_usage.
  FIELD-SYMBOLS <ls_message>  LIKE LINE OF et_messages.

  TRY.
    "Initialization - track any changes applied to the dataset:
    me->mo_editor->start_recording( ct_data ).
    GET REFERENCE OF ct_data INTO lr_data.
    ASSIGN lr_data->* TO <lt_data>.

    "Apply updates to the role data as needed:
    CASE iv_eventid->mv_event_id.
      WHEN zcl_user_info_form=>co_user_selected_event.
        "Load the table for the first time:
        APPEND LINES OF me->mt_user_roles TO <lt_data>.
        ev_data_changed = abap_true.
      WHEN co_add_role_event.
        "Add a new blank line to the table:
        ls_role-from_dat = sy-datum.
        ls_role-to_dat = '99991231'.

        APPEND ls_role TO <lt_data>.
        APPEND ls_role TO me->mt_user_roles.

        ev_data_changed = abap_true.
      WHEN co_remove_role_event.
        "Remove the selected role from the table:
        IF cv_lead_index GT 0 AND
           cv_lead_index LE lines( <lt_data> ).
          DELETE <lt_data> INDEX cv_lead_index.
          DELETE me->mt_user_roles INDEX cv_lead_index.

          ev_data_changed = abap_true.
        ENDIF.
      WHEN if_fpm_constants=>gc_event-cancel.
        REFRESH: <lt_data>, me->mt_user_roles.
        ev_data_changed = abap_true.
      WHEN if_fpm_guibb_list=>gc_guibb_list_on_cell_action.
        "Update a role record (text) as needed:
        update_role_record(
          EXPORTING
```

```
          io_evt_params = iv_eventid->mo_event_data
        CHANGING
          cv_data_changed = ev_data_changed
          ct_data = <lt_data> ).
      WHEN OTHERS.
        "Sync up changes made in the UI - as necessary:
      IF iv_raised_by_own_ui EQ abap_true.
        "Look for key changes:
        LOOP AT <lt_data> ASSIGNING <ls_data>.
          READ TABLE me->mt_user_roles INDEX sy-tabix
           ASSIGNING <ls_role>.
          IF <ls_role>-agr_name NE <ls_data>-agr_name.
            me->mo_editor->key_changed(
              line_before = <ls_role>
              line_after  = <ls_data> ).

            <ls_role>-agr_name = <ls_data>-agr_name.
          ENDIF.
        ENDLOOP.
      ENDIF.
    ENDCASE.

    "Record the updates in the change log - as necesary:
    me->mo_editor->stop_recording( ).
    IF ev_data_changed EQ abap_true.
      eo_itab_change_log = me->mo_editor.
    ELSE.
      CLEAR eo_itab_change_log.
    ENDIF.
  CATCH cx_root.
  ENDTRY.
endmethod.
```

Listing 6.6: Implementing the GET_DATA() Method

Since we're allowing sorting and filtering on the role assignment data, we need to keep track of the changes made in the GET_DATA() method using the EO_ITAB_CHANGE_LOG parameter. As you can see in Listing 6.6, this basically requires that we create an object reference of type IF_SALV_ITAB_CHANGE_LOG and use its START_RECORDING() and STOP_RECORDING() methods to track any changes made during the course of the GET_DATA() method. More details on how this works can be found in the *FPM Developer's Guide*. You can also find a more complete implementation of this feeder class in the book's source code bundle.

Configuring the List ATS Component

The configuration of the list ATS component in this instance is quite straightforward. Here, we simply create the component configuration, plug in our feeder class, and define the table columns as shown in Figure 6.39. As a finishing touch, we then need to add in the ADD ROLE and REMOVE ROLE buttons on the list component toolbar.

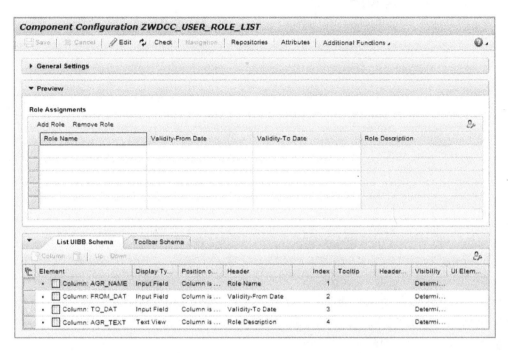

Figure 6.39: Configuring the List ATS Component © Copyright 2013. SAP AG. All rights reserved

6.3.4 Finishing Touches

Once we've configured our form and list UIBBs, we're ready to put the finishing touches on our sample application. First, we need to create a component configuration for the FPM_TABBED_UIBB component. As shown in Figure 6.40, we've placed the user selection form in the master area and the role maintenance list in the tab area.

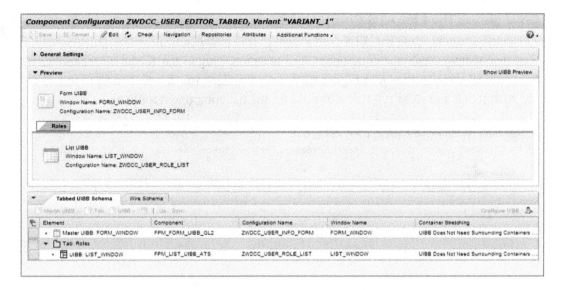

Figure 6.40: Configuring the Tabbed Component © Copyright 2013. SAP AG. All rights reserved

Then, we need to embed the tabbed component into the OVP floorplan configuration as shown in Figure 6.41. Once we save our changes, we're ready to fire up our application and start editing user master records. When you think about what might have been involved if you were to try and create a similar application from scratch using freestyle UIBBs, it becomes pretty obvious that GUIBBs offer a highly productive alternative for filling in the content areas of FPM applications.

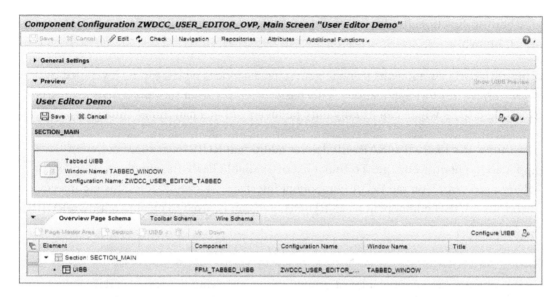

Figure 6.41: Configuring the OVP Floorplan Component © Copyright 2013. SAP AG.
All rights reserved

6.4 Reuse UIBBs (RUIBBs)

Before we wrap up our discussion in this chapter, we would be remiss if we didn't
highlight a new class of UIBBs that have cropped up with the SAP NetWeaver 7.03
release: *Reuse UIBBs* (RUIBBs). Unlike GUIBBs which simply provide a template for
implementing a particular UI pattern, RUIBBs are positioned as finished products which
can pretty much be used as-is. This is to say that RUIBBs not only provide a UI, but also
the corresponding business logic needed to define a complete and reusable component.

At the time of this writing, there are two standard RUIBB components provided by SAP:

➢ **Attachment Component**

This component renders a table control in which users can add, edit, remove, or
display attachments (or links to attachments). It's implemented by the
FPM_ATTACHMENT_WRAPPER WDA component which provides built-in functionality
for saving attachments using the *Knowledge Provider* (KPro) or *Enterprise Content
Management* (ECM) frameworks.

➢ **Notes Component**

This component renders a table control which users can use to maintain long text
notes (similar to the ones created in the SAP GUI using SAPscript). It's
implemented by the FPM_NOTES_WRAPPER WDA component which also provides

built-in functionality for interfacing with the aforementioned KPro and ECM frameworks.

These RUIBBs components provide generalized services which can be leveraged by a wide variety of FPM applications. This basic criteria is what sets an RUIBB apart from freestyle UIBBs which can usually only be leveraged in a handful of situations.

Over time, it's likely that SAP will deliver additional RUIBBs as more common application patterns emerge. To find a list of available RUIBBs, simply perform a where-used search on the WDA component interface `IF_FPM_RUIBB`. This tag interface identifies a UIBB component as an RUIBB, and can be used to create your own RUIBBs as desired.

6.5   Summary

In this chapter, we covered a lot of ground while surveying the various GUIBB components provided by the FPM framework. Hopefully the demonstration provided in Section 6.3 showed you the power of GUIBBs as it relates to the development of FPM applications. As you start to get more hands on with FPM application development, you'll likely find yourself working quite a bit with the various GUIBB types.

In the next chapter, we'll look at another feature of the FPM framework that can make it even easier to rapidly develop UI content using GUIBBs: the *wire model*.

Chapter 7

Working with the Wire Model

In Chapter 6, we observed how GUIBBs make it easy to rapidly create UI content based on various template components (e.g. the form component, the list component, and so on). For the most part, we can rely on these components to take care of rendering the UI, allowing us to focus our attention on getting the business logic right behind the scenes. For ABAP developers who live and breathe server-side application development, this sort of feeder class development is right in their wheelhouse. In practice though, the actual implementation details can be quite tedious.

Since frameworks like the FPM are designed to reduce the slack in day-to-day development tasks, it's not surprising to learn that the FPM framework also provides a mechanism for integrating application models using declarative techniques. This abstraction is known as the *wire model*. In this chapter, we'll explore the concepts surrounding the wire model and see how it can be used to create FPM applications almost exclusively through configuration.

7.1   Getting Started

In many ways, the wire model represents a natural extension of the floorplan concepts described in introductory part of this book. Indeed, if we think back to the building metaphor introduced in Chapter 1, we can envision wires as a means of connecting various rooms/compartments together - not unlike the Ethernet cables that run through the walls of corporate offices. In an FPM application context, wires connect UIBBs together by providing a conduit for data exchange. In the upcoming sections, we'll unpack all this and see how the wire model works from both a conceptual and technical point of view.

7.1.1 What is the Wire Model Used For?

Before we begin digging into the wire model and it's surrounding APIs, we first need to understand its positioning in the FPM application hierarchy. Earlier, we noted that the goal of the wire model is to make it possible to integrate with backend application models through configuration as opposed to manual ABAP development. This capability naturally speeds up the development process since we can define and configure applications almost exclusively via WYSIWYG tools like FLUID.

Of course, all this doesn't happen by magic. Obviously, there has to be ABAP code somewhere along the way to make this work. The difference with the wire model approach is that the majority of the application integration logic is factored into separate and reusable classes which encapsulate the model dependency semantics centrally. We'll take a closer look at the nature of these classes in Section 7.1.3, but for now, the major take-away from all this is that these reusable classes abstract away a lot of the tedious model integration code that normally goes into custom feeder classes. Indeed, in many cases, we can leverage these classes right out-of-the-box to meet basic UIBB requirements.

In order for such seamless integration to work, the backend object model must have a rather generic access interface. After all, we can't expect the framework to automatically integrate with just any old application model; there has to be some kind of common interface to work with. By default, SAP provides support for a couple of standard object models: the *Business Object Layer* (BOL) and the more recent *Business Object Processing Framework* (BOPF). As developers, we also have the option of building our own wire models - we just have to create the necessary wire model classes to support the integration.

7.1.2 How does Wiring Work?

So far, we've talked about wiring and the wire model in fairly abstract terms. Now, let's shift gears a bit and take a look at how wiring works from a conceptual point of view. Here, our goal is to paint a picture so that you can have a frame of reference to draw upon as we approach more advanced concepts in later sections.

As we mentioned earlier, wires provide a conduit for data to be exchanged between two UIBBs. The data flow occurs in one direction: from a source UIBB to a target UIBB. For the most part, the FPM framework doesn't place any restrictions on the type of data that gets transmitted over the wire[21]. Regardless of how the data is packaged, it's ultimately funneled through one of the source UIBB's *outports*. Here, a given source UIBB can define several different types of outports:

➢ **Lead Selection (LS)**

This type of outport can be used to transmit changes to the lead selection element in a collection of elements. For example, we might use this outport in a list UIBB to let an interested form UIBB know of a change in row selection. This scenario often comes into play when building applications to edit multi-tiered business objects such as sales orders. Here, we might use a list UIBB to display sales order line items and a form UIBB to edit the selected line item. As you can see in Figure 7.1, the lead selection outport allows the list UIBB to forward the lead selection element to the form UIBB so that it can respond to the selection and refresh itself accordingly.

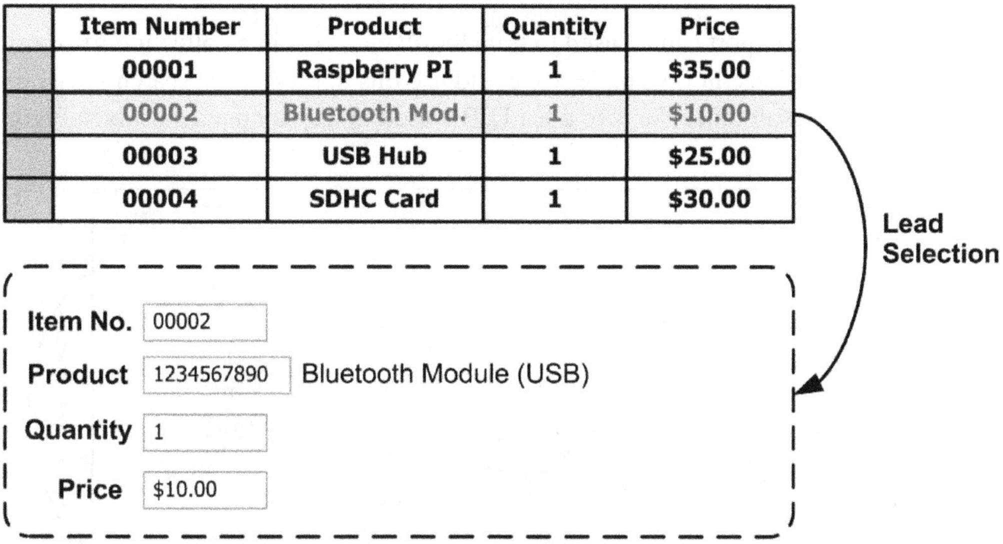

	Item Number	Product	Quantity	Price
	00001	Raspberry PI	1	$35.00
	00002	Bluetooth Mod.	1	$10.00
	00003	USB Hub	1	$25.00
	00004	SDHC Card	1	$30.00

Lead Selection

Item No. 00002

Product 1234567890   Bluetooth Module (USB)

Quantity 1

Price $10.00

Figure 7.1: Example Scenario Using the Lead Selection Outport

➢ **Selection (SE)**

This type of outport can be used in multi-selection scenarios where we need to pass multiple selected elements to a downstream UIBB. This port type can be useful in situations where we need implement a "browse-and-collect" UI pattern like the one provided with the `shuttle` UI element defined by the WDA framework. Figure 7.2 depicts this scenario for an FPM application used to edit user master records. Here,

---

[21] For performance reasons though, most implementations prefer to pass the relevant object keys as opposed to the objects themselves.

you can see how selected role records from the source UIBB are being collected into the target UIBB.

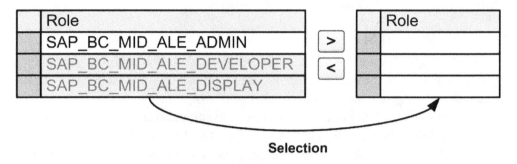

Selection

Figure 7.2: Example Scenario Using the Selection Outport

> **Collection (CO)**

This type of outport can be used to transfer *all* elements in a collection irrespective of user selections. For example, we could use this port type in a search UIBB to pass the search result object keys to a list UIBB used to display the results (see Figure 7.3).

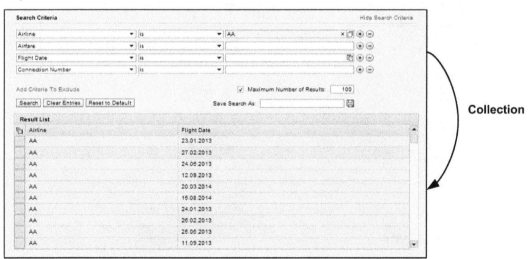

Collection

Figure 7.3: Example Scenario Using the Collection Outport © *Copyright 2013. SAP AG. All rights reserved*

We can also use the collection port type to model parent-child relationships between business object nodes. For instance, in the aforementioned sales order application example, we might use a form UIBB to edit header-level data and a list UIBB to edit sales order line items. In this scenario, we would use the collection outport on the form UIBB to pass the selected sales order record down to the list UIBB so that it's able to load the corresponding line items. Depending on how nested the business object in question is, we can recursively apply this approach to lower-level nodes such that the relevant UIBBs are effectively daisy chained together.

Once we determine how we want to link a pair of UIBBs together, the wiring configuration itself is pretty straightforward. Here, we simply open up an FPM application's floorplan configuration in FLUID and navigate to the WIRE SCHEMA tab (see Figure 7.4). From here, we can create new wire connections by clicking on the WIRE button in the toolbar directly above the wire connections.

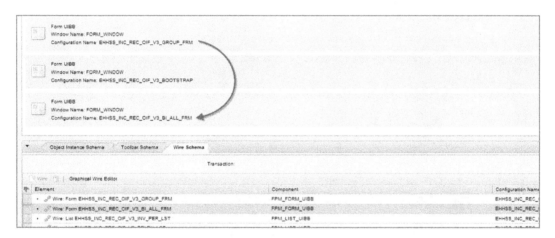

Figure 7.4: Wire Configuration in the FPM Configuration Editor - Part 1 © Copyright *2013. SAP AG. All rights reserved*

In order to complete a wire connection definition, there are a number of attributes that we need to specify (see Figure 7.5 below):

➤ **Source Component/Configuration**

These attributes specify the source UIBB along with its corresponding configuration (assuming it has one). In Section 7.1.3, we'll look at the requirements for a UIBB to be cast in this role.

➤ **Target Component/Configuration**

These attributes specify the receiver UIBB that will be the recipient of the wire data. In Section 7.1.3, we'll look at the requirements for a UIBB to be cast in this role.

➢ **Port Type/Port Identifier**

With this attribute, we can choose from a list of available outports provided by the source UIBB. Within the configuration, an outport is uniquely identified by its *type* (e.g. collection, lead selection, or selection) and an arbitrary identifier assigned by the source UIBB.

➢ **Connector Class**

At runtime, the connector class acts as an intermediary between the source and target UIBBs, facilitating data transfer. We'll learn more about connector classes in Section 7.1.3.

➢ **Connector Parameters**

In some cases, connector classes may define parameters which are used to parameterize the connector behavior at runtime.

Attributes of Wire: Form EHHSS_INC_REC_OIF_V3_BI_ALL_FRM			
Standard Attributes			
Component: *	FPM_FORM_UIBB	Srce Inst. ID:	
Configuration Name:	EHHSS_INC_REC_OIF_V3_BI_ALL_FRM	Port Type:	Collection
Instance ID:		Port Identifier:	CO
Source Component:	FPM_FORM_UIBB	Connector Class: *	CL_EHFND_FBI_CONNECTOR
Source Config Name:	EHHSS_INC_REC_OIF_V3_GROUP_FRM		
Connector Parameters			
SRC_NODE_ASSOC:	BASIC_INFO_ALL		

Figure 7.5: Wire Configuration in the FPM Configuration Editor - Part 2 © Copyright 2013. SAP AG. All rights reserved

Collectively, these attributes provide the FPM framework with the information it needs to wire a pair of UIBBs together at runtime. Of course, in order for this wiring to have any effect, there must be some foundation-level code in place to process the data behind the scenes. With that in mind, let's turn our attention to the nitty-gritty details of the wire model and look at its underlying API.

7.1.3 Understanding the Wire Model API

In order for UIBB components to be a part of the wire model, they must implement the IF_FPM_MODEL WDA component interface. This component interface defines a single method called GET_MODEL_API() which passes the FPM framework an object reference of type IF_FPM_FEEDER_MODEL. At runtime, the FPM framework can use this object reference to facilitate the data exchange.

The IF_FPM_FEEDER_MODEL Interface

From the FPM framework's point of view, the provided feeder model reference could be coming from a freestyle UIBB component or a GUIBB component; it doesn't care one way or the other. The only real difference between approaches lies in where the feeder model interface is implemented. With GUIBBs, the feeder model interface is implemented by the associated feeder class. With freestyle UIBBs, the implementation has to come from a separate ABAP Objects class (e.g. the assistance class). For the purposes of this book, our focus will be more on the GUIBB-based approach as this is the most common scenario you'll see in practice.

Table 7.1 describes the methods defined by the IF_FPM_FEEDER_MODEL interface. These callback methods are used by the FPM framework both at design time and at runtime to establish wire linkages.

Method	Description
get_namespace()	This design time method returns the namespace of the model implementation being utilized by the UIBB. For example, the wire model implementation based on the BOL uses the namespace BOL.
	Since the wire model API is necessarily generic, namespaces help the FPM framework to identify compatible wire model artifacts (i.e. feeder model classes and connector classes) at design time. Here, the FPM framework can assume that classes within the same namespace will handle data/object references consistently. This knowledge makes it possible for the FPM Configuration Editor tool to provide us with input helps and configuration checks during the wire configuration process.
get_outports()	This method is called at design time by the FPM Configuration Editor. Among other things, it provides a value help which allows us to choose from the available outports exposed by a given source UIBB.
get_inport_key()	In some respects, this method is the analog of the GET_OUTPORTS() method in that it identifies the *inport* of a target UIBB at design time. Specifically, it returns a reference to an object key that characterizes the metadata type expected to be received at runtime.

Method	Description
set_connector()	This method is invoked by the FPM framework at runtime whenever a UIBB is instantiated. The provided connector reference (of type IF_FPM_CONNECTOR_RUN) can be cached within the implementing feeder class and then used later on to retrieve data at the appropriate time (i.e. in the GET_DATA() method, for instance).
get_outport_data()	This method is invoked by the FPM framework at runtime during the data transfer process. Here, the source UIBB returns an object reference containing the data linked to a given outport. This data is then copied into the connector class instance so that it can be subsequently retrieved by the target UIBB.

Table 7.1: Methods of the IF_FPM_FEEDER_MODEL Interface

If the underlying object model has a generic access interface, we can oftentimes get away with defining a default implementation for the IF_FPM_FEEDER_MODEL interface in a base class that can be used as the foundation for creating new feeder classes based on a given object model. Here, the subclass can focus on FPM-related development concerns, delegating model integration concerns to the superclass. We'll see an example of this in Section 7.3 when we take a look at some of the standard feeder classes provided by the *FPM BOPF Integration* (FBI) framework.

The IF_FPM_CONNECTOR Interface

The UML class diagram contained in Figure 7.6 illustrates the roles played by the IF_FPM_FEEDER_MODEL interface in a particular wire configuration scenario. Here, we can see that there are three wire model classes involved in a given wire exchange: the wire model implementations for the source/target UIBBs and the *connector class* which effectively glues them together.

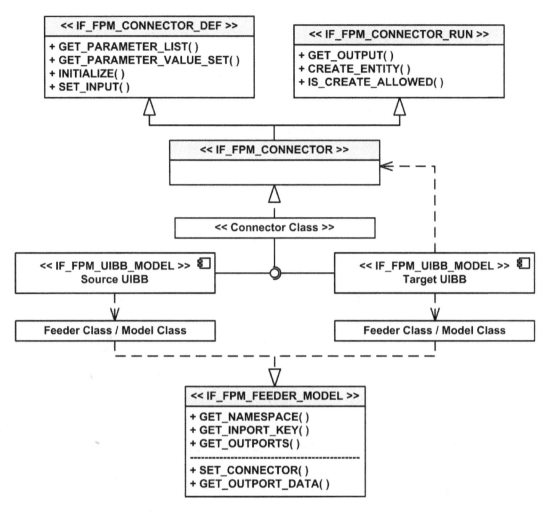

Figure 7.6: UML Class Diagram Depicting Wire Model API

As you can see in Figure 7.6, connector classes within the wire model implement the IF_FPM_CONNECTOR interface which, in turn, inherits from the IF_FPM_CONNECTOR_DEF and IF_FPM_CONNECTOR_RUN interfaces, respectively. Collectively, the methods defined by the IF_FPM_CONNECTOR interface allow the FPM framework to meet a pair of UIBBs in the middle, facilitating data exchange on both sides.

Table 7.2 describes each of the methods provided by the IF_FPM_CONNECTOR interface in more detail. Normally, these methods need only be implemented one time by a given wire model implementation. Indeed, all of the standard wire model implementations provided by SAP have a base connector class which can generally be used out-of-the-box without any customizations.

Method	Description
`get_parameter_list()`	In order to maximize flexibility, connector classes can be *parameterized*. As the name suggests, this method allows us to build a parameter list which is used by the FPM Configuration Editor to dynamically build the CONNECTOR PARAMETERS section shown at the bottom of Figure 7.4.
	Each parameter in the list is defined by its name, data type, and an optional descriptive text. What parameters we choose to define here is really up to us. The intent is to collect any and all needed configuration metadata at design time so that the connector class can function autonomously at runtime.
`get_parameter_value_set()`	This design time method supplements the `GET_PARMAETER_LIST()` method by allowing us to define input helps for the custom parameters that we define. The resultant value sets will then be used to assist users in the wire configuration process within the FPM Configuration Editor tool.
`initialize()`	This method is invoked by the FPM framework at runtime during the connector creation process. It is passed two parameters:
	❖ `IT_PARAMETER_VALUE` This table parameter contains the list of parameter values used to configure the wire connection at design time. The parameter types correspond with the parameters defined by the `GET_PARAMETER_LIST()` method.
	❖ `IV_PORT_TYPE` This parameter tells the connector class which port type is being used in the wire connection (e.g. `LS`, `SE`, or `CO`).

Method	Description
set_input()	This method is invoked by the FPM framework at runtime whenever data is transferred between a pair of UIBBs. Here, data from the source UIBB's outport is copied into the connector class instance so that it can be subsequently retrieved by the target UIBB.
get_output()	This method is the analog of the SET_INPUT() method, allowing the target UIBB to pick up data that was passed into the connector instance by the FPM framework.
is_create_allowed()	In some cases, the data represented on the receiver end of a wire connection may not exist at runtime. For example, imagine an FPM application used to edit purchase orders. Here, suppose we have a wire connection from a form UIBB used to represent the header-level data down to a list UIBB used to represent the item-level data (e.g. using the collection (CO) port type). During the PO creation process, whenever this wire connection is fired, the PO item data will not exist. In this case, the target UIBB must decide whether or not to create the PO line items on the fly. However, depending on the nature of the underlying application model, we may or may not want this to happen automatically. This is where the IS_CREATE_ALLOWED() method comes into play. Basically, the IS_CREATE_ALLOWED() method returns a Boolean indicating whether or not entity creation is supported by the wire model implementation. Target UIBBs can use this method to control their behavior accordingly.
create_entity()	Assuming entity creation is allowed, this method allows a given target UIBB to request the creation of an entity at runtime (e.g. in response to an FPM event). This is another example of how the wire model abstracts the interface to the underlying application model.

Table 7.2: Methods of the IF_FPM_CONNECTOR Interface

7.1.4 Putting it All Together

Having seen how the wire model API is organized in the previous section, let's now take a look at how these entities are used to facilitate data exchange between a pair of UIBBs at runtime. This data flow is depicted in the UML sequence diagram contained in Figure 7.7.

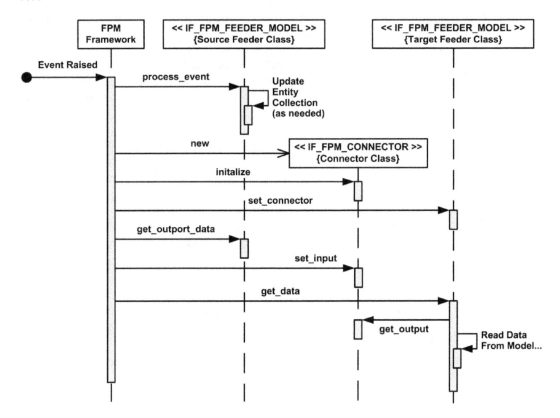

Figure 7.7: UML Sequence Diagram Depicting Data Exchange in the Wire Model

As you can see in Figure 7.7, the data exchange process is driven almost exclusively through the FPM framework during the FPM event loop. Internally, the FPM framework keeps tabs of the UIBBs in context and determines when/where a wire connection should be established. Whenever it determines that a connection is needed, the basic call flow proceeds as follows:

1. First, the FPM framework creates an instance of the appropriate connector class.

2. Shortly after the connector class is instantiated, the FPM framework follows up with a call to the INITIALIZE() method so that the connector instance can initialize itself as needed.

3. Once the connector is initialized, its object reference is passed to the target UIBB via the SET_CONNECTOR() method of the IF_FPM_FEEDER_MODEL interface (where it is cached internally for subsequent use later on).

4. Next, the FPM framework pulls the data from the source UIBB's configured outport using the GET_OUTPORT_DATA() method.

5. The outport data is then passed to the connector instance via the SET_INPUT() method.

6. Finally, the target UIBB can pick up the outport data via FPM event loop callback methods such as GET_DATA() or PROCESS_EVENT(). Since most wire model implementations pass object keys around as opposed to actual object references, it's usually up to the target UIBB to retrieve the referenced data[22]. If the data in question doesn't exist, then the target UIBB can use the IS_CREATE_ALLOWED() and CREATE_ENTITY() methods to potentially create the data on the fly.

As you can see in Figure 7.7, the data flow process associated with a given wire connection has a lot of moving parts. However, the good news for us as FPM developers is that most of these complexities are abstracted away within the FPM framework. Once we isolate the various classes and understand their roles, the methods themselves are fairly straightforward to understand and implement. And, if we're lucky enough to be working with a wire model implementation provided by SAP, then there's even less to worry about on the development side.

7.2 Advanced Wire Configuration Concepts

In Section 7.1.2, we learned a little bit about how wire connections are established between a pair of UIBBs. Now that we have a sense for how this works technically, let's now take a step back and see how these wire connections come together at the FPM application level.

As we noted earlier, wire connections are defined on the level of the floorplan configuration as opposed to individual UIBB configurations. This centralized approach makes it possible for the FPM framework to construct a graph of wire connections like the one shown in Figure 7.8. Behind the scenes, this metadata is used by the FPM

---

[22] This data lookup process is also generally abstracted by the base feeder class(es) provided by a given wire model implementation.

framework and the floorplan component to instantiate UIBBs and fill them with data in ad hoc fashion.

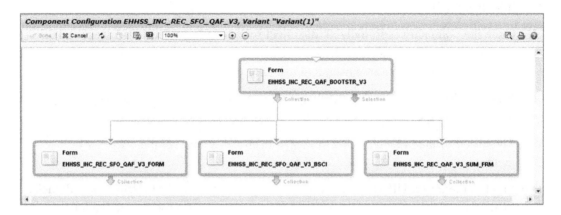

Figure 7.8: Viewing Wire Configurations in the Graphical Wire Editor Tool

Most of the time, wire connection hierarchies like the one shown in Figure 7.8 are rooted by a faceless UIBB whose role is to *bootstrap* the wire model at runtime. In this scenario, the faceless UIBB may use application parameters, input from an initial selection screen and so on as a key for loading a particular business object into context. From here, data can flow downstream from the faceless UIBB's outport to subordinate UIBBs which are daisy-chained together using wire connections.

As we noted in Section 7.1.2, wire configurations are maintained on the WIRE SCHEMA tab in FLUID. As you can see in Figure 7.9, this editor tab page allows us to create wire connections in one of two ways:

➢ We can use the ATTRIBUTES form at the bottom of the editor page to manually fill in the various connection details.

➢ Alternatively, the FLUID editor allows us to edit the wire connections using a graphical editor like the one shown in Figure 7.8. This graphical editor can be accessed by clicking on the GRAPHICAL WIRE EDITOR button highlighted in Figure 7.9.

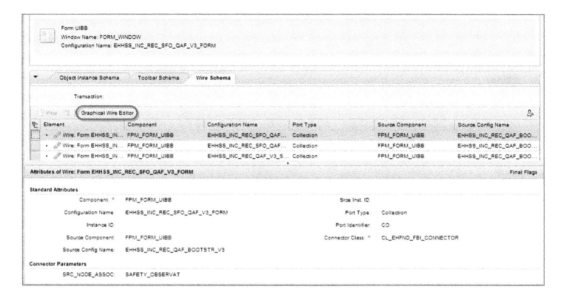

Figure 7.9: Maintaining the Wire Schema in the FPM Configuration Editor

Regardless of the approach we take, we should be able to construct a wire graph which supplies a floorplan instance's constituent UIBBs with the data they need to render their content areas.

7.2.1 Working with Composite Components

Earlier, we noted that wire connections are defined at the floorplan configuration level. This begs the question: how do we connect embedded UIBBs contained in composite components? After all, since composite components aren't associated with a feeder class, there's no way for us to define an inport to funnel the data through. Fortunately, the FPM framework allows us to get around this limitation through the definition of a *wire plug* in the composite component.

Within a composite component configuration, we can define a wire plug on the WIRE SCHEMA tab as shown in Figure 7.10. Here, we simply edit the pre-defined WIRE PLUG element and select one of the embedded UIBBs (usually a master UIBB) to serve as the external connection port for the composite component. Once a wire plug is established, we can then define wire connections to the wire plug UIBB within the floorplan configuration as per usual.

*Figure 7.10: Working with Wire Plugs in a Composite Component © Copyright 2013.
SAP AG. All rights reserved*

Once we establish connectivity to the wire plug, we can broadcast data to the rest of the
embedded UIBBs in the composite component by filling out the composite component's
wire schema as shown in Figure 7.10. Here, we can define wires using the same process
applied to the floorplan configuration. Naturally, the wire plug UIBB serves as the
starting point for establishing a configuration, playing a similar role to the "bootstrap"
component described earlier. Other than that, it's business as usual.

7.3   Case Study: Editing Sales Orders Using the BOPF

Before we wrap up our discussion on the wire model, we thought it would be useful to
see a live example which shows how all the various pieces fit together in real-world
applications. Here, our object model of choice will be the aforementioned BOPF. This
object model has come into vogue in recent years as it has been rolled out with new SAP
Business Suite applications such as *Environment, Health, and Safety Management* (SAP
EHSM) and *Transportation Management* (SAP TM).

7.3.1   BOPF and FBI Introduction

First things first, if we're going to build an FPM application using the BOPF, then we
need to spend a little bit of time coming up to speed with the BOPF. As the name
suggests, the BOPF is a processing framework which makes it easy for developers to

model and deploy *business objects* (BOs). These BO definitions are abstractions on top of well-known business entities such as customers and products, sales orders, etc.

Anatomy of a Business Object in the BOPF

Since the term *business object* is thrown around quite a bit in and around the SAP landscape, some further clarification is needed to understand what a BO is from a BOPF perspective. According to the online help documentation, a BO within the BOPF is "a representation of a type of uniquely identifiable business entity described by a structural model and an internal process model". This is to say that BOPF business objects:

➢ Have a well-defined component model.

➢ Have a defined process model which governs the business object lifecycle, behaviors, and so forth.

➢ Execute within a container-like environment which handles low-level tasks such as caching, object-relational mapping (ORM), transaction management, and so on.

In this regard, BOs in the BOPF are not unlike objects developed in other component architectures (e.g. EJBs in Java, Microsoft COM+, etc.).

From a modeling perspective, BOs are made up of several different types of entities:

➢ **Nodes**

○ Nodes are the basis of the BO object model. Each node definition is kind of like an OO class in that it encapsulates data and behavior into a self-contained package.

○ Nodes are used to model a BO's data. Here, nodes are arranged hierarchically underneath a single root node to reflect the various dimensions of the BO data (similar to XML).

○ Nodes can be classified as either *persistent nodes* or *transient nodes*. Persistent nodes are backed by a database table while transient nodes are loaded on demand at runtime.

○ Each node consists of one or more attributes which describe the type of data stored within the node. The attributes are defined in terms of structure definitions from the ABAP Dictionary.

○ At runtime, a BO node is like a container which may have zero, one, or many rows. In this sense, BO nodes are similar to context nodes in the Web Dynpro programming model.

➢ **Actions**

Actions define the services (or behavior) of a BO node. As such, they are analogous to methods in an ABAP Objects class.

➢ **Associations**

In order to maximize reuse, it's possible for a BO node to define *associations* to other BOs. For example, a sales order BO might define an association between its header node and a customer BO. This approach has much richer semantics than if we were to simply define a foreign key in a database table.

➢ **Determinations**

Determinations are kind of like specialized user exits which allow us to insert custom logic to respond to certain lifecycle events related to a BO node (e.g. during the loading of a BO node, whenever a BO node is being saved, and so on).

➢ **Validations**

Validations are like internal consistency checks on a BO node. These checks are carried out before a node's data is saved to ensure that the node data remains consistent with the overall business model.

➢ **Queries**

Query definitions encapsulate tedious selection logic so that external clients can quickly and easily search for BO instances without having to write complex SQL joins, etc.

Collectively, these entity types allow us to encapsulate every aspect of a business entity within a unified model. Of course, such a high-level introduction barely scratches the surface of what we can do with BOs. For the purposes of this book though, we'll stick to the basics and focus on FPM integration using pre-delivered BOs. If you're interested in learning more about what the BOPF has to offer, we would recommend that you check out the SAP Help Library online at *http://help.sap.com*. The author has also published a blog series for this topic on the SAP SDN called *Navigating the BOPF* which covers the framework in great detail.

FPM BOPF Integration (FBI)

Once a BO has been defined within the BOPF, we can access it via an object-oriented API which is quite generic in nature. So, whether we're working with a sales order BO or a product BO, the API call sequence is largely the same. Behind the scenes, the BOPF framework will use BO metadata to determine how to carry out generic requests to create new object instances, save changes to an object, and so on. This layered approach to request processing is illustrated in Figure 7.11.

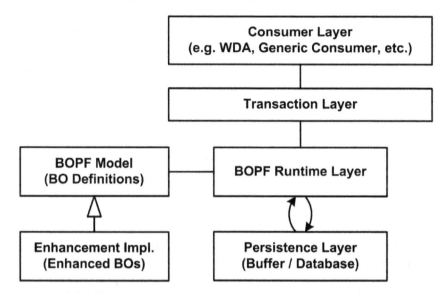

Figure 7.11: Simplified Diagram Depicting BOPF Framework Architecture

As you might expect, the generic nature of the BOPF API lends itself well to integrating with the FPM wire model. In fact, SAP provides a default wire model implementation that can be used straight out of the box in most cases: the *FPM BOPF Integration* (FBI) framework. Within the FBI, we can find a default connector class (/BOFU/CL_FBI_CONNECTOR) as well as base-level feeder classes which provide GUIBB-specific implementations of the IF_FPM_FEEDER_MODEL interface. We'll look at some practical examples which demonstrate how these classes are used in Section 7.3.2.

Working with the /BOBF/DEMO_SALES_ORDER Business Object

For the purposes of our demonstration, we will be working with a sample BO that comes preinstalled in SAP NetWeaver systems: the /BOBF/DEMO_SALES_ORDER business object. As you can see in Figure 7.12, this BO provides a simplified model of a sales order transaction. Here, the sales order data is organized under a ROOT node which contains header-level data. Underneath the ROOT node, child nodes are arranged in hierarchical fashion to model sales order items, the sold-to customer information, and so on.

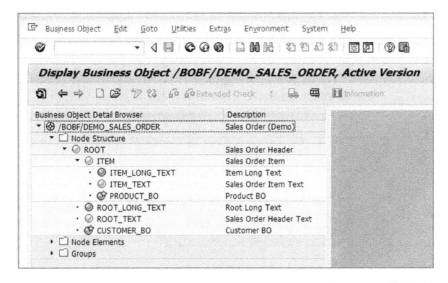

Figure 7.12: Viewing the /BOBF/DEMO_SALES_ORDER Business Object © Copyright 2013. SAP AG. All rights reserved

Within the FBI framework, we have two basic options for displaying BO node data:

➢ Most of the time, we'll use the default feeder class implementations to display the data from a single BO node in a UIBB. For instance, in our sample application, we've used the /BOFU/CL_FBI_GUIBB_FORM as the basis for building a form UIBB to display sales order header data from the ROOT node. We're also using the /BOFU/CL_FBI_GUIBB_LIST class to display sales order line items in a list UIBB.

➢ Occasionally, we may need to include data from several nodes in a single UIBB layout. In these situations, we can employ the use of *FBI views* to join several nodes together into a combined structure which can be consumed by various UIBB types.

To build our sales order editor application, we'll use the former approach to access the data. As we'll see in Section 7.3.2, this approach will require no custom BOPF development; all we have to know is which node(s) in the /BOBF/DEMO_SALES_ORDER business object to retrieve the data from and the FBI framework will take care of the rest.

7.3.2 Designing the Application

Now that we have a basic understanding of what the BOPF is all about, let's turn our attention towards the development of our sample FPM application. For brevity's sake, we'll touch on the high points, focusing mostly on wire model-specific concerns. However, if you're curious about how a particular component was configured, you can review the finished product in the book's source code bundle by opening the WDA application called ZWDA_SALESORD_WIRE_DEMO.

UI Design Approach

In order to keep things simple, we'll loosely pattern our sales order editor off of the familiar sales order editor transactions used in SAP® ERP systems (e.g. Transaction VA02). Using the OIF floorplan type, we'll provide an initial screen which allows users to select a pre-existing sales order record (see Figure 7.13).

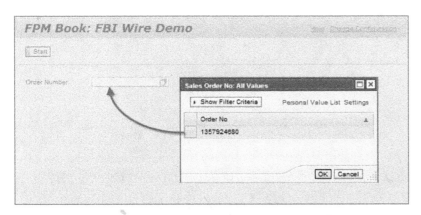

Figure 7.13: Selection Screen for the Sales Order Editor Demo Application © Copyright 2013. SAP AG. All rights reserved

Once a sales order record has been selected, users can enter the main editor screen by clicking on the START button (see Figure 7.13). This will take them to an editor screen like the one shown in Figure 7.14. Here, the sales order data is organized within a tabbed UIBB such that header-level data is displayed in the master area and items/text data is displayed in the tab area.

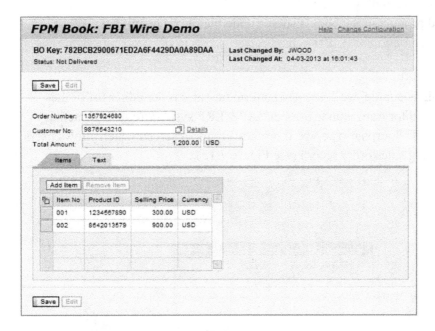

Figure 7.14: Main Editor Screen for the Sales Order Editor Demo © Copyright 2013. SAP AG. All rights reserved

The component diagram contained in Figure 7.15 illustrates how the OIF content area has been laid out. In the next section, we'll take a closer look at how the constituent GUIBB components are configured.

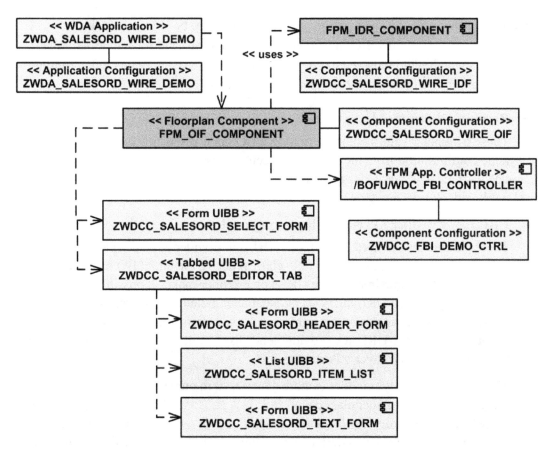

Figure 7.15: Component Architecture of the Sales Order Editor Application

7.3.3 Configuring the UIBB Components

In this section, we'll take a look at the steps required to integrate various GUIBB components with data from the /BOBF/DEMO_SALES_ORDER BO. Here, we'll see that most of the heavy lifting is performed by pre-delivered FBI feeder classes: all we have to do is provide the right parameters and the feeder classes will take care of the rest.

Configuring the Bootstrap Form

The first UIBB component that we'll look at is the form UIBB which provides the application's selection screen as shown in Figure 7.13. Unlike the other UIBB components that we'll look at in this section, this particular form UIBB is unique in the sense that it's also responsible for bootstrapping the wire model. Therefore, its feeder class is defined as a subclass of the FBI standard class /BOFU/CL_FBI_GUIBB_BOOTSTRAP.

In order for the `/BOFU/CL_FBI_GUIBB_BOOTSTRAP` class to be able to load the `/BOBF/DEMO_SALES_ORDER` BO into context, we need to provide several design time parameters which will be passed to the feeder class' `INITIALIZE()` method at runtime. As you can see in Figure 7.16, these parameters include:

> **Business Object / Node**

> These parameter values combine to form a BO node key which is used to obtain BO node configuration from the BOPF (via factory class `/BOPF/CL_FRW_FACTORY`). The obtained metadata provides the generic feeder class with the information it needs to work with BOs of any type.

> **URL Key Provider / Pre-Selection Key Provider**

> These parameters are used to configure FBI key provider classes which are used by the `/BOFU/CL_FBI_GUIBB_BOOTSTRAP` class to derive the target BO instance's key at runtime. As the name implies, the URL key provider makes it possible to pass a BO instance key using a URL query string parameter called `KEY`. Whenever this key is passed, the application will skip right over the selection screen and jump right into the editor. Thus, the URL key provider lends itself well to integrating applications using the SAP NetWeaver® Portal.

> The pre-selection key provider is more generic, so in our sample application, we created a custom provider class called `ZCL_FBI_BOOTSTRAP_PRESEL_PROV` to copy the selected sales order key from the selection screen into context. At runtime, the bootstrap class will use this derived value along with the metadata derived via the BUSINESS OBJECT and NODE parameters to load the target BO instance. From here, data is passed downstream to other UIBBs as per usual via the bootstrap class' implementation of the `IF_FPM_FEEDER_MODEL` interface.

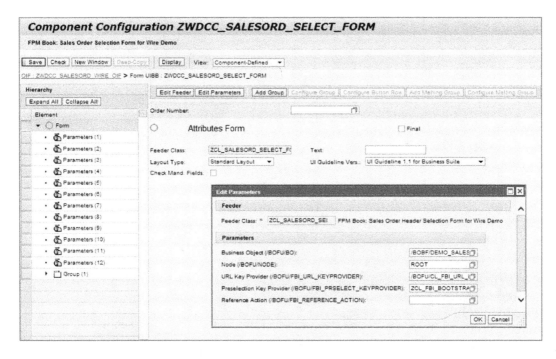

Figure 7.16: Configuring the Bootstrap Form Parameters © Copyright 2013. SAP AG.
All rights reserved

In our custom ZCL_SALESORD_SELECT_FORM feeder class, we have deferred almost
everything to the /BOFU/CL_FBI_GUIBB_BOOTSTRAP superclass. Indeed, the only
customization worth noting is with the redefined FLUSH() method shown in Listing 7.1.
Here, we are taking the selected order number, using it to lookup the target sales order
BO node key, and storing the results in the pre-selection provider's key cache. That way,
the bootstrap class will find it whenever it processes the GET_DATA() and
PROCESS_EVENT() methods in response to the user confirming their selection.

```
method IF_FPM_GUIBB_FORM~FLUSH.
  DATA ls_key LIKE LINE OF me->mt_keys.
  DATA lo_key_provider TYPE REF TO zcl_fbi_bootstrap_presel_prov.

  FIELD-SYMBOLS <ls_search_fields> TYPE zsales_order_search.
  FIELD-SYMBOLS <ls_key_provider>  LIKE LINE
                                   OF me->mt_key_providers.

  "Use the provided search criteria to find the
  "appropriate sales order:
  ASSIGN is_data->* TO <ls_search_fields>.
  IF <ls_search_fields> IS ASSIGNED.
    SELECT SINGLE db_key
```

```
        INTO ls_key-key
        FROM /bobf/dm_sord_rt
       WHERE order_id EQ <ls_search_fields>-order_id.

    IF sy-subrc EQ 0.
      "Store the target BOPF node record key in context:
      APPEND ls_key TO me->mt_keys.

      "Also add the key to the FPM application parameters
      "so that we can read it in the FBI controller:
      me->mo_fpm->mo_app_parameter->set_value(
        iv_key   =
          /bofu/if_fbi_runtime_c=>sc_application_parameters-key
        iv_value = ls_key-key ).
    ENDIF.
  ENDIF.

  "Use our custom preselection provider class to cache
  "the selected object key:
  READ TABLE me->mt_key_providers ASSIGNING <ls_key_provider>
       WITH KEY provider_type = 'PRESELECTION_PROVIDER'.
  IF <ls_key_provider> IS ASSIGNED.
    IF <ls_key_provider>-provider IS BOUND.
      lo_key_provider ?= <ls_key_provider>-provider.
      lo_key_provider->set_keys( me->mt_keys ).
    ENDIF.
  ENDIF.
endmethod.
```

Listing 7.1: Storing the Selected Sales Order Key in Context

Configuring the Header Details Form

Compared to the bootstrap selection form, the configuration of the header details form is a piece of cake. As you can see in Figure 7.17, there are two main parameters that we have to specify: the source BOPF business object and the target BO node. With this information, the base FBI form feeder class /BOFU/CL_FBI_GUIBB_FORM is able to dynamically load the node data into context without any further customization. Of course, this assumes that the target node key will be provided via the wire model.

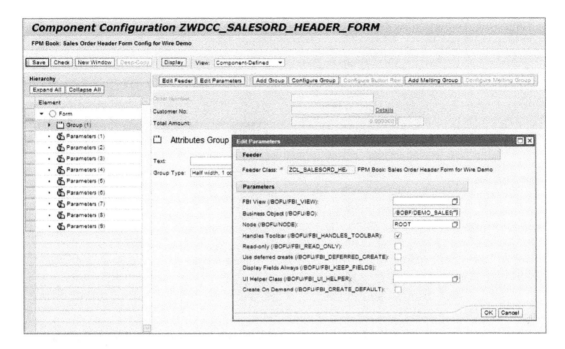

Figure 7.17: Configuring the Header Details Form © Copyright 2013. SAP AG. All rights reserved

Configuring the Items List

Configuration-wise, the process of setting up the sales order item list is quite similar to the one used to configure the sales order header data form. Here, we simply create a new list UIBB instance and associate it with the standard FBI feeder class `/BOFU/CL_FBI_GUIBB_LIST`. Once again, the two main parameters of interest are the BOPF business object and target BO node (`/BOBF/DEMO_SALES_ORDER` and `ITEM` in this case).

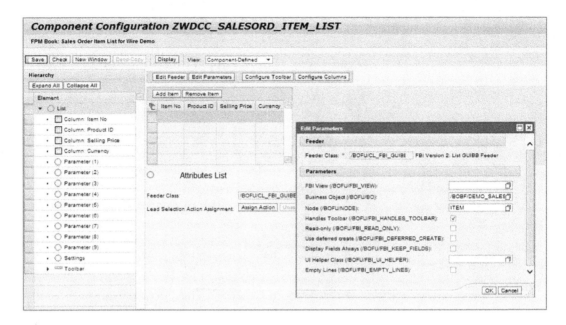

Configuring the Long Text Form

For all intents and purposes, the configuration of the long text form used to fill in the TEXT tab page (see Figure 7.14) is a repeat of what we did to configure the header details form. The only real difference here is that we're referencing the sub-ordinate ROOT_TEXT node in lieu of the ROOT node used to configure the header details form. Otherwise, it's business as usual with the form component and the /BOFU/CL_FBI_GUIBB_FORM feeder class.

7.3.4 Defining the Wire Configuration

Once all of the relevant UIBBs are in place, the wire configuration itself is pretty straightforward. Figure 7.19 provides a bird's eye view of what the configuration looks like at the component level.

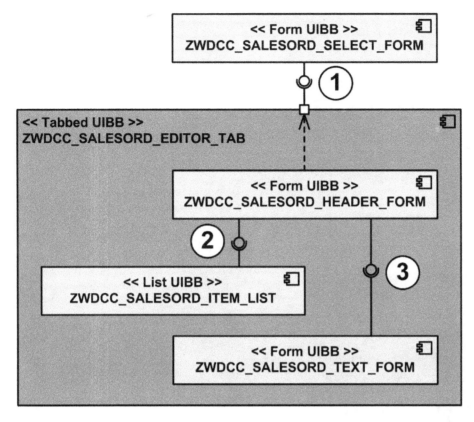

Figure 7.19: Wire Configuration for the Sales Order Example Application

As you can see in Figure 7.19, there are three wire connections that must be configured:

1. First, we need to configure a wire connection between the selection screen form and the sales order header details form. Here, notice how the header details form was selected as the wire plug for the surrounding tabbed component. Since both of these components are working with the ROOT node of the /BOBF/DEMO_SALES_ORDER BO, no connection parameters are required to make this connection work.

2. Once we've established a connection to the header details form, we can begin configuring wire connections within the tabbed component. Figure 7.20 shows how we've established the connection between the header form and the line items list. Here, notice how we've filled in the SRC_NODE_ASSOC connection parameter with the target ITEM node in order to define a linkage between the header ROOT node and the sub-ordinate ITEM node.

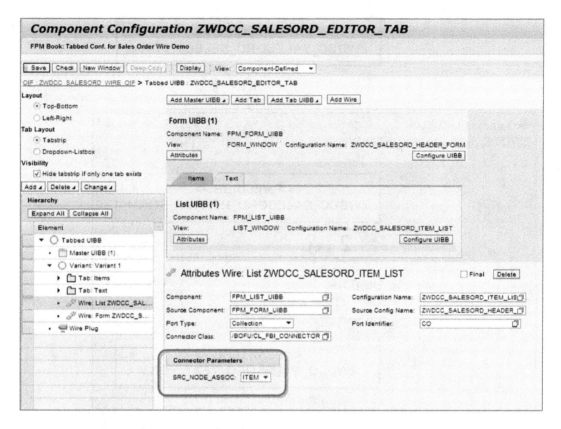

Figure 7.20: Configuring a Wire Connection to the Items List © Copyright 2013. SAP AG. All rights reserved

3. Finally, our last connection links the header form with the text form. Here, we link the ROOT node with the sub-ordinate ROOT_TEXT node (see Figure 7.21).

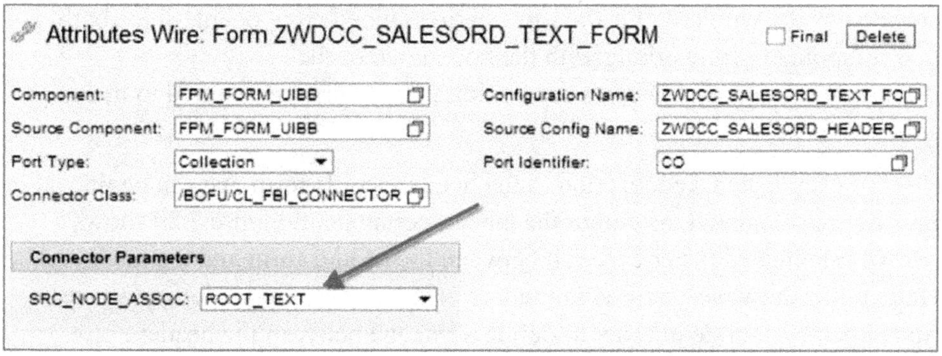

Figure 7.21: Configuring a Wire Connection to the Text Form © Copyright 2013. SAP AG. All rights reserved

7.3.5 Finishing Touches

After the wire configuration is in place, all that's left is the specification of the FBI application controller. Since we haven't yet had much opportunity to discuss application controllers, suffice it to say for now that this application controller is tasked with maintaining the transactional state of the BOPF business object(s) during the course of the FPM application session. Therefore, it's a required element if we're going to be working with the FBI framework.

Figure 7.22 shows how we've linked in the FBI controller component /BOFU/WDC_FBI_CONTROLLER in the floorplan configuration of our sales order editor application. This is the standard controller component of the FBI framework, and can be customized as needed by plugging in a component configuration in the CONFIGURATION NAME field.

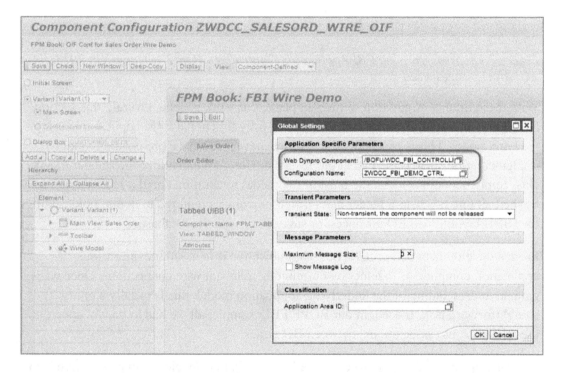

Figure 7.22: Specifying the FBI Application Controller - Part 1 © Copyright 2013. SAP AG. All rights reserved

In our sample application, we've specified a component configuration called ZWDCC_FBI_DEMO_CTRL. Within this configuration, we've plugged in a custom FBI application controller class called ZCL_DEMO_FBI_CONTROLLER (see Figure 7.23). This class inherits from the SAP standard class /BOFU/CL_FBI_CONTROLLER_NEW, which provides all of the necessary plumbing on the backend to enable the transfer of data over wire connections. Other than that, we've just added a few tweaks to fill in the IDR with sales order details - something we'll learn how to do in Chapters 8 and 9.

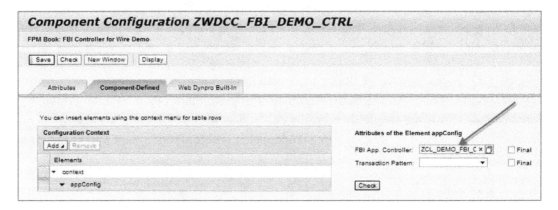

Figure 7.23: Specifying the FBI Application Controller - Part 2 © Copyright 2013. SAP AG. All rights reserved

With these final configuration settings in place, our work is done. Overall, this section has shown us just how easy it can be to create fully functional FPM applications using the wire model. This is especially the case whenever we have a pre-existing model implementation such as the FBI at our disposal. Here, we can utilize the standard feeder class implementations to handle most of the model integration details. This is evidenced by the fact that no custom feeder class development was required to define field catalogs for UIBB layout, load BO instances, or save changes to the database.

From a development perspective, our main objective is to assemble the various application components together by defining the relevant wire connections. Once we gain an understanding of the underlying application model, this is usually a pretty straightforward task. Indeed, in our BOPF/FBI example, all we had to do was specify the relationships (associations) between BO nodes.

After the basic plumbing in place, all that's left is from a development perspective is to lay out the UIBB content areas and implement any custom behaviors that were included with the application requirements. In these situations, even though custom feeder class logic is required, our task is generally simpler since we can leverage the model integration that's in place already to perform more advanced tasks (e.g. invoking actions on BO nodes, triggering validations, and so on).

7.4 Summary

In this chapter, we've shown you how the wire model can take generic UIBB components and infuse them with data from a backend data model. This approach allows us to avoid having to switch back and forth between the declarative and imperative development paradigms, which in turn increases productivity. Indeed, depending on the robustness of a given wire model implementation, it's possible to create fully functional FPM applications without having to write hardly any custom ABAP code.

In the next chapter, we'll shift our focus away from individual UIBBs and begin looking more broadly at application-level development concepts. In particular, we'll look at some of the standard APIs which can be used to handle requirements which span multiple UIBBs.

Chapter 8
Influencing Application Behavior

Throughout the course of this book, we've demonstrated how FPM applications come together by assembling various WDA components together via configuration. Though this is an accurate portrayal of the basic process, it doesn't tell the whole story. In real-world application scenarios, we will often run into requirements which cut across multiple UIBB components. It's here that we discover that there's more to FPM application development than just gluing a series of UIBB components together.

In this chapter, we'll take a step back and look at FPM application development from a holistic point of view. In particular, we'll introduce the concept of *application controllers* which provide us with a place for consolidating application-wide functions. Then, once we understand how application controllers are positioned, we'll look at some standard FPM APIs which can be used to enable transaction management, data sharing, and more.

8.1   Working with Application Controllers

In the past several chapters, our focus has been on developing individual UIBBs. Here, we've seen how UIBBs participate in the FPM event loop and collaborate with one another by raising FPM events.

Though it is technically possible to achieve most application-level requirements through FPM event coordination between UIBBs, this is not an ideal way to go about designing our FPM applications. To do so would be to encumber individual UIBBs with too many responsibilities and thus reduce their reusability. Our goal with UIBB development is to create components which are both *modular* and *cohesive*. This is to say that the functions encapsulated by our UIBBs should be closely related. If we add in functionality which helps coordinate between specific UIBBs, we irrevocably couple the

UIBBs together and end up back where we started before the FPM framework was brought into the picture.

In the upcoming sections, we'll discover that the FPM framework provides us with a much better alternative for defining global behaviors like this as we explore the notion of *application controllers*.

8.1.1 What are Application Controllers?

Right off the bat, you're probably wondering what application controllers are and how they're positioned within the FPM framework. To a certain extent, it's appropriate to think of application controllers as being like *user exits* which allow us to insert custom behaviors as specific points within the FPM application flow. This is evidenced by the UML sequence diagram contained in Figure 8.1. Here, we can see how the FPM framework invokes a series of callback methods on the application controller at specific points during the FPM event loop. Within these methods, we can insert custom logic to steer the application in different directions as needed.

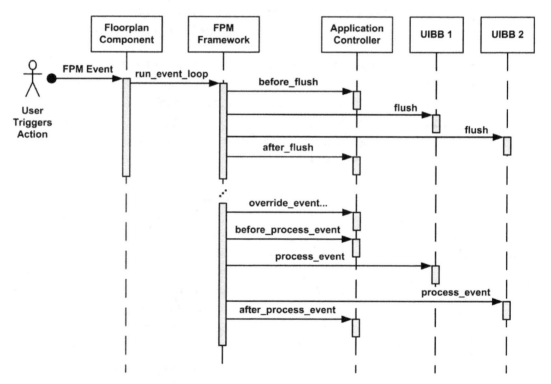

Figure 8.1: Revised FPM Event Loop Incorporating an Application Controller

In terms of positioning within the FPM framework, application controllers are aligned as extensions of a floorplan component[23]. We'll see how this relationship is established within a floorplan configuration in Section 8.1.2.

When we think about application controllers in this context, we can begin to see how they can also be used to share data between UIBBs, handle complex transactions, and even adjust the layout of specific floorplan types. In essence, they provide us with a centralized location for filling in the gaps and rounding out our FPM application designs.

8.1.2 Controlling Application Flow with FPM Application Controllers

Technically speaking, there are two different classes of application controllers supported by the FPM framework: the *FPM Application Controller* and the *Application-Specific Configuration Controller* (AppCC). In this section, we'll look at the FPM Application Controller. We'll then follow up with AppCCs in Section 8.1.3.

Implementing an FPM Application Controller

Technically speaking, there are two ways to implement an FPM Application Controller:

➢ We can either create a faceless WDA component that implements the `IF_FPM_APP_CONTROLLER` component interface.

➢ Or, we can define an ABAP Objects class that implements the `IF_FPM_APP_CONTROLLER` OO interface.

For the most part, which approach we choose to take is up to us as developers. However, as we'll see in upcoming sections, there are certain advantages to defining the application controller as a WDA component. Figure 8.2 illustrates how the `IF_FPM_APP_CONTROLLER` interface is being implemented in a WDA component.

---

[23] Technically, it's also possible to define application controllers on composite components such as the tabbed component. Here, the principles are the same; the only difference in this context is that the controller has a much more limited scope.

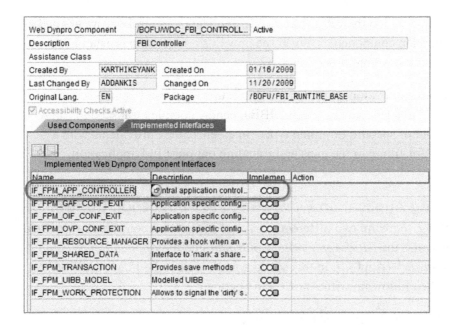

Table 8.1 describes the methods defined by the IF_FPM_APP_CONTROLLER interface (which are the same regardless of whether or not you're using the WDA component interface or the ABAP OO interface). As you can see, these methods correspond with the UIBB callback methods defined by the IF_FPM_UI_BUILDING_BLOCK component interface. Looking back at the sequence diagram contained in Figure 8.1, you can see that these methods are called before/after the UIBB-level methods are invoked. This allows us to interject custom application-wide logic before/after control is handed off to the UIBBs.

Method	Description
`before_flush()` `after_flush()`	These methods are used to allow the application controller component to synchronize any shared data it might contain with dependent UIBBs.
`before_needs_confirmation()` `after_needs_confirmation()`	These methods allow the application controller to react to requests for a confirmation dialog box from UIBBs.
`before_process_event()` `after_process_event()`	These methods allow the application controller to interject pre/post-processing for specific event types which might be of interest to the application as a whole.
`before_after_failed_event()` `after_after_failed_event()`	These methods allow the application controller to respond to failed events which are triggered from individual UIBBs.
`before_process_before_output()` `after_process_before_output()`	These methods can be used to sync up any shared data before the UIBBs are rendered in the UI.

Table 8.1: Methods of the IF_FPM_APP_CONTROLLER Interface

Associating an Application Controller with a Floorplan Configuration

Once we define our FPM Application Controller, we can add it to our FPM application by assigning it in the corresponding floorplan configuration. This can be achieved in the GENERAL SETTINGS section of the FLUID tool by choosing the FLOORPLAN SETTINGS → APPLICATION CONTROLLER SETTINGS menu option. This will open up the CHANGE APPLICATION-SPECIFIC PARAMETERS dialog box shown in Figure 8.3. Here, we can plug in the implementing WDA controller/class in the WEB DYNPRO COMPONENT/CLASS input field. This is all that's needed in order to establish a link between a floorplan configuration and a specific application controller.

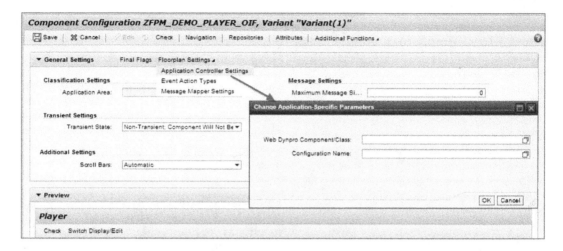

Figure 8.3: Assigning an Application Controller in a Floorplan Configuration

The CONFIGURATION NAME field is used whenever we want to specify a component configuration for an application controller component. This feature can come in handy whenever we want to *parameterize* application controller implementations using attributes defined by a component-defined adaptation. For more information on how to define such adaptations, check out the Web Dynpro ABAP documentation available in the SAP Help Library online at *http://help.sap.com*. Within your current SAP NetWeaver release, you can find the information you're looking for by searching on the term *Web Dynpro ABAP Configuration Framework*.

8.1.3 Overriding Behavior with AppCCs

In addition to the more generic application controller introduced in the previous section, the FPM framework also provides us with a more floorplan-specific type of controller: the so-called *Application-Specific Configuration Controller* (AppCC). AppCCs give us more fine-grained control over floorplan layout at runtime. Here, we can:

➤ Obtain information about the current state of the floorplan layout (e.g. the number of main views in an OIF floorplan, the number of main/sub-steps in a GAF floorplan, etc.).

➤ Adjust and manipulate the floorplan layout by adding in UIBBs/wires, hiding floorplan elements, and so forth.

➤ Intercept, update, and even cancel FPM events.

➤ And much more...

In the upcoming sections, we'll see how AppCCs are implemented in FPM applications.

Implementing an AppCC Component

From a technical perspective, the process of implementing an AppCC component mirrors that of the FPM Application Controller. Here, once again, we can choose between:

➢ Defining a faceless WDA component that implements one of the following WDA component interfaces:

❖ IF_FPM_OIF_CONF_EXIT for OIF floorplans

❖ IF_FPM_GAF_CONF_EXIT for GAF floorplans

❖ IF_FPM_OVP_CONF_EXIT for OVP floorplans

➢ Defining an ABAP Objects class that implements one of the following ABAP OO interfaces:

❖ IF_FPM_OIF_CONF_EXIT for OIF floorplans

❖ IF_FPM_GAF_CONF_EXIT for GAF floorplans

❖ IF_FPM_OVP_CONF_EXIT for OVP floorplans

Normally, it makes sense to combine the implementation of these interfaces with an FPM Application Controller, but this is not a hard requirement. If you just want to define an AppCC component, you can create a standalone WDA component/ABAP Objects class and associate it with a floorplan configuration using the same procedure described in Section 8.1.2.

Each of the floorplan-specific AppCC interfaces define a single method whose name is of the form OVERRIDE_EVENT_<Floorplan Type>(). So, if we were defining an AppCC component for an OIF floorplan, this method would be called OVERRIDE_EVENT_OIF(). At runtime, this method will be passed an object reference that implements a floorplan specific interface: IF_FPM_OIF for OIF floorplans, IF_FPM_GAF for GAF floorplans, and IF_FPM_OVP for OVP floorplans. Within the floorplan-specific method implementation, we can use the provided object reference parameter to manipulate the floorplan layout as needed.

For the most part, you'll find that the methods provided by these interfaces are pretty intuitive. For example, if you want to manipulate main steps in a GAF floorplan, you'll find that the IF_FPM_GAF interface defines methods such as GET_MAINSTEPS(),

ENABLE_MAINSTEP(), and HIDE_MAINSTEP(). Since the list of available methods is long and the usage possibilities are endless, we won't go through each method in detail here[24]. However, we would be remiss if we didn't at least provide a couple of examples to demonstrate how AppCCs are used in practice. Therefore, in the next couple of sections, we'll show you how AppCCs can be used to dynamically adjust floorplan layouts at runtime.

Case Study: Working with Variants

One very common requirement for AppCCs is the handling of *variants* in floorplan configurations. Since we haven't had a chance to work with variants yet, a brief introduction is in order. As the name suggests, variants provide us with a way of defining alternate screen layouts within a floorplan configuration (or within a composite component). This feature can come in handy whenever we're building an FPM application which will be utilized in different ways. Here, we can variants to:

➤ Define different screen layouts for specific user types (e.g. power users vs. casual users).

➤ Adjust the floorplan layout according to application modes (e.g. edit mode vs. display mode).

➤ Re-organize floorplan elements into different configurations based on certain runtime conditions.

From a configuration perspective, variants are rather like folders in that they group together related screen elements. This relationship is demonstrated in Figure 8.4 for an OIF floorplan. Here, we should point out that every floorplan configuration implicitly defines at least one (default) variant. Whether we choose to define additional variants is up to us.

---

[24] Such details can be found in the Class Builder documentation and in the *FPM Developer's Guide*.

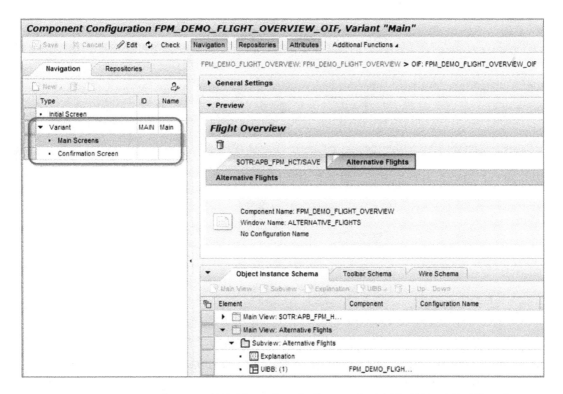

Figure 8.4: Variants within an OIF Floorplan © Copyright 2013. SAP AG. All rights reserved

We can define new variants using the relevant toolbar functions in the FLUID tool. As you can see in Figure 8.5, a variant definition consists of a variant ID and variant name. Once a new variant is created, we can use it to group together related screen types just like we've been doing all along with the default variants.

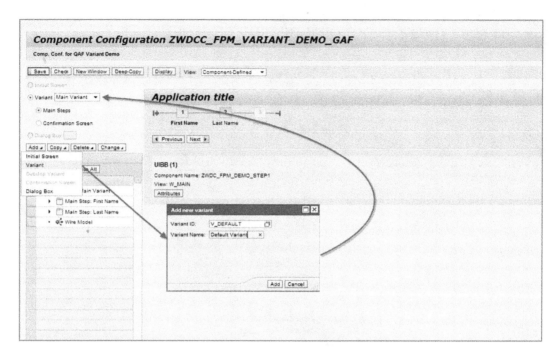

Figure 8.5: Configuring Variants within a Floorplan Configuration © Copyright 2013. SAP AG. All rights reserved

By default, any new variants we create will be ignored the next time we fire up our FPM application. This is because variant selection is something that must be controlled programmatically within an AppCC controller. To demonstrate how this works, we've re-worked the "Hello, World!" GAF demo application from Chapter 2 to define two variants: the original default variant and a new variant which derives the person's name via their SAP user name. A contrived example to be sure, but it serves our purpose.

To drive the variant selection in our example application (which can be found in the book's source code bundle), we've introduced an initial screen which allows users to choose between the two different application modes (see Figure 8.6). Alternatively, we could have driven the selection via URL query string parameters (which are also supported in this instance) or some other custom logic that's evaluated behind the scenes.

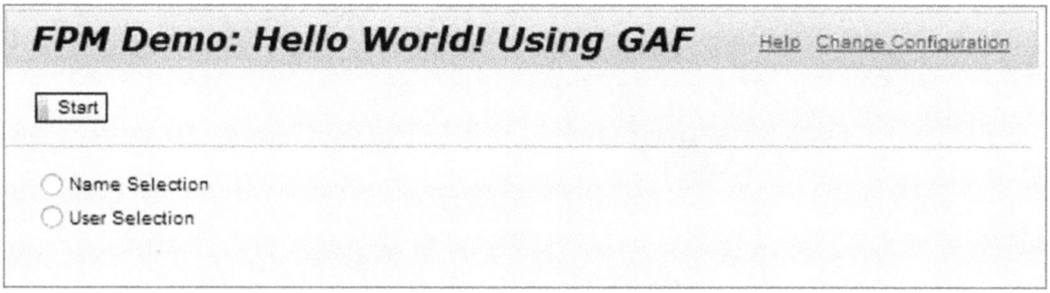

Figure 8.6: Providing an Initial Screen in our Variant Selection Demo © Copyright 2013. SAP AG. All rights reserved

Once the user makes their selection, they can hit the START button to load the application. Behind the scenes, the UIBB used to build the initial screen stores the variant selection in an FPM application parameter called VARIANT. When the FPM framework kicks off the FPM event loop for the FPM_LEAVE_INITIAL_SCREEN event, the OVERRIDE_EVENT_GAF() method of AppCC controller for the application gets invoked, allowing us to react to the selection and dynamically choose the appropriate variant. This logic is demonstrated in Listing 8.1. Here, notice how we're using the SET_VARIANT() method of the IF_FPM_GAF interface to control the variant selection.

```
method OVERRIDE_EVENT_GAF.
  DATA lo_fpm TYPE REF TO if_fpm.

  "Override selected GAF floorplant events:
  CASE io_gaf->mo_event->mv_event_id.
    WHEN if_fpm_constants=>gc_event-start.
      "Retrieve the variant from the application parameters:
      lo_fpm = cl_fpm_factory=>get_instance( ).
      lo_fpm->mo_app_parameter->get_value(
        EXPORTING
          iv_key  = 'VARIANT'
        IMPORTING
          ev_value = wd_this->mv_variant ).

      "If a variant is provided in the application parameters,
      "skip over the initial screen and go right into the
      "application:
      IF wd_this->mv_variant IS NOT INITIAL.
        lo_fpm->raise_event_by_id(
          if_fpm_constants=>gc_event-leave_initial_screen ).
      ENDIF.
    WHEN if_fpm_constants=>gc_event-leave_initial_screen.
      "Retrieve the selected variant from the
```

```
       "application parameters:
       lo_fpm = cl_fpm_factory=>get_instance( ).
       lo_fpm->mo_app_parameter->get_value(
         EXPORTING
           iv_key   = 'VARIANT'
         IMPORTING
           ev_value = wd_this->mv_variant ).

       "Set the target variant in the GAF floorplan:
       TRY.
         io_gaf->set_variant( wd_this->mv_variant ).
       CATCH cx_fpm_floorplan.
       ENDTRY.
   ENDCASE.
endmethod.
```

Listing 8.1: Implementing the OVERRIDE_EVENT_GAF() Method

Looking over the example code contained in Listing 8.1, you'll notice that the
OVERRIDE_EVENT_GAF() method also contains logic to respond to the FPM_START event.
Here, as we noted earlier, we've included support for variant selection via URL-based
application parameters (the VARIANT parameter in this case). The logic in this case is
pretty straightforward. If a variant is provided via the application parameters, then we
raise the FPM_LEAVE_INITIAL_SCREEN event so that we can bypass the initial screen
altogether and jump right into the application. Since we already have logic in place to
handle this event, the variant selection is the same in either case.

One last thing we should note is that, although this particular example was geared
towards GAF floorplans, the same principles apply to OIF or OVP floorplans. Using the
OVERRIDE_EVENT_*() method, we can listen for pertinent events and adjust the floorplan
variant/layout accordingly. We can exert even finer-grained control by combining an
AppCC with a regular FPM Application Controller so that we can trace state changes in
the relevant BEFORE_...() and AFTER_...() methods from the
IF_FPM_APP_CONTROLLER interface.

Case Study: Activating Substeps in GAF Applications

As we learned in Chapter 3, we can expand on the data collected in the main step of a
GAF floorplan by defining one or more *substeps*. These substeps are optional steps
along the roadmap which allow users to plug in additional information as needed. For
example, in Figure 8.7, you can see how we've enhanced the "Hello, World!" demo
program to include a substep which allows users to enter their middle name as desired.

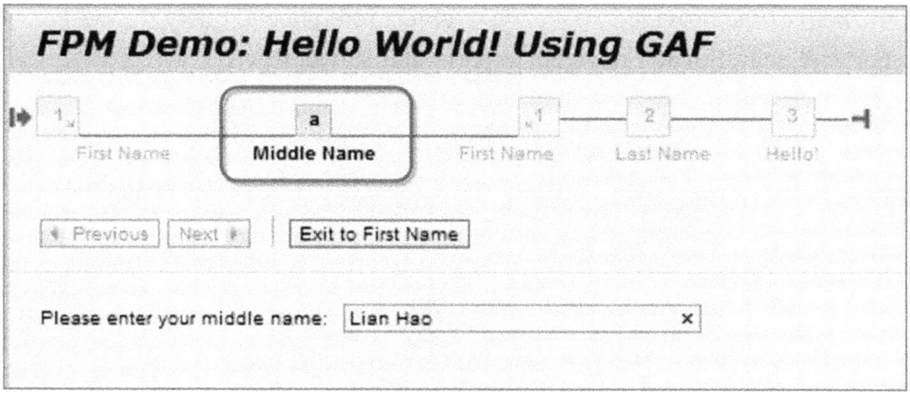

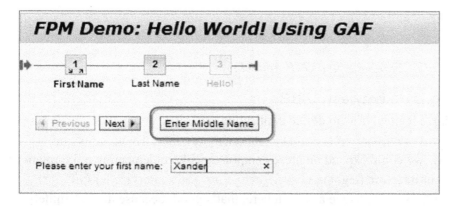

Figure 8.7: Working with Substeps in GAF Applications © *Copyright 2013. SAP AG. All rights reserved*

Since proposing a middle name is an optional step in our application, we need to provide a mechanism for allowing users to traverse over to that substep as needed. In Figure 8.8, you can see how we've provided a button called ENTER MIDDLE NAME in the GAF page toolbar which allows users to navigate to this substep. This seems straightforward enough, but you're probably wondering what happens when the user actually pushes the button. In other words, how do we trigger the actual navigation?

Figure 8.8: Activating a Substep in a GAF Application © *Copyright 2013. SAP AG. All rights reserved*

As it turns out, we're able to perform this navigation function pretty easily from within the AppCC controller using the OVERRIDE_EVENT_GAF() method. Listing 8.2 provides the particulars, but it basically boils down to raising an FPM change step event. Because this is an application-wide navigation request, it makes logical sense to put the event handling code in the OVERRIDE_EVENT_GAF() method. In more advanced scenarios, we might enlist the help of the provided IF_FPM_GAF object reference to query the GAF application state and conditionally navigate to particular substeps, etc.

```
method OVERRIDE_EVENT_GAF.
  DATA lo_event TYPE REF TO cl_fpm_event.

  "Override selected GAF floorplant events:
  CASE io_gaf->mo_event->mv_event_id.
    WHEN 'NAV_MIDDLENAME'.
      "Raise an event to open up the sub-step:
      lo_event = cl_fpm_event=>create_by_id(
        cl_fpm_event=>gc_event_change_step ).

      lo_event->mo_event_data->set_value(
        iv_key   = cl_fpm_event=>gc_event_param_mainstep_id
        iv_value = 'MAINSTEP_FIRST' ).

      lo_event->mo_event_data->set_value(
        iv_key   = cl_fpm_event=>gc_event_param_substep_id
        iv_value = 'SUBSTEP_MIDDLE' ).

      lo_event->mo_event_data->set_value(
        iv_key   = cl_fpm_event=>gc_event_param_subvariant_id
        iv_value = 'DEFAULT' ).

      wd_this->mo_fpm->raise_event( io_event = lo_event ).
  ENDCASE.
endmethod.
```

Listing 8.2: Activating Sub-Steps in a GAF Application

8.1.4 Sharing Data between UIBBs

In Section 8.1.2, we learned how to define application controller components by implementing the IF_FPM_APP_CONTROLLER component interface. Then, in Section 8.1.3, we saw how we could expand on these components by implementing a floorplan-specific component interface (e.g. the IF_FPM_OIF_CONF_EXIT interface for OIF floorplans). If you're starting to see a pattern here, that's good, because there definitely is one.

Due to their global stature, application controller components are uniquely positioned to act as an intermediary between the FPM framework and the UIBB components embedded within an FPM application. Therefore, in addition to the more generalized application controller interfaces noted earlier, there are several other key WDA component interfaces that we can implement to enhance an FPM application's functionality.

One example of these component interfaces is the IF_FPM_SHARED_DATA interface used to share data between UIBBs. If this component interface sounds vaguely familiar, it's because we've actually seen this interface before back in Chapter 2. Since we've covered a lot of ground since then though, a refresher is definitely in order.

Unlike the other component interfaces we've seen in this chapter, the IF_FPM_SHARED_DATA interface is somewhat unique in the fact that is merely a *tag interface*. This is to say that it's a marker interface that doesn't define any methods, events, etc. So why even bother defining an interface like this? To understand the reasoning, we have to dig a little deeper into component usage relationships in Web Dynpro.

Figure 8.9 provides a simplified UML component diagram which shows the relationship between an application controller component that implements the IF_FPM_SHARED_DATA interface and a series of UIBB components which share the application controller's data (e.g. via Web Dynpro context mappings). In order to establish this relationship, we must go into each of the sharing UIBB components and define a usage to the application controller (see Figure 8.10). Under normal circumstances, such component usage relationships would call for a separate instance of the used component to be loaded into context at runtime – one per using UIBB component. This is where the IF_FPM_SHARED_DATA tag interface comes into play.

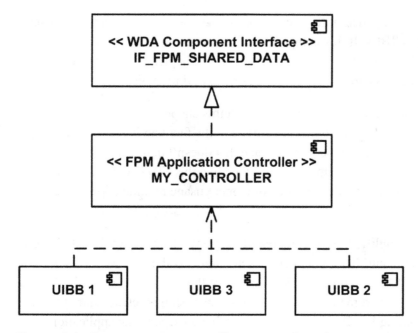

Figure 8.9: Component Diagram Illustrating Shared Data Scenario

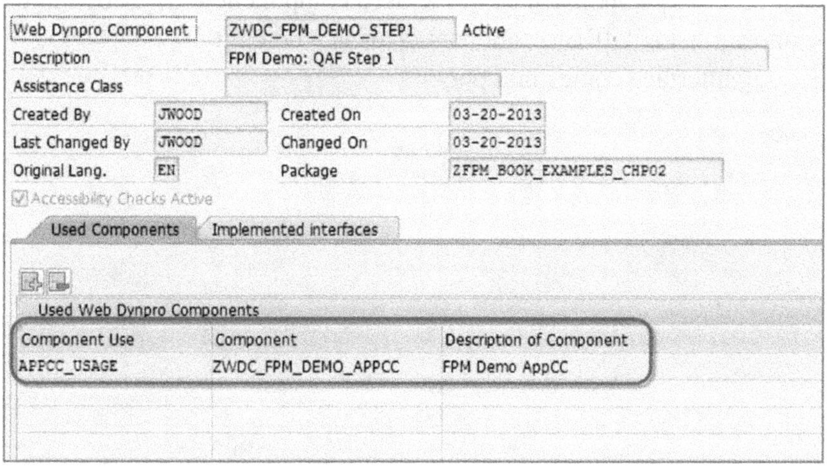

Figure 8.10: Defining a Component Usage to an Application Controller © Copyright 2013. SAP AG. All rights reserved

Whenever the FPM framework detects a usage pointing to a component that implements the `IF_FPM_SHARED_DATA` tag interface, it associates a singleton instance of the shared data component with the UIBB. Not only does this reduce memory overhead, it also ensures that the shared data is localized within the application controller of an FPM application.

An added benefit to having the FPM framework manage all this is that it makes it very easy for UIBBs to consume the shared data provided by the application controller. If you look back at Chapter 2, you can see how we defined sharing relationships to a series of freestyle UIBBs using Web Dynpro context mappings.

For GUIBB instances, we can achieve data sharing by wrapping up the data in a singleton instance managed by the application controller. That way, feeder classes can come along and read the data as needed within the various callback methods. You can find a working example of this with the FBI framework introduced in Chapter 7. Here, the default /BOFU/WDC_FBI_CONTROLLER application controller and corresponding /BOFU/CL_FBI_CONTROLLER_NEW controller class provide the basic infrastructure for data sharing between FBI-based GUIBB instances.

8.1.5 Transaction Management

Another optional component interface that we can implement in an application controller is the IF_FPM_TRANSACTION interface. This component interface is used to provide an FPM application with more fine-grained control over transactions. Table 8.2 describes the methods provided by this interface.

Method	Description
check_before_save()	As the name suggests, this method is invoked right before the FPM_SAVE event is processed. Here, we can perform any global-level checks to ensure that the application is in a consistent state before we start the save process.
	If the consistency check fails, then we can convey this information on to the FPM framework using EV_REJECTED exporting parameter. This will halt the processing of the FPM_SAVE event so that the user can correct the issues and move on.

Method	Description
save()	Assuming the consistency checks performed in the CHECK_BEFORE_SAVE() method (if any) go off without a hitch, then this method will be called next to actually carry out the save process. Here, we can consolidate any save logic that would normally be carried out within the PROCESS_EVENT() method of each of the FPM application's constituent UIBBs. This approach is particularly effective when used in conjunction with business object frameworks like the BOPF framework introduced in Chapter 7. You can get a feel for how this works by looking at the default application controller provided by the FBI framework: the /BOFU/WDC_FBI_CONTROLLER component. Here, you can see how the application controller manages the BOPF transactional context, allowing individual UIBBs to freely manipulate BO nodes without worrying about event coordination issues, etc. As was the case with the CHECK_BEFORE_SAVE() method, the SAVE() method also defines a Boolean exporting parameter called EV_REJECTED which can be used to notify the FPM framework of a failed save process.
after_commit()	This method is called whenever the save process is successful. Here, we can release any held resources (e.g. database/enqueue locks) and also optionally raise FPM events to notify interested UIBBs that the transaction was successful.
after_rejected_save()	If the SAVE() method fails (i.e. it returns a true value in the EV_REJECTED parameter), this method will be invoked allowing us to clean up the mess. Here, we can release any held resources, rollback any database updates, etc.

Table 8.2: Methods of the IF_FPM_TRANSACTION Component Interface

8.1.6 Enabling Work-Protection Mode

If the FPM application we're building is going to be deployed in the SAP NetWeaver Portal or the SAP NetWeaver Business Client (NWBC), then another component interface that might be of interest is the IF_FPM_WORK_PROTECTION interface. As the name suggests, this interface allows us to enable "work-protection mode" in our applications. This mode makes it possible for us to prompt users to save their changes if they attempt to navigate away from the application while editing a business object, etc.

From an implementation perspective, all we have to do to enable work-protection mode is implement the IF_FPM_WORK_PROTECTION interface in our application controller and then fill in the IS_DIRTY() method; the FPM framework will take care of invoking it at the right times. Within the IS_DIRTY() method, it's essentially up to us to determine whether or not the application is in a volatile state and needs to be saved before navigating away.

8.2 Managing Resources

When building larger FPM applications, it's not uncommon for us to occasionally run into performance issues. Most of the time, poor performance in FPM applications can be directly attributed to heavy memory consumption – most notably in the embedded UIBB components. Fortunately, there are steps that we can take in our FPM application designs to reduce this memory footprint and improve runtime performance.

8.2.1 Configuring the Transient Settings on a Floorplan Definition

It all starts with an attribute which was added to floorplan configurations with enhancement package 1 of the SAP NetWeaver 7.0 release: the TRANSIENT STATE attribute. As you can see in Figure 8.11, this Boolean attribute has two different settings:

➢ **Transient**

Whenever this setting is selected, the managing floorplan component has the option of *releasing* UIBB component references whenever the UIBBs are not visible on the display (or about to become visible during a navigation sequence). Here, the term *release* implies that the floorplan component will release any references it has to dynamically-instantiated UIBB components that have become invisible. This in turn makes it possible for the garbage collector to re-coup the unused resources.

As you might expect, this behavior can lead to significant reductions in the overall memory footprint of large FPM applications. For example, imagine an OIF or GAF application with multiple main views or main steps. Here, it's the difference between having all of the embedded UIBB components in scope at all times vs. having only the visible UIBBs in scope.

➤ **Non-Transient**

In this (default) mode, all embedded UIBB components will remain in context no matter what.

Figure 8.11: Setting the Transient State Attribute on a Floorplan Configuration

8.2.2 Understanding the Impacts of Transient Behavior Settings

Although transient behavior concepts sound pretty straightforward on paper, there are some challenges involved in making it all work in practice. Indeed, there are some cases where we may not want the floorplan component to release a referenced UIBB component. Specific scenarios include:

➤ Cases where a given UIBB component is embedded multiple times. Here, the component reference can only be removed whenever all of the interface views of the given UIBB component pass out of scope.

➤ The UIBB component happens to implement one of the following component interfaces:

❖ IF_FPM_SHARED_DATA

❖ IF_FPM_TRANSACTION

❖ IF_FPM_APP_CONTROLLER

❖ IF_FPM_OIF_CONF_EXIT / IF_FPM_GAF_CONF_EXIT

❖ IF_FPM_TABBED_CONF_EXIT

> The UIBB component in question is being used by another component.

In these situations, the managing floorplan component will not delete the UIBB component reference since it could have severe impacts on application functionality.

As developers, we also have another option for blocking the release of a component: we can have the component implement the IF_FPM_RESOURCE_MANAGER component interface. This interface defines a single method called ON_HIDE() which gives us the option to effectively veto the release of a component at runtime by passing a value back in the EV_VETO_RELEASE Boolean exporting parameter. How we determine whether or not the component should be released is entirely up to us. This functionality can be useful in situations where a component needs to stay in context for reasons specific to the application at hand.

8.2.3 Performance Tradeoffs

In many cases, a quick flip of the switch on the TRANSIENT STATE attribute can work wonders performance-wise in our FPM applications. However, it's important to remember that this setting is not a cure-all. In fact, there are some significant trade-offs that must be taken into account whenever we consider turning on transient behavior in UIBBs:

> First of all, we really need to understand the nature of the performance problem(s) we're facing. If the latency experienced by users is mostly due to UIBBs taking forever to initialize themselves, then it's possible that turning on transient behavior may actually make things worse since this initialization logic will need to be executed repeatedly as UIBBs pass in and out of context.

> If the memory overhead is limited to a handful of UIBB components which mostly remain visible, then it's better to let these components remain in context since there's probably more overhead in having to unload/reload them.

> If some of the UIBB components maintain internal state information that's hard to reconstruct as UIBBs pass in an out of context, then we should probably look at using the IF_FPM_RESOURCE_MANAGER component interface to conditionally block context switches since the resources required to reconstruct this state may offset any performance gains we might see otherwise.

8.3 Navigating within OVP Applications

As we learned in Chapter 3, OVP floorplans allow us to model our applications using a variety of different page types. Using this assortment of page types, we can layout our applications in much the same way that we might develop a site map for an external-facing web application. Of course, in order for this type of design to work, we need to provide navigation links which allow users to navigate between pages.

In this section, we'll take a look at ways of navigating within OVP applications. Along the way, we'll also explore the notion of *application modes* within FPM applications in general and OVP applications in particular.

8.3.1 Conceptual Overview

Navigation within OVP applications is achieved by raising FPM events. Here, there are many standard OVP-related FPM events which can be used to perform routine navigation tasks such as navigating from the main page to a sub-overview page, re-routing a user back to the initial page, and so forth.

In general, these navigation events can be triggered in one of two ways:

➢ Frequently, we'll want to link the navigation events to buttons in the in page/UIBB toolbars or `LinkToAction` elements within the UIBB content. This approach gives the user control over when specific navigation sequences occur.

➢ Alternatively, we can raise the events programmatically within feeder class methods, application controllers, etc. This approach gives developers more control over when the navigation should occur, which can come in handy whenever another FPM event might force a state transition. For example, within the event handler associated with a deletion event, we probably want to automatically re-route the user to the confirmation page rather than leave them on the current editor screen.

In the upcoming sections, we'll see how these navigation links are established in a real and tangible way. To guide us through this discussion, we'll use the `S_EPM_FPM_PO` purchase order (PO) editor application provided as part of SAP's new *Enterprise Procurement Model* (EPM) demo model[25] as our working reference. Figure 8.12 illustrates the various page types used within this application.

---

[25] For more information on the EPM, we recommend that you read through the SDN whitepaper entitled *The NetWeaver Enterprise Procurement Model – An Introduction*.

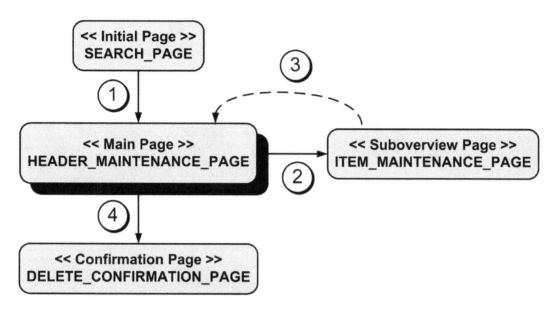

Figure 8.12: Page Schema for the S_EPM_FPM_PO Demo Application

As you can see in Figure 8.12, there is a very specific page flow within the
S_EPM_FPM_PO application. Here, users can traverse back and forth between the
following page types:

> **Initial Page**

  From the initial landing page, users can search for relevant POs using the search
  screen shown in Figure 8.13. This screen was built using the FPM_SEARCH_UIBB and
  FPM_LIST_UIBB_ATS components, respectively. Within the search results, users can
  click on a PO number in the PURCHASE ORDER ID column to open that specific PO
  in the (main) editor page. Alternatively, they can click on the NEW button in the
  toolbar above the search result list to launch a separate instance of the PO editor in
  create mode.

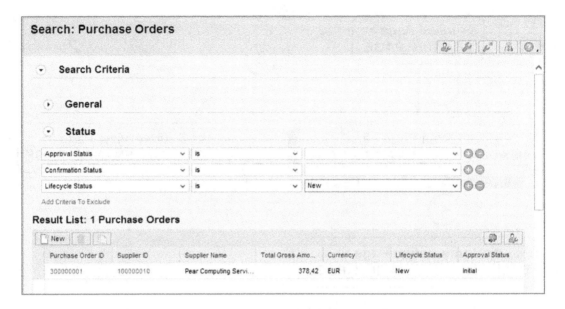

Figure 8.13: Searching for POs on the Initial Page © Copyright 2013. SAP AG. All rights reserved

➤ Main Page

On the main page, users can edit and/or display a given PO document. As you can see in Figure 8.14, this editor screen is divided up into various sections which organize the PO data along different dimensions (e.g. header vs. line item details).

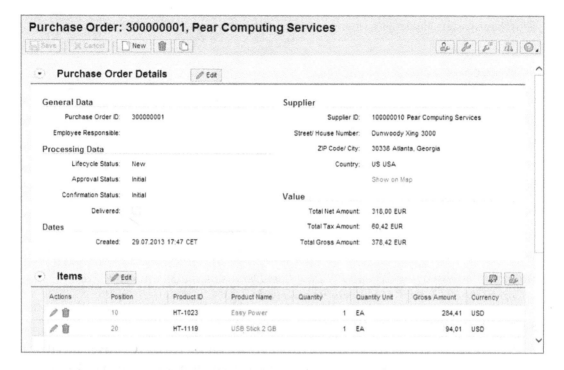

Figure 8.14: Displaying/Editing a PO on the Main Page © Copyright 2013. SAP AG. All rights reserved

➤ **Sub-Overview Page**

If we look closely at the bottom of Figure 8.14, we can see that each PO line item within the ITEMS table contains a hyperlink in the POSITION column. This hyperlink can be used to navigate from the main editor page to a sub-overview page that's used to edit/display PO line item information. As you can see in Figure 8.15, this sub-overview page contains further details about a selected PO line item.

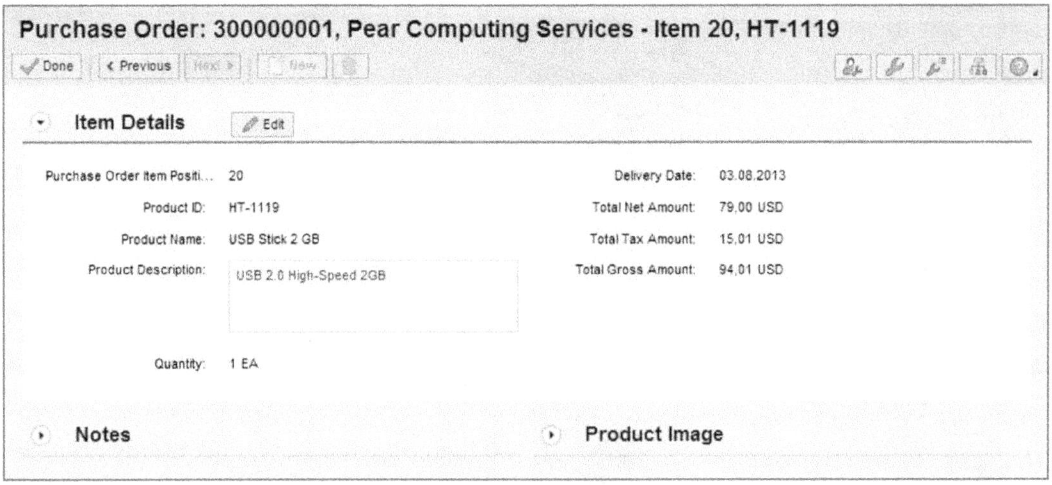

Purchase Order: 300000001, Pear Computing Services - Item 20, HT-1119

✓ Done   ‹ Previous   Next ›   New   🗑   ⚙ 🔧 🔨 🔍 ⓘ

▾   **Item Details**   ✎ Edit

Purchase Order Item Positi...	20	Delivery Date:	03.08.2013
Product ID:	HT-1119	Total Net Amount:	79.00 USD
Product Name:	USB Stick 2 GB	Total Tax Amount:	15.01 USD
Product Description:	USB 2.0 High-Speed 2GB	Total Gross Amount:	94.01 USD
Quantity:	1 EA		

▸   **Notes**   ▸   **Product Image**

Figure 8.15: Displaying/Editing PO Line Item Details on the Suboverview Page

➤ **Confirmation Page**

Finally, if a user decides to delete a given PO record from the main page, then the user will be routed to a confirmation page which confirms the deletion and also provides links to start the process over. Here, users can choose to create a new PO record (which takes them to the main page) or search for other PO records (which takes them back to the initial page).

8.3.2 Defining Navigation Links

Whenever an OVP application is started, the FPM_OVP_COMPONENT must determine which page to route the user to. Since a given OVP application may have many different pages to choose from, there is a defined search sequence which governs the selection process:

1. First, the FPM_OVP_COMPONENT checks to see if the FPM_START_PAGE_ID application parameter was provided. If so, then that page ID is selected as the start page and the search is halted right then and there.

2. If a start page was not proposed, then the next step is to look for any initial pages that may be configured. If there is more than one initial page types configured, then the FPM_OVP_COMPONENT will select the *default* initial page.

3. Otherwise, if no initial pages are found, the next step is to look for the default main overview page.

4. Finally, if each of the previous three steps fails to locate a start page, then the search halts and a hard error is issued on the screen.

Regardless of how we get there, once we arrive at the start page, we can begin laying out our navigation schema. As we noted earlier, this amounts to wiring up various FPM navigation events. Which FPM event types we choose depends on the navigation context. If we're navigating to external applications (or launching the same application in a different mode/perspective), then we'll usually want to wire up the FPM_NAVIGATE event. For all other internal navigation scenarios, we can choose from a series of OVP-related FPM events. In the upcoming sections, we'll see how to work with both of these event types.

Navigating with the FPM_NAVIGATE Event

To understand how to work with the FPM_NAVIGATE event, let's take a closer look at a couple of navigation links provided on the initial page of the S_EPM_FPM_PO application introduced in Section 8.3.1. Looking back at Figure 8.13, we can see that users have a couple of options for navigating to specific PO documents:

➢ Within the search results, users can click on the hyperlink in the PURCHASE ORDER ID column to open up a given PO record on the main editor page.

➢ Or, within the toolbar of the result list table, users can click on the NEW button to open up a new PO record on the main editor page.

In the latter case, the navigation link is configured in such a way that it causes a *separate instance* of the same S_EPM_FPM_PO application to be loaded in a new window/tab. While this may seem a bit strange at first glance, it's actually a fairly common design idiom based on recommendations from the current set of UI guidelines prescribed by SAP.

For the most part, you'll find that configuring the FPM_NAVIGATE event is pretty straightforward. For example, in Figure 8.16 you can see how the link in the PURCHASE ORDER ID column is configured. Here, SAP has defined the PO_ID column as a LinkToAction element which is bound against the FPM_NAVIGATE event (see Figure 8.16). The navigation details are specified in the EVENT PARAMETERS panel directly beneath.

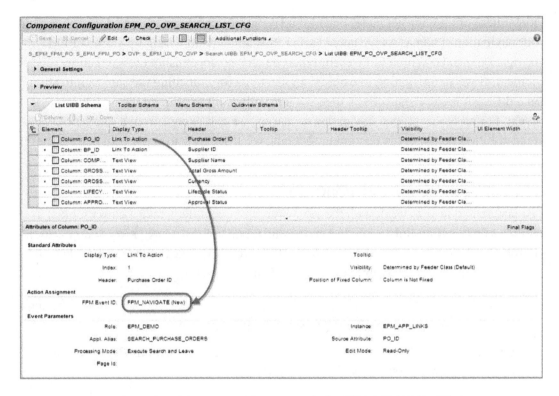

Figure 8.16: Binding a LinkToAction Element with the FPM_NAVIGATE Event
© *Copyright 2013. SAP AG. All rights reserved*

As you can see in Figure 8.16, the FPM_NAVIGATE event defines a number of event parameters which direct the navigation. Table 8.3 describes each of these parameters in further detail. You can find the technical details for these parameters by looking at the FPM_S_EXTERNAL_NAVIGATION_INFO structure type in the ABAP Dictionary (via Transaction SE11).

Parameter Name	Description
Role / Instance / Application Alias	These parameters point to a launchpad created in Transaction LPD_CUST. Figure 8.17 shows how the launchpad selected in Figure 8.16 is defined. Note that the specification of a launchpad here is optional: whenever a launchpad is omitted, it's assumed that we're executing an internal navigation. Refer back to Chapter 6 for a refresher on launchpads.
Source Attribute	This parameter points to the field that contains the target object's key. For example, in Figure 8.16, you can see how the PO number is being pulled from the PO_ID field in the search results. At runtime, this key value will be used to queue up the selected PO record in the search results so that it can be loaded into the main editor page.

Parameter Name	Description
Processing Mode	Whenever the `FPM_NAVIGATE` event is triggered from within a Search GUIBB, this parameter defines the processing mode of the Search GUIBB whenever a navigation request is initiated. Here, we can choose between the following values: ❖ **(Blank) - Normal** Whenever this mode is selected, it's as if the application is simply started over from scratch. In other words, there's no special navigation logic which bypasses the initial screen, etc. ❖ **E - Execute Search** This mode is used whenever we're processing launchpad-based navigation requests. Here, a navigation request causes the Search GUIBB to trigger the `FPM_EXECUTE_SEARCH` FPM event in the background, using parameters from the derived URL as search parameters. After the search is complete, there is no further navigation. This mode can be used to build specialized refresh functions which refine the search results, etc. ❖ **L - Execute Search and Leave** This mode works in much the same way as the Execute Search mode. The primary difference is that, after the search is complete, the `FPM_LEAVE_INITIAL_SCREEN` event will be raised in order to navigate away from the initial page. If you look closely at Figure 8.16, you can see that SAP selected this mode for the link from the search results to the PO editor page. ❖ **C - Create** This mode causes the OVP application to be started anew. Here, the target page is specified with the Page ID parameter described below. Naturally, this mode makes sense for the NEW button used to create new POs from the initial search page.
Edit Mode	The Edit Mode parameter determines the edit mode for the target page in the navigation sequence. We'll learn more about the effects of this parameter in Section 8.3.3.

Parameter Name	Description
Page ID	As noted earlier, this parameter can be used to specify the target page ID whenever we're re-opening the OVP application in create mode. Here, the configured page ID will be passed as the value of the FPM_START_PAGE_ID parameter.

Table 8.3: Parameters of the FPM_NAVIGATE Event

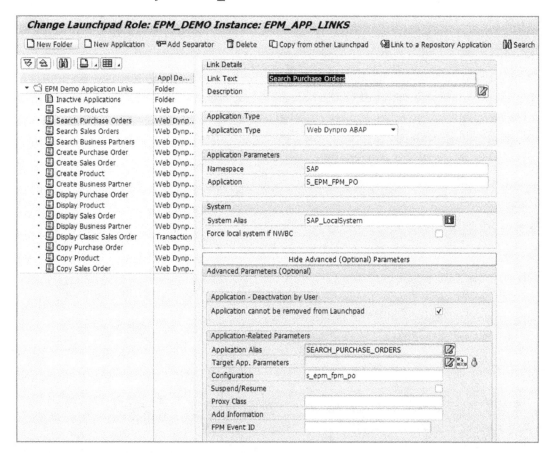

Figure 8.17: Launchpad for the S_EPM_FPM_PO Application © Copyright 2013. SAP AG. All rights reserved

Once we configure the relevant event parameters for the FPM_NAVIGATE event, our work is basically done; the FPM framework will take care of the rest. However, there is one code-level requirement in order to be able to use the FPM_NAVIGATE event. Within the GET_DEFINITION() method of our target feeder class, we must configure a feeder class action which points to the FPM_NAVIGATE event (see Listing 8.3).

```
METHOD if_fpm_guibb_list~get_definition.
  FIELD-SYMBOLS <ls_action> LIKE LINE OF et_action_definition.

  APPEND INITIAL LINE TO et_action_definition[]
            ASSIGNING <ls_action>.
  <ls_action>-id = if_fpm_constants=>gc_event-navigate.
  <ls_action_definition>-event_param_strukname =
    'FPM_S_EXTERNAL_NAVIGATION_INFO'.
ENDMETHOD.
```

Listing 8.3: Adding the FPM_NAVIGATE Event as a Feeder Class Action

Navigating Using OVP-Related FPM Events

As we noted earlier, internal navigation scenarios within OVP applications can be implemented using a series of OVP-related FPM events. Table 8.4 provides an overview of the available event types and their typical usage. You can find a more detailed listing of the available event types in the *FPM Developer's Guide* in the section entitled *OVP-Related FPM Events for Navigation*.

FPM Event ID	Usage
FPM_LEAVE_INITIAL_SCREEN	This event is used to navigate from an initial page to the default main overview page. If desired, we can override the default selection by specifying the target page ID in the TARGET_CONTENT_AREA event parameter.
FPM_BACK_TO_MAIN	This event is used to navigate from an edit page back to the last main overview page. Here, we should note that any changes applied on the edit page are NOT saved.
FPM_CALL_DEFAULT_DETAILS_PAGE	This event is used to trigger navigation to the default details page configured for a given UIBB instance. This default page type is configured within the UIBB's attributes as highlighted in Figure 8.18.
FPM_CALL_DEFAULT_EDIT_PAGE	This event is used to trigger navigation to the default edit page configured for a given UIBB instance. This default page type is configured within the UIBB's attributes as highlighted in Figure 8.18.

FPM Event ID	Usage
FPM_CALL_FULL_SCREEN	This event is used to navigate to the default edit page for the OVP application. Or, alternatively, we can specify a different edit page using the TARGET_CONTENT_AREA event parameter.
FPM_CALL_SUBOVERVIEW_PAGE	This event is used to navigate from a main overview page to its default sub-overview page. Alternatively, we can specify the target sub-overview page by specifying the TARGET_CONTENT_AREA event parameter.
FPM_CHANGE_CONTENT_AREA	This event type can be used to navigate over to any page within the OVP application. Here, the target page is specified with the TARGET_CONTENT_AREA event parameter.
FPM_DELETE_CURRENT_OBJECT	This event type is used to navigate to the default confirmation page after an object is deleted.
FPM_DONE_AND_BACK_TO_MAIN	This event is used in the same capacity as the FPM_BACK_TO_MAIN event described earlier.
FPM_SAVE_AND_BACK_TO_MAIN	This event type is triggered after an FPM_SAVE event has been processed on an edit page. Here, we leave the edit page and navigate back to the last main overview page.

Table 8.4: OVP-Related FPM Events

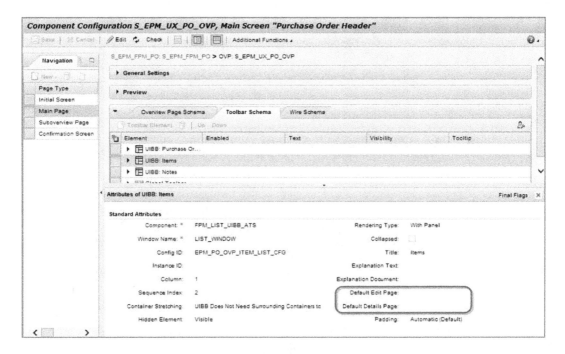

Figure 8.18: Selecting the Default Edit/Details Page on a UIBB Embedded in an OVP Page © Copyright 2013. SAP AG. All rights reserved

As you can see in Table 8.4, the OVP-related events at our disposal cover just about any state transition that could occur within our OVP applications. For our part, all we have to do is raise the FPM events within the relevant event handler methods of our feeder classes and/or application controllers. Listing 8.4 demonstrates how this works for the FPM_CHANGE_CONTENT_AREA event type. Using this event type, we can navigate over to any page within our OVP application.

```
METHOD navigate_to_page.
  DATA lo_event TYPE REF TO cl_fpm_event.

  lo_event = cl_fpm_event=>create_by_id(
    cl_fpm_event=>gc_event_change_content_area ).

  lo_event->mo_event_data->set_value(
    iv_key   =
      if_fpm_constants=>gc_event_param-target_content_area
    iv_value = iv_page ).

  cl_fpm_factory=>get_instance( )->raise_event( lo_event ).
ENDMETHOD.
```

Listing 8.4: Navigating between OVP Pages

8.3.3 Working with Application Modes

As we've seen, the content model of OVP floorplan is flexible enough to support any of the four basic use cases associated with business object editor applications: **C**reate, **R**emove, **U**pdate, and **D**isplay (i.e. CRUD operations). As a result, it makes good sense to combine these operations underneath a single multi-function OVP application since this approach promotes the reuse of page content, simplifies navigation scenarios, and so on. Of course, at the same time, this combined approach does add some complexity to the application logic since we now have to handle the transition between different *application modes*. In this section, we'll look at ways of dealing with this complexity[26].

State Transition Concepts

To put the notion of application modes into perspective, let's take a look back at the S_EPM_FPM_PO application described earlier in this section. This PO editor application supports each of the 4 basic CRUD operations, following a state transition like the one shown in Figure 8.12. As users navigate back and forth between pages, the application context naturally changes. This is to say that as users access individual page types, they might be accessing them in create mode, edit mode, or display mode; it all depends on what sort of task the user's trying to accomplish at the time.

For example, consider the main overview page illustrated in Figure 8.14. Here, we have a header details form as well as an items table which contains the PO line item data. Whenever we're in create mode or change mode, most (if not all) of the fields contained within various UIBBs should be open for input. In display mode, however, the fields should be grayed out and any toolbar functions which support changes to the business object should be disabled.

To complicate matters further, we have to contend with the fact that, during the course of an application session, it's possible that a user might toggle back and forth between these states many times. For example, immediately after a PO creation, the user might discover that they need to go back in and make further changes. Or, while reviewing a PO in display mode, they may determine that they need to make a change right then and there. Here, the user might click on the EDIT button in the page toolbar to switch over to edit mode.

At any of these transition points, we must make sure that the state of the UI is consistent with the selected application mode. This requires that we be able to detect the

---

[26] Note: Although this section is focused on application mode handling with the OVP floorplan, most of the concepts that we'll discuss apply with the OIF floorplan as well.

application mode and then apply the necessary UI property changes in real time. In the upcoming sections, we'll see how this is accomplished.

Specifying the Edit Mode of an OVP Application

Technically speaking, OVP applications maintain an internal "edit mode" which drives the behavior of various application elements: buttons in the page toolbar, embedded UIBB components, and so on. This edit mode can be set in several different ways:

➤ By specifying the SAP standard FPM_EDIT_MODE application parameter in the application URL.

➤ By configuring the EDIT MODE parameter in the GENERAL SETTINGS section of the OVP floorplan configuration (see Figure 8.19).

Figure 8.19: Explicitly Setting the Edit Mode for an OVP Floorplan Configuration

➤ If either of the previous two methods are utilized to pre-select the OVP application's edit mode, then the FPM_OVP_COMPONENT component will automatically adjust the edit mode whenever users click on the EDIT/DISPLAY, SAVE, and CANCEL buttons in the page toolbar. For example, if a user's editing a business object and hits the SAVE button, the changes would be saved and the OVP application would revert back to display mode. From here, the user could toggle back and forth between modes by clicking on the EDIT and DISPLAY buttons, respectively.

If we don't use any of the aforementioned options for explicitly setting the edit mode for our OVP application, then the default edit mode will be "No Mode Handling". Whenever this default setting is turned on, this is no specialized application mode handling within the FPM_OVP_COMPONENT component. Since this kind of behavior is almost never what we want in real-world situations, we would recommend that you pre-select the "Read-Only" edit mode within the OVP floorplan configuration at design time. This is in line with best practices which call for overview pages to be initially opened in display mode.

As you think about setting the default edit mode for your OVP application at design time, keep in mind that the default settings can be overridden by the aforementioned FPM_EDIT_MODE application parameter at runtime. So, for example, even if we set the default edit mode to "Read-Only", we can still provide users with direct application links to jump right in and create new business object instances or edit existing ones by specifying the correct edit mode in the FPM_EDIT_MODE application parameter.

Responding to Changes to the Edit Mode

Whenever we work with explicit edit modes in our OVP applications, we must careful to define our application logic in such a way that we detect and react to state transition changes. For complex applications, this likely requires a two-fold approach:

➤ At the application controller level, we may need to reserve and/or release transaction resources at different points. We can normally coordinate these sync points with the standard FPM lifecycle events: FPM_START, FPM_EDIT, FPM_SAVE, and so forth.

➤ At the UIBB level, we must detect any edit mode changes that might occur and then adjust the properties of UI elements accordingly.

Since we've already observed how application-wide logic is applied with application controllers earlier in this chapter, our focus here in this section will be on UIBB development concerns - specifically UIBBs based on GUIBB components[27].

Generally speaking, our approach to edit mode handling at the GUIBB level involves the following:

---

[27] For the most part, the concepts that follow can be adapted to work with freestyle UIBBs as well. For example, we can use the GET_UIBB_EDIT_MODE() method of the IF_FPM interface to determine the edit mode of a freestyle UIBB and react accordingly. The primary difference in this case is that there's no standard procedure for applying UI-level changes from here. This becomes a design detail that's implemented at the Web Dynpro development layer.

1. To detect changes to the edit mode, we can introspect the value of the IV_EDIT_MODE parameter passed to the GET_DATA() method of our feeder class[28].

2. Then, once this mode is selected, we can adjust the properties of relevant UI elements by modifying entries in the CT_FIELD_USAGE and CT_ACTION_USAGE parameters of the GET_DATA() method.

To demonstrate how this works, let's take a look at some example code. In Listing 8.5, you can see how we've implemented the GET_DATA() method for a form UIBB component. In this simplified implementation, we are toggling the READ_ONLY property of the form fields and the ENABLED property of any form actions based on the value of the IV_EDIT_MODE parameter. In real world implementations, additional logic might be required to filter out certain actions which might need to be enabled in display mode, etc., but you get the basic idea.

```
method IF_FPM_GUIBB_FORM~GET_DATA.
  DATA lv_read_only TYPE boole_d.
  DATA lv_actions_enabled TYPE boole_d.

  FIELD-SYMBOLS <ls_field> LIKE LINE OF ct_field_usage.
  FIELD-SYMBOLS <ls_action> LIKE LINE OF ct_action_usage.

  "Regular data processing goes here...
  cs_data-field1 = ???.
  ...

  "Track the edit mode locally in order to avoid
  "unnecessary UI element updates:
  IF me->mv_edit_mode EQ iv_edit_mode.
    RETURN.
  ELSE.
    me->mv_edit_mode = iv_edit_mode.
  ENDIF.

  "Test the edit mode to see where we are:
  CASE iv_edit_mode.
    WHEN 'E'.                         "Edit Mode
      lv_read_only = abap_false.
      lv_actions_enabled = abap_true.
    WHEN 'R'.                         "Read Only Mode
      lv_read_only = abap_true.
```

[28] Note: This parameter was added with the SAP NetWeaver 7.03 release. So, for older SAP NetWeaver releases (e.g. the 7.02 release), you'll have to implement your own logic for tracking the edit mode (e.g. using application parameters).

```
      lv_actions_enabled = abap_false.
    WHEN OTHERS.
      RETURN.
  ENDCASE.

  "Apply UI element updates based on the current edit mode:
  LOOP AT ct_field_usage ASSIGNING <ls_field>.
    <ls_field>-read_only = lv_read_only.
  ENDLOOP.

  ev_field_usage_changed = abap_true.

  LOOP AT ct_action_usage ASSIGNING <ls_action>.
    <ls_action>-enabled = lv_actions_enabled.
  ENDLOOP.

  ev_action_usage_changed = abap_true.
endmethod.
```

Listing 8.5: Adjusting the Edit Mode of a UIBB

In general, we would recommend that you design the majority of your UIBBs to be aware of their edit mode. That way, you can get more reuse out of your UIBBs while resting comfortably knowing that they're smart enough to be used in varying contexts. This approach is particularly effective when combined with the use of a generic business object access layer and the wire model introduced in Chapter 7. Here, we can delegate transactional level concerns to the application controller and keep our UIBB implementations simple and straightforward.

8.4   Summary

In this chapter, we learned about some of the different ways that we could steer the behavior of FPM applications at a macro level. This is one of those areas of FPM application development where we can really round out the design and offer the user a rich and rewarding experience.

In the next chapter, we'll continue along these lines by taking a look at some of the more interactive elements of the FPM framework. You know, those little bells and whistles that make applications shine. Once we understand how to utilize these elements, our journey from novice to FPM master will be almost complete.

Chapter 9

Interactive Elements of the FPM

As we've seen throughout the course of this book, FPM applications are built using a layered approach. Here, we define/assemble a series of UIBB components, weave them together in a floorplan configuration, and then from there all that's left is to fill in any remaining gaps at the application level. In the previous chapter, we learned how application controllers are used to handle many application-level requirements. Now, we're ready to turn our attention towards some of the other framework elements that can be used to round out our FPM applications. Specifically, we'll focus in on those FPM framework elements that make our applications more interactive.

9.1 Working with Toolbars

Up to now, our coverage of toolbars in FPM applications has been tangential at best. This omission has been purposeful on our part since we felt like we needed to cover other related topics such as FPM event processing and application controllers before we could really dig in and describe all of the features that FPM toolbars have to offer. Now, we have what we need to get started.

In many respects, toolbars are to FPM applications what remote controls are to TV sets: they provide users with a set of controls which allow them to control the application experience. Since the toolbar UI pattern has been used so extensively in software over the past 30 years, it requires little introduction to developers and end users alike. When a user needs to perform a particular application function, they instinctively look to toolbars to find the functions they're looking for. In this section, we'll learn how to build intuitive toolbars which make it easy for users to maneuver within our FPM applications.

9.1.1 Configuration Concepts

Within the FPM framework, there are two classes of toolbars that we can configure[29]:

➢ **Application/Page Toolbar**

This toolbar is the main toolbar that shows up near the top of the floorplan layout. It is used to group together functions which affect the application as a whole (e.g. SAVE, EDIT, and so on).

In the case of GAF applications, keep in mind that there is no top-level toolbar, per se. Rather, each main step (and substep) within a given variant has its own toolbar. This allows us to adjust the toolbar configuration at each roadmap step, as needed. Fortunately, the FPM Configuration Editor takes care of plugging in the NEXT and PREVIOUS buttons automatically, so our configuration efforts here are limited to adding in custom application functions on an as-needed basis.

➢ **GUIBB-Level Toolbars**

These toolbars are defined within a given GUIBB configuration. Here, the integration points vary depending on the GUIBB component that we're working with. In general though, these toolbars are like lightweight versions of the application toolbar. The only difference in this case is that the scope of the embedded functions is limited to the UIBB itself. For example, we might use a toolbar in a list component to control the addition/removal of list elements at runtime.

For the most part, the basic configuration concepts are essentially the same for both toolbar types. However, in the case of GUIBB-level toolbars, we're limited in the types of functions that we can provide. When you think about it, this makes sense since certain operations don't really apply in a local UIBB context (e.g. a SAVE button, for instance). These differences are outlined in Table 9.1, which describes the kinds of elements that we configure within a given toolbar definition.

---

[29] This point refers to framework-based toolbars which are configured using the FPM Configuration Editor. Toolbars in freestyle UIBBs are configured outside of the FPM (i.e. in the Web Dynpro View Designer tool).

Element Type	Description	Page Toolbar	GUIBB Toolbar
Standard Function Buttons	These buttons provide some of the common global functions that you'd expect to find in any application definition (e.g. SAVE, EDIT, CHECK and CLOSE). By default, these buttons are linked with standard FPM event types. You can get a feel for the types of events that are supported by looking at the global GC_EVENT constant defined in the IF_FPM_CONSTANTS interface.	X	
Application-Specific Function Buttons	As the name implies, these button types are used to implement application-specific functions. Such functions can be defined globally in the page toolbar or locally within a GUIBB configuration. In the latter case, the application-specific buttons must be associated with FPM events defined in the GET_DEFINITION() method of the GUIBB's feeder class. At the application/page toolbar level, we have the option of assigning *precedence* to selected functions by defining an *Activation Function* and an optional *Alternative Function*. These functions are placed at the first and second positions in the application toolbar, respectively, to signify their importance. For example, in OIF/OVP applications, the FPM Configuration Editor will automatically define the SAVE button as the activation function since it's the most important and commonly used function on the screen.	X	X

Element Type	Description	Page Toolbar	GUIBB Toolbar
Navigation Menus	These built-in menus are available for configuration within the page toolbar. Here, we can provide navigation links to related applications of various types. We'll see how this works in Section 9.1.2.	X	

Table 9.1: Elements of FPM Toolbars

The screenshot contained in Figure 9.1 highlights some of the various toolbar element types described in Table 9.1. As you can see, in addition to regular buttons, we also have the option of defining button choice elements which aggregate related events together in a *button menu*. Here, each menu option corresponds with an FPM event ID which will be fired upon user selection.

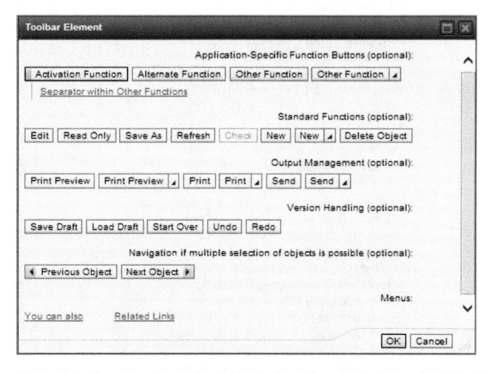

Figure 9.1: Choosing Among Available Toolbar Elements © Copyright 2013. SAP AG. All rights reserved

Regardless of a button's type (i.e. standard vs. application-specific), the basic configuration attributes are largely the same. As you can see in Figure 9.2, a button definition consists of an FPM event ID assignment, a text label, and various other display parameters. Collectively, these attributes provide the FPM framework with the information it needs to render a button and wire it up to an FPM event. Here, notice that we also have the option of defining event parameters which will be passed along with the configured FPM event at runtime. We can respond to these events in feeder classes, freestyle UIBBs, and application controllers as per usual.

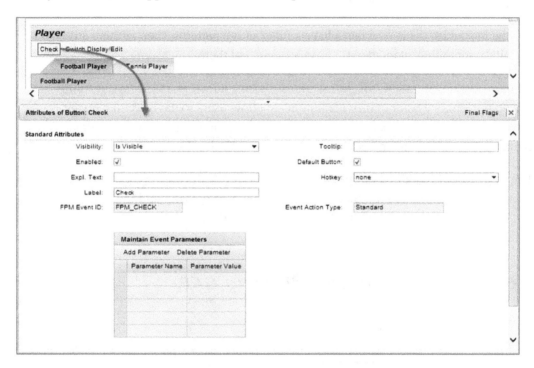

Figure 9.2: Configuring Toolbar Elements © Copyright 2013. SAP AG. All rights reserved

9.1.2 Dynamically Adjusting the Toolbar Layout

Now that we have a handle on how toolbars are configured *statically*, let's now see how we can manipulate them *dynamically* at runtime. In the upcoming sections, we'll see how this is achieved at both the page toolbar and GUIBB toolbar levels.

Adjusting the Page Toolbar Using the CNR APIs

In order to be able to dynamically adjust the page toolbar of an FPM application, we must enlist the services of the *context navigation region* (CNR) API. The CNR API is split into three separate floorplan-specific interfaces:

➢ `IF_FPM_CNR_OIF` for OIF floorplans

➢ `IF_FPM_CNR_GAF` for GAF floorplans

➢ `IF_FPM_CNR_OVP` for OVP floorplans

For the most part, these interfaces have similar usage patterns, though there are definitely some floorplan-specific nuances here and there.

To demonstrate how the CNR API works, let's take a look at a GAF application example. Here, we want to provide buttons to allow users to navigate to relevant substeps as they are made available during a user's journey through the roadmap. We caught a glimpse of this in Section 8.1.3 with our "Hello, World!" example.

The screenshots contained in Figure 9.3 and Figure 9.4 illustrate the changes that we want to make to the page toolbar. Here we want to strategically add in the ENTER MIDDLE NAME and EXIT TO FIRST NAME buttons at the proper locations within the roadmap flow.

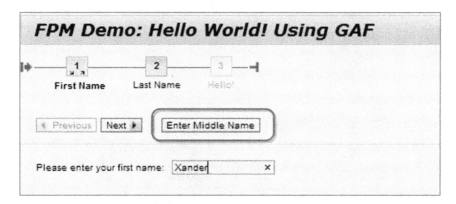

Figure 9.3: Adding Buttons to Control Access to a GAF Substep – Part 1 © Copyright 2013. SAP AG. All rights reserved

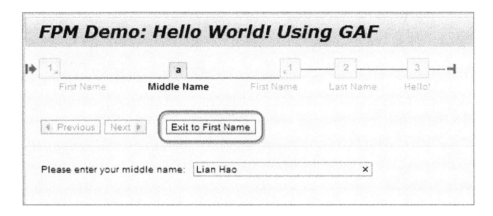

Figure 9.4: Adding Buttons to Control Access to a GAF Substep – Part 2 © Copyright 2013. SAP AG. All rights reserved

So how do we achieve this? Well, as it turns out, the CNR API makes this pretty easy. Basically, it's a two-step process:

1. First, we use the GET_SERVICE() method of the IF_FPM interface to obtain a reference to the CNR API for the floorplan type that we're working with.

2. Then, we use the appropriate method in the CNR API to create the buttons. For GAF/OIF floorplans, the method of choice is the DEFINE_BUTTON() method. For OVP floorplans, we must use the ADD_TOOLBAR_BUTTON() method.

This process is illustrated in the code excerpt contained in Listing 9.1. Here, you can see that we're defining the buttons in the WDDOINIT() method of the application controller for our "Hello, World!" application. By specifying the target mainstep/substep IDs, we can determine when and where these dynamically-created buttons will show up in the GAF page toolbar. Once the buttons are defined, we can respond to the FPM event defined in the IV_ON_ACTION parameter as per usual.

```
method WDDOINIT.
  DATA lo_fpm TYPE REF TO if_fpm.
  DATA lo_cnr TYPE REF TO if_fpm_cnr_gaf.

  "Initialize the controller:
  lo_fpm = cl_fpm_factory=>get_instance( ).
  lo_cnr ?=
    lo_fpm->get_service(
      cl_fpm_service_manager=>gc_key_cnr_gaf ).

  "Define a button to navigate to/from our custom sub-step:
```

```
lo_cnr->define_button(
  iv_variant_id   = 'V_NAME'
  iv_mainstep_id  = 'MAINSTEP_FIRST'
  iv_function     = if_fpm_constants=>gc_button-other_function
  iv_text         = 'Enter Middle Name'
  iv_enabled      = abap_true
  iv_on_action    = 'NAV_MIDDLENAME' ).

lo_cnr->define_button(
  iv_variant_id    = 'V_NAME'
  iv_mainstep_id   = 'MAINSTEP_FIRST'
  iv_subvariant_id = 'DEFAULT'
  iv_substep_id    = 'SUBSTEP_MIDDLE'
  iv_function      =
    if_fpm_constants=>gc_button-exit_to_mainstep
  iv_text          = 'Exit to First Name'
  iv_enabled       = abap_true
  iv_on_action     = 'NAV_FIRSTSTEP' ).
endmethod.
```

Listing 9.1: Dynamically Adding Buttons to the GAF Page Toolbar

Adjusting GUIBB Toolbars Using Feeder Classes

When it comes to adjusting the toolbar of GUIBB components, we have to get a little more creative. Here, we need to statically define the superset of buttons that we want to provide up front, and then we can toggle their visibility at runtime using the GET_DATA() method of the corresponding feeder class. Here's the step-by-step rundown:

1. First, we need to define the actions that will be used as the basis for building the buttons in the GET_DEFINITION() method of the associated feeder class. These actions are defined via the ET_ACTION_DEFINITION exporting table parameter of this method. Here, we can use the ENABLED and VISIBILITY attributes to control the initial visibility of the buttons at runtime.

2. Next, we need to configure the GUIBB component in the FPM Configuration Editor, statically defining all of the buttons that we want to eventually expose at runtime.

3. Finally, we must encode logic in the GET_DATA() method of the feeder class to toggle the ENABLED and VISIBILITY attributes which were initialized in the GET_DEFINITION() method. Here, we can use the provided IO_EVENT parameter to determine when and where to apply the changes.

9.1.3 Providing Navigation Menus

Frequently, we may have a requirement to provide users with navigation links which allow them to navigate to pertinent online help documentation, related applications, and so forth. Though we could probably conceive of several ways to achieve this requirement using standard WDA programming techniques, it turns out that the FPM provides a much easier alternative based on *launchpads*.

Conceptual Overview

As you may recall from Chapter 6, launchpads are defined as a collection of related navigation links that are grouped together and stored as a separate technical object in the system (using Transaction LPD_CUST). Within a launchpad definition, we can create links which point to all kinds of different applications: 3rd-party web applications (using URL-based access), classic Dynpro-based transactions, WDA/WDJ applications, and so on. There are several advantages to defining our navigation menus this way:

➤ First of all, the links configured within a launchpad definition are *parameterizable*. Among other things, this implies that we can define links in a system-independent way. Here, for example, we can use system aliases to bypass hard-coding of host names and ports in URL definitions. That way, a given link will point to the right host which corresponds with the current environment (e.g. Dev → Dev, QA → QA, and so on).

➤ Secondly, since launchpad definitions are maintained outside of FPM, they can be transported independently without requiring changes to the FPM application.

➤ Finally, use of a standard technology should make the maintenance process easier in the long run than if we were to build a custom solution on our own.

With all this in mind, let's now turn our attention to the configuration of navigation menus using the FPM Configuration Editor.

Adding Navigation Menus to the Page Toolbar

In order to add a navigation menu to the page toolbar, we must proceed as follows:

1. First, we need to open up the floorplan configuration for the target FPM application and open up the TOOLBAR SCHEMA tab. Here, we can press the TOOLBAR ELEMENT button to open up the dialog box shown in Figure 9.5.

2. Within the TOOLBAR ELEMENT dialog box shown in Figure 9.5, we can add a navigation menu to the page toolbar by clicking on the RELATED LINKS or YOU

CAN ALSO links provided in the menus section at the bottom of the dialog box (see Figure 9.5).

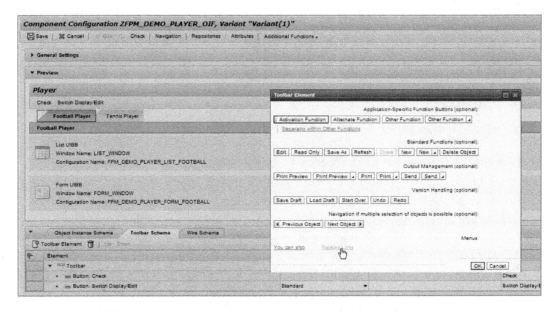

Figure 9.5: Creating Navigation Menus - Part 1 © Copyright 2013. SAP AG. All rights reserved

3.   Once the navigation menu has been added to the toolbar schema, we can edit its properties in the ATTRIBUTES panel shown in Figure 9.6. Here, the two main attributes of interest are the ROLE and INSTANCE attributes which point to a launchpad[30] definition in Transaction LPD_CUST.

---

[30] We covered launchpads in detail in Section 6.2.8.

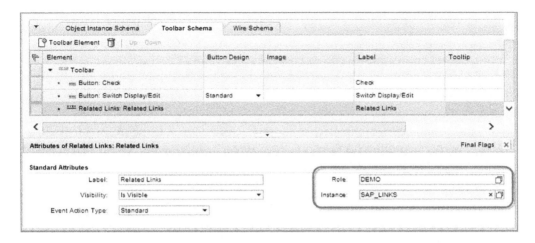

4. Finally, once we save our changes, we can see the new navigation menu show up in the page toolbar of our FPM application as shown in Figure 9.7. Here, the rendering process is 100% defined by the overarching floorplan component.

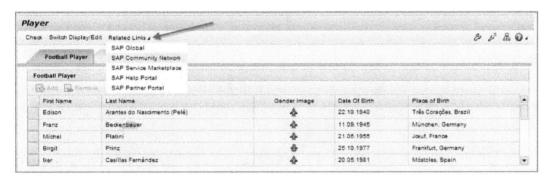

Runtime Behavior

Now that we've seen how navigation menus are configured in the FPM Configuration Editor, you might be wondering how all this works whenever users select navigation links at runtime. Well, by default, the floorplan component uses the metadata from the launchpad configuration to derive the target link URL and then launches the application in a separate browser window/tab. From a developer's perspective, there's nothing we have to do to make this happen. However, there are times whenever we may want to add in our own tweaks here or there. For this, we can enlist the services of the IF_FPM_NAVIGATION interface.

If you look at the IF_FPM_NAVIGATION interface in the Class Builder tool, you'll find that it defines a number of utility methods which allow us to modify a navigation menu at runtime. Here, we can add or remove application links, modify existing links, or even add in dynamic application parameters at runtime. Collectively, these utility methods provide us with the flexibility we need to adjust the navigation menu layouts such that they remain in step with the state of our FPM application at runtime.

To demonstrate how the IF_FPM_NAVIGATION interface is used in practice, let's take a look at an example. Figure 9.8 shows a sample launchpad which contains a URL-based application link which points to Google's search tool. What we'd like to do is have this application link drive a dynamic search based on key words derived somewhere within the application. So, for example, if we wanted to perform a search on the term *Floorplan Manager*, then we'd need to adjust the application URL to look like this: *https://www.google.com/search?q=Floorplan+Manager*. This can be accomplished using the MODIFY_PARAMETERS() method of the IF_FPM_NAVIGATION interface.

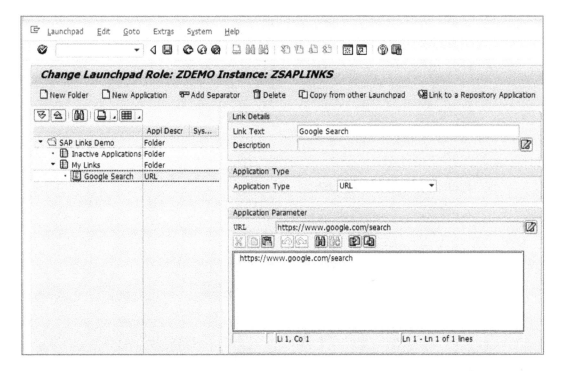

Figure 9.8: Adjusting the Query String Parameters of a URL-Based Application
© Copyright 2013. SAP AG. All rights reserved

As you might have guessed, this kind of page-level toolbar manipulation belongs within an application controller. The code excerpt contained in Listing 9.2 provides an example of how we can use the IF_FPM_NAVIGATION interface to perform this task. Here, we're obtaining the navigation reference from the FPM event instance, though we could have just as easily grabbed it using the GET_NAVIGATION() method of the IF_FPM interface. In any case, we can simply compile the list of parameters and pass it to the MODIFY_PARAMETERS() method and the URL will be adjusted prior to navigation.

```
method OVERRIDE_EVENT_OIF.
  DATA lo_nav_event TYPE REF TO cl_fpm_navigation_event.
  DATA lo_navigation TYPE REF TO if_fpm_navigation.
  DATA lt_params TYPE apb_lpd_t_params.
  FIELD-SYMBOLS <ls_target> TYPE if_fpm_navigation=>s_target.
  FIELD-SYMBOLS <ls_param> LIKE LINE OF lt_params.

  "Process global events of interest:
  CASE io_oif->mo_event->mv_event_id.
    WHEN if_fpm_constants=>gc_event-navigate.
      "Isolate the selected navigation target:
      lo_nav_event ?= io_oif->mo_event.
```

```
    lo_navigation = lo_nav_event->mo_navigation.
    READ TABLE lo_navigation->mt_targets
      ASSIGNING <ls_target>
        WITH KEY key = lo_nav_event->mv_target_key
                alias = lo_nav_event->mv_target_alias.
    IF sy-subrc NE 0.
      RETURN.
    ENDIF.

    "Process the selected navigation target:
    CASE <ls_target>-text.
      WHEN 'Google Search'.
        "Update the URL query string parameters to point
        "to a search target:
        APPEND INITIAL LINE TO lt_params ASSIGNING <ls_param>.
        <ls_param>-key = 'q'.
        <ls_param>-value = 'Floorplan Manager'.

        lo_navigation->modify_parameters(
          EXPORTING
            id_target_key = lo_nav_event->mv_target_key
            it_business_parameter = lt_params ).
    ENDCASE.
  ENDCASE.
endmethod.
```

Listing 9.2: Updating the Parameters of a URL Link

An Alternative to Launchpads

Sometimes, we may want to provide a navigation link outside of the provided YOU CAN ALSO and RELATED LINKS navigation menus. For example, we might just want to have a button to open up another application in a separate window. Whatever the situation might be, there is an alternative to using launchpads: the IF_FPM_NAVIGATE_TO interface.

If you look at the IF_FPM_NAVIGATE_TO interface in the Class Builder tool, you can see that it defines a number of methods whose name starts with the term "launch" (e.g. LAUNCH_URL(), LAUNCH_WEBDYNPRO_ABAP(), and so on). These methods make it pretty easy to launch an external application on the fly. Compared to the launchpad-based approach though, there is a twist: we have to come up with the navigation parameters on our own.

To access this alternative navigation API, we must invoke the GET_NAVIGATE_TO() method of the IF_FPM interface. Much like the launchpad-based example contained in

Listing 9.2, this navigation logic belongs in an application controller. You can find some examples that demonstrate the use of this API in the *FPM Developer's Guide*.

9.2 Messaging in FPM Applications

During the course of an FPM application session, there will be times whenever we need to display messages on the screen so that users understand what's going on behind the scenes. For example, if an error occurs during the application processing, we need to display an error message providing information about what went wrong. Similarly, if an operation is successful, we should display a success message so that users can see that their request was processed. Within the FPM framework, we can generate such messages using the *FPM Message Manager*.

The FPM Message Manager exists in two parts:

➢ **Message Region**

The message region (also sometimes referred to as the *message area*) is a content area that is dynamically placed towards the top of a floorplan layout. Here, users can interactively process through any messages raised by the application.

➢ **IF_FPM_MESSAGE_MANAGER Interface**

This interface provides the programmatic part of the FPM Message Manager. Here, methods are provided which allow us to create various types of messages, raise exceptions, and clear the message log as needed.

In this section, we'll learn how to use these elements to handle messaging requirements in FPM applications.

9.2.1 Configuring the Message Region

Even though the message region is a content area owned by the floorplan component, we do have some options for configuring its layout. We can configure these settings in the GENERAL SETTINGS section of a floorplan configuration as shown in Figure 9.9.

*Figure 9.9: Configuring the Message Region © Copyright 2013. SAP AG. All rights
reserved*

Within the MESSAGE SETTINGS section, we can configure the following attributes:

➤ **Maximum Message Size**

This parameter determines how many messages are displayed in the message area
before scrolling begins.

➤ **Display Message Log**

Whenever this checkbox is turned on, users have the option of viewing messages in
a *message log*. Figure 9.10 and Figure 9.11 show the differences the normal view of
the message region and the message log view. In the latter case, messages are
displayed in a table along with information about when they were issued, etc.

➤ **Message Area Design**

We can use this attribute to influence the display of the message region on the
screen (e.g. displaying a thin border, etc.). Most of the time, we'll want to stick with
the default setting here.

➤ **Message Area Display**

This attribute influences when the message area should be displayed (e.g. always vs.
whenever a message is in context, etc.).

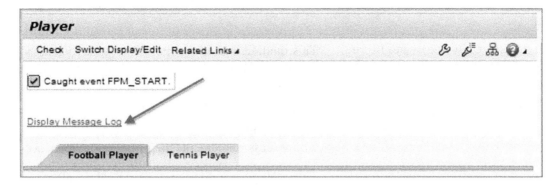

Figure 9.10: Accessing the Message Log View of the Message Region – Part 1

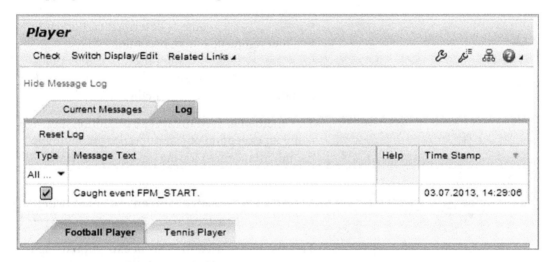

Figure 9.11: Accessing the Message Log View of the Message Region – Part 2

9.2.2 Working with the IF_FPM_MESSAGE_MANAGER Interface

Now that we have a feel for how messages are displayed, let's turn our attention to how they're created in the first place. As we noted earlier, this is achieved using the IF_FPM_MESSAGE_MANAGER interface. Table 9.2 describes the methods provided by this interface.

Method	Description
report_message()	This method is used to report free-form text messages.

Method	Description
report_t100_message()	This method is used to report T100 type messages defined in Message Maintenance using Transaction SE91.
report_object_message()	This method is used to report exceptions. Here, the object being referenced is an exception object whose class implements the IF_MESSAGE interface.
report_bapiret2_message()	This method is used to report BAPIRET2 style messages returned from BAPI functions.
raise_exception()	This method is used to raise an exception message using a free text message of our choosing. Unlike the REPORT_*() methods described earlier, calling this method results in an exception of type CX_FPM_EXCEPTION being raised. This can put a halt to request processing, so it carries a bit more bite than the REPORT_*() methods.
raise_cx_root_exception()	This method is used to raise an exception message using an exception object reference belonging to the inheritance tree for the CX_ROOT root exception type.
raise_t100_exception()	This method is used to raise an exception using a T100 type message.
raise_bapiret2_exception()	This method is used to raise an exception using a structure of type BAPIRET2 as the message description.
clear_messages()	Since messages created using the REPORT_*() and RAISE_*() methods can potentially have a long-term duration in the message log, this method exists for housekeeping purposes. For example, we might use this method to clear out any error messages after a user corrects input errors and resubmits their request.

Table 9.2: Methods of the IF_FPM_MESSAGE_MANAGER Interface

If we open up the IF_FPM_MESSAGE_MANAGER interface in the Class Builder tool and look around at the method signatures, we can see that most of the methods described in Table 9.2 come with quite a few parameters. Though you can find details about the function of these parameters in the Class Builder documentation, we thought we would highlight some of the more prominent parameters so that you can get a feel for what we can achieve with the IF_FPM_MESSAGE_MANAGER interface:

➤ IV_SEVERITY

This parameter determines the severity of the message (i.e. success vs. warning vs. errors).

➤ IV_LIFETIME

This parameter determines how long the message remains in scope within the message log. The various options are described in the GC_LIFE_VISIBILITY* constants defined within the IF_FPM_MESSAGE_MANAGER interface.

➤ IO_ELEMENT / IV_ATTRIBUTE_NAME

These parameters can be used to link a message to a particular WDA controller context element/attribute. These parameters can come in handy whenever we're using the IF_FPM_SHARED_DATA interface to store data centrally within the WDA controller context of an application controller component.

➤ IS_NAVIGATION_ALLOWED

This Boolean parameter can be used to determine whether or not users can navigate to the next roadmap step in a GAF application in situations where errors exist.

Accessing the Message Manager at Runtime

Now that we have a feel for how the IF_FPM_MESSAGE_MANAGER interface is structured, let's see how we can use it to create messages within our FPM applications. As you can see in Listing 9.3, the IF_FPM interface makes this pretty easy to accomplish anywhere within our FPM application (e.g. in an application controller, a freestyle UIBB component, GUIBB components, and so on). Basically, all we have to do is use the CL_FPM_FACTORY class to obtain a reference to the IF_FPM interface and then access the message manager from its MO_MESSAGE_MANAGER instance attribute. With this object reference in hand, we can create messages to our heart's content using the methods outlined in Table 9.2.

```
method someMethod.
  DATA lo_fpm     TYPE REF TO if_fpm.
  DATA lo_msg_mgr TYPE REF TO if_fpm_message_manager.
  DATA lv_message TYPE string.

  lo_fpm = cl_fpm_factory=>get_instance( ).
  lo_msg_mgr = lo_fpm->mo_message_manager.
  lv_message = |Record is locked by user { sy-uname }.|.
```

```
  lo_msg_mgr->raise_exception( lv_message ).
endmethod.
```

Listing 9.3: Reporting a Message Using the Message Manager

What about the Message Parameters in Feeder Class Methods?

As you may recall from Chapter 6, a number of the feeder class interface methods define exporting parameters in which we can pass back various kinds of messages. Given this, you might be wondering how those messages relate to the messages maintained within the message manager. As it turns out, there is a direct correlation between these message types.

If you dig into the guts of the various wrapper methods of the GUIBB component definitions, you can see that the messages returned from these feeder class methods are passed into the message manager using methods of the IF_FPM_MESSAGE_MANAGER interface. Thus, the feeder class parameters are merely convenience mechanisms which make it easier to implement feeder classes.

9.2.3 Message Mapping

Oftentimes, we're at the mercy of the underlying application model when it comes to generating messages. Here, we can think of the model as a black box: we pass data from the UI into it, and it spits back some results. Sometimes though, the returned results are rather cryptic (or occasionally in a different language). This is often the case with BAPI calls where the BAPIRET2 return messages could be coming from just about anywhere in the system. In these situations, we have a dilemma on our hands as it could be argued that no error message at all is better than one that makes absolutely no sense to the user.

One way of getting around this issue is to employ the use of the *Message Mapper* feature introduced with the SAP NetWeaver 7.03 release. As the name suggests, this feature can be used to map cryptic messages to more generalized messages so that users have a better sense of what might have gone wrong. Such mappings are defined in a series of customizing tables which are used internally by the FPM framework to handle the message translations. For more information about how to setup these tables and access this feature, we recommend that you read through the section entitled *Message Mapper* in the *FPM Developer's Guide*.

9.3   Dialog Boxes

In this section, we'll look at how to implement another familiar UI element within our FPM application designs: *dialog boxes*. Dialog boxes are used in many different ways in

FPM applications: to solicit information from the user, to provide a popup window containing additional information about a selected element, and so forth. For the most part, when and how we choose to utilize dialog boxes is left up to us as developers. From the FPM framework's perspective, dialog boxes are basically just a specialized page type that's only opened in special circumstances. In the upcoming section, we'll learn how to work with dialog boxes.

9.3.1 Configuring Dialog Boxes

For the most part, dialog boxes are created just like any other page type within a floorplan configuration. Indeed, it's one of the page type options that show up whenever we select the NEW button menu in the NAVIGATION panel of FLUID (see Figure 9.12).

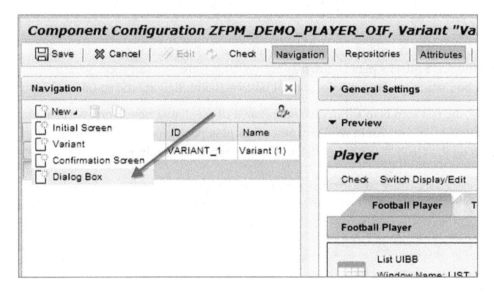

Figure 9.12: Creating a Dialog Box - Part 1 © Copyright 2013. SAP AG. All rights reserved

In order to complete the dialog box definition, there are three items that we must configure:

1. First, we need to configure a unique ID for the dialog box using the DIALOG BOX ID attribute shown at the top of Figure 9.13. This ID represents a unique handle that we'll use to reference the dialog box from a programmatic context.

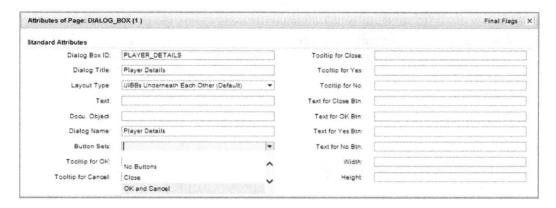

Figure 9.13: Creating a Dialog Box - Part 2 © Copyright 2013. SAP AG. All rights reserved

2. Next, we need to fill in the various visual attributes of the dialog box definition using the ATTRIBUTES panel shown in Figure 9.13. Here, we can specify the dialog box's title, its layout type, control buttons, width/height, and so on.

3. Finally, the last step is to fill in the content area of the dialog box. Here, we can proceed just like we would with any other floorplan page type by embedding UIBBs on the OBJECT INSTANCE SCHEMA tab page as shown in Figure 9.14.

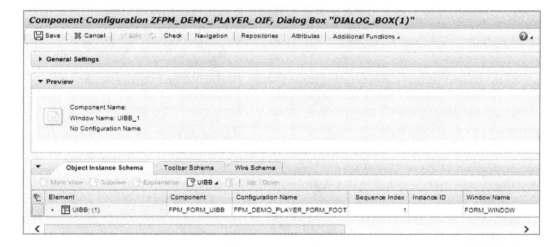

Figure 9.14: Creating a Dialog Box - Part 3 © Copyright 2013. SAP AG. All rights reserved

9.3.2 Opening Dialog Boxes at Runtime

Once we've defined our dialog boxes in the FPM Configuration Editor, there are two different ways for us to open them at runtime:

➢ We can use the OPEN_DIALOG_BOX() method of the IF_FPM interface to open them within an event handler method (e.g. in a feeder class or application controller).

➢ We can use the pre-defined FPM_OPEN_DIALOG event to link the dialog box to a toolbar button.

In the upcoming sections, we'll see how both approaches are used to open up dialog boxes.

Opening Dialog Boxes Programmatically

To open up a dialog box from a programmatic context, all we have to do is obtain a reference to the FPM framework handle (which is of type IF_FPM) and call the OPEN_DIALOG_BOX() method. As you can see in Listing 9.4, the main driver for this method is the IV_DIALOG_BOX_ID parameter which corresponds with the dialog box ID that was assigned to the dialog box in the FPM Configuration Editor. Besides that key bit of information, we also have the option of overriding the dialog box visual properties using the IS_DIALOG_BOX_PROPERTIES parameter. Also of note is the optional IO_EVENT_DATA parameter which can be used to pass parameters to the dialog box at runtime.

```
method myEventHandler.
  DATA lo_fpm TYPE REF TO if_fpm.
  DATA ls_props TYPE fpm_s_dialog_box_properties.

  ls_props-title = 'Customer Details'.
  "ls_props-...

  lo_fpm = cl_fpm_factory=>get_instance( ).
  lo_fpm->open_dialog_box(
    EXPORTING
      iv_dialog_box_id = 'CUSTOMER_DETAILS'
      is_dialog_box_properties = ls_props ).
endmethod.
```

Listing 9.4: Opening a Dialog Box Using the IF_FPM Interface

Behind the scenes, the OPEN_DIALOG_BOX() method packages up the parameters that we pass to it in an instance of the CL_FPM_EVENT class and raises the FPM_OPEN_DIALOG event. Internally, the FPM framework keys off this event to determine when and how to open up a dialog box. In Section 9.3.3, we'll see how UIBBs that are embedded in the dialog box can also key off this event in order to initialize themselves.

Opening a Dialog Box from a Toolbar Button

To open up a dialog box directly from a toolbar button, all we have to do is assign the FPM_OPEN_DIALOG event to the button's FPM EVENT ID attribute as shown in Figure 9.15. Here, we can specify the target dialog box using the DIALOG_BOX_ID parameter maintained in the MAINTAIN EVENT PARAMETERS table shown at the bottom of Figure 9.15. At runtime, the FPM framework will use this event as a means for opening the target dialog box automatically; we don't have to write any custom event handler logic to make this happen.

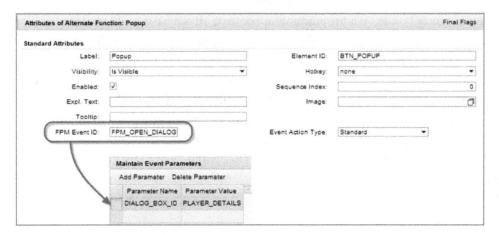

Figure 9.15: Linking a Button from the Page Toolbar to a Dialog Box © Copyright 2013. SAP AG. All rights reserved

9.3.3 Communicating with Dialog Boxes

Both of the techniques for opening dialog boxes described in the previous section ultimately result in the same FPM event being fired at runtime: the FPM_OPEN_DIALOG event. Though this is mostly a housekeeping detail for the FPM framework itself, it also has some significance on the development side. This is because this particular event is often used to facilitate communication with dialog boxes at runtime.

So how does this work? Well, as we noted in Section 9.3.2, we can pass all kinds of different event parameters along with the FPM_OPEN_DIALOG event. Some of these parameters are needed by the FPM framework in order to determine which dialog box to open, the launch context, and so on. However, there's nothing stopping us from passing along additional parameters as needed. For example, if we wanted to display the details of a particular customer in a dialog box, then it would make sense to pass the customer's ID as a parameter.

On the flip side of the exchange, we can consume these parameters within the event handler methods of the feeder classes associated with UIBBs that are embedded within the dialog box. Listing 9.5 demonstrates how this works in the GET_DATA() method of some form UIBB that's embedded in a dialog box. As you can see, there's nothing really special going on here - it's just FPM event processing as per usual.

```
METHOD if_fpm_guibb_form~get_data.
  DATA lv_customer_id TYPE /bobf/demo_customer_id.

  CASE io_event->mv_event_id.
    WHEN cl_fpm_event=>gc_event_open_dialog_box.
      "Read the event parameters into context:
      io_event->mo_event_data->get_value(
        EXPORTING iv_key   = 'CUSTOMER_ID'
        IMPORTING ev_value = lv_customer_id ).

      "Initialization code goes here...
  ENDCASE.
ENDMETHOD.
```

Listing 9.5: Retrieving Parameters from the FPM_OPEN_DIALOG Event

In addition to event-based communication, UIBBs that are embedded in dialog boxes can also receive data from some of the other data sources reviewed in earlier chapters of the book (e.g. wire connections, shared data instances, etc.). Which of these options you choose to implement is up to you as a developer. However, depending on the context, we would encourage you to think long and hard about how tightly you want to couple a dialog box to a particular application instance. Frequently, the UIBBs embedded in dialog boxes are reusable in a wide variety of contexts, so the more autonomous we can make them, the better.

9.4   Displaying Information in the Information Area (IDR)

As we learned in Chapter 3, both the OIF and GAF floorplan layouts contain a top-level *information area*[31] which can be used to display information about the current object instance/process. In this section, we'll learn how to fill in this dynamic content area.

9.4.1 Anatomy of the Information Area

Before we begin looking at ways of filling in the information area, we first need to take a quick look at the anatomy of this area so that we can understand the various elements

---

[31] In previous releases, the information area was referred to as the *identification region* (IDR).

in play. As you can see in Figure 9.16, the information area is broken up into two distinct areas:

➢ On the left-hand side, we have the *ticket area* which is further split into two sub-areas: the *ticket top* and *ticket bottom*.

➢ On the right-hand side, we have the *items area* in which we can plug in a series of name-value pairs which provide additional information of interest to the user.

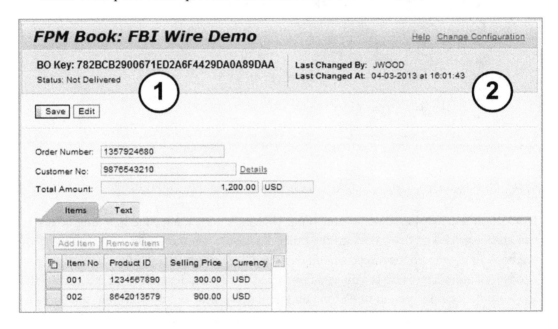

Figure 9.16: Anatomy of the Information Area © Copyright 2013. SAP AG. All rights reserved

As we go to layout the information area at design time, it's up to us as to which areas we choose to fill in. We could fill in both areas, just the ticket or items area, or just part of the left-hand ticket area. At runtime, the IDR component will take care of rendering the information area to accommodate the data that we've filled in.

9.4.2 Working with the IF_FPM_IDR Interface

In order to fill in the contents of the information area, we must enlist the services of the IF_FPM_IDR interface. We can obtain an object reference which implements this interface using the GET_SERVICE() method of the IF_FPM interface. Once we have an IF_FPM_IDR reference in hand, we can use its methods to fill in pertinent sections of the information area.

Listing 9.6 demonstrates how this works in practice. Here, you can see how we're filling in the information area using two methods defined by the IF_FPM_IDR interface:

➤ The ticket area is being filled in using the aptly named SET_TICKET() method.

➤ The items area is being filled in using the ADD_ITEM_GROUP_BY_VAL() method. Here, the various item name-value pairs are passed using a table parameter of type IF_FPM_IDR=>T_ITEMS_VAL.

```abap
method FILL_OIF_INFO_AREA.
    DATA lo_fpm       TYPE REF TO if_fpm.
    DATA lo_idr       TYPE REF TO if_fpm_idr.
    DATA lv_key       TYPE string.
    DATA lv_status    TYPE string.
    DATA lt_idr_items TYPE if_fpm_idr=>t_items_val.

    FIELD-SYMBOLS <ls_idr_item> TYPE if_fpm_idr=>s_items_val.

    lo_fpm = cl_fpm_factory=>get_instance( ).
    lo_idr ?= me->mo_fpm->get_service(
      cl_fpm_service_manager=>gc_key_idr ).

    "lv_key = ...
    "lv_status = ...

    lo_idr->set_ticket( iv_top = lv_key
                        iv_bottom = lv_status ).

    APPEND INITIAL LINE TO lt_idr_items ASSIGNING <ls_idr_item>.
    <ls_idr_item>-label_name = `User Name:`.
    <ls_idr_item>-value = sy-uname.

    APPEND INITIAL LINE TO lt_idr_items ASSIGNING <ls_idr_item>.
    <ls_idr_item>-label_name = `Current Date:`.
    <ls_idr_item>-value = sy-datum.

    APPEND INITIAL LINE TO lt_idr_items ASSIGNING <ls_idr_item>.
    <ls_idr_item>-label_name = `Current Time:`.
    <ls_idr_item>-value = sy-uzeit.

    lo_idr->add_item_group_by_val( it_items = lt_idr_items ).
endmethod.
```

Listing 9.6: Manipulating the Information Area

As you might expect, this kind of code normally belongs in an application controller since we're manipulating an application-level content area. Here, we can use the

OVERRIDE_EVENT...() method of IF_FPM_OIF_CONF_EXIT / IF_FPM_GAF_CONF_EXIT interfaces to control when and where specific updates are applied.

9.5 Drag-and-Drop

Throughout the course of this book, we've observed several mechanisms for sharing data between UIBBs: FPM eventing, context mapping, shared memory techniques, etc. From a user's perspective, these data sharing methods are rather *passive* in nature. This is to say that data is normally transferred in an indirect manner as a result of some other operation. Sometimes though, we might want to let users to take on a more active role in the data transfer process, allowing them to visualize the data as it's being passed back and forth between UIBBs. One of the most intuitive ways of achieving this in the FPM framework is to utilize its built-in drag-and-drop support. In this section, we'll see how to utilize this feature in our FPM applications.

9.5.1 Enabling Drag-and-Drop

Within the FPM application development context, drag-and-drop is something that occurs between a pair of GUIBB components. For example, we might drag a row from a list UIBB and drop it on a form UIBB used to display row details. This is demonstrated in the sample application shown in Figure 9.17.

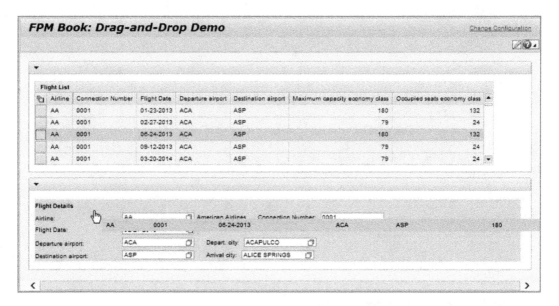

Figure 9.17: Using Drag-and-Drop to Copy a List Record to a Details Form

Whenever we talk about drag-and-drop within the FPM development context, we're talking about the built-in framework-level support for drag-and-drop between GUIBB components. Since the underlying WDA framework also provides support for drag-and-drop, it's also possible to implement drag-and-drop scenarios between freestyle UIBB components. In this case, however, we cannot rely on the FPM framework to do any of the heavy lifting; we're 100% on our own.

To enable drag-and-drop support for a given GUIBB instance, we simply need to fill in the ET_DND_DEFINITION table parameter provided by the GET_DEFINITION() method of the GUIBB instance's feeder class. Each record within this table specifies a drag or drop scenario from the perspective of the GUIBB component. These scenarios are defined by the following fields:

➢ **Type**

In this field, we can specify the type of drag-and-drop scenario we want to configure. Here, we can choose between one of two values: DRAG for drag scenarios and DROP for drop scenarios.

➢ **Enabled**

In this Boolean field, we can specify whether or not the drag-and-drop scenario is enabled at runtime. In Section 9.5.2, we'll see how this default setting can be overridden.

➢ **Tags**

Tags are string-based labels used to define *matches* in drag-and-drop scenarios. For example, in Figure 9.18, you can see how a match is established between a list UIBB that has a drag record with the tag FLIGHT_CONN and a form UIBB that has a drop record with the tag FLIGHT*. Here, the asterisk (*) character is used as a wild card. So, in this example, the target form UIBB can receive drag data from any source UIBB that has a tag that begins with the FLIGHT prefix. Had we tried to drag data from a source UIBB with the tag OTHER, then the mouse cursor would have shown up with an invalid drop target icon and the drop operation would not have been possible.

Within a given ET_DND_DEFINITION record, we can specify multiple tag values in the TAGS column by separating the individual tags with a space character. What we choose to encode in this column is really up to us. However, we'd highly recommend that you adopt a naming convention that has semantic meaning within the source/target GUIBB component itself rather than encoding scenario-specific tags such as FROM_SOURCE_UIBB_A. By keeping the tags generic, we have a better opportunity for reuse in other UIBB placement scenarios.

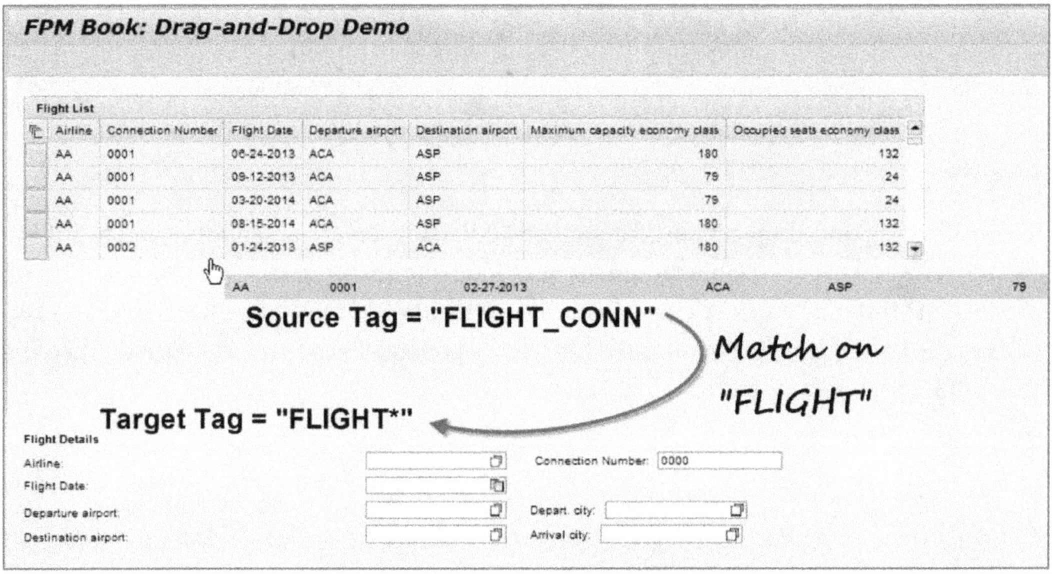

Figure 9.18: Understanding the Tag Concept in Drag-and-Drop Scenarios © Copyright 2013. SAP AG. All rights reserved

➢ **Scope**

The SCOPE field determines the scope of a drag or drop operation. Here, we can choose between two values: G for global scope and L for local scope. What's the difference? Well, if a drag/drop record has global scope, then it can be used in inter-UIBB drag-and-drop scenarios. On the other hand, local scope only allows for intra-UIBB drag-and-drop scenarios. Most of the time, we'll prefer the global scope setting.

➢ **Name**

This field is used to define an optional name for the drag/drop scenario.

➢ **Override**

This Boolean field allows us to determine whether or not the default settings defined in the GET_DEFINITION() method can be later overwritten at design time and/or runtime. We'll learn more about how this works in Section 9.5.2.

Listing 9.7 shows how we've configured the drag scenario for the list UIBB used in the example application shown in Figure 9.17. Here, you can see how we've defined a drag record with global scope that has the tag FLIGHT_CONN. Then, in Listing 9.8, you can see how we configured a drop record in the form UIBB to receive this data.

```
method IF_FPM_GUIBB_LIST~GET_DEFINITION.
  DATA lo_line_def TYPE REF TO cl_abap_structdescr.
  FIELD-SYMBOLS
    <ls_dnd_definition> LIKE LINE OF et_dnd_definition.

  lo_line_def ?=
    cl_abap_structdescr=>describe_by_name( 'SFLIGHTS' ).
  eo_field_catalog =
    cl_abap_tabledescr=>create( p_line_type = lo_line_def ).

  APPEND INITIAL LINE TO et_dnd_definition
                ASSIGNING <ls_dnd_definition>.
  <ls_dnd_definition>-type     = 'DRAG'.
  <ls_dnd_definition>-enabled  = abap_true.
  <ls_dnd_definition>-tags     = 'FLIGHT_CONN'.
  <ls_dnd_definition>-scope    = 'G'.
  <ls_dnd_definition>-override = abap_true.
endmethod.
```

Listing 9.7: Creating a Drag Record in a List Feeder Class

```
method IF_FPM_GUIBB_FORM~GET_DEFINITION.
  FIELD-SYMBOLS
    <ls_dnd_def> LIKE LINE OF et_dnd_definition.

  eo_field_catalog ?=
    cl_abap_structdescr=>describe_by_name( 'SFLIGHTS' ).

  APPEND INITIAL LINE TO et_dnd_definition
                ASSIGNING <ls_dnd_def>.
  <ls_dnd_def>-type    = 'DROP'.
  <ls_dnd_def>-enabled = abap_true.
  <ls_dnd_def>-tags    = 'FLIGHT*'.
  <ls_dnd_def>-scope   = 'G'.
endmethod.
```

Listing 9.8: Creating a Drop Record in a Form Feeder Class

Since both of the drag-and-drop records are enabled by default, the only thing left for us to do to complete the drag-and-drop scenario is figure out what to do with the dropped data at runtime. Here, we must implement some event handling logic to respond to the FPM_DROP_COMPLETED event that is triggered by the FPM framework whenever the user completes a drag-and-drop gesture using their mouse cursor. Listing 9.9 shows how we responded to this event in the GET_DATA() method of the form UIBB's feeder class in our sample scenario. The code itself can be broken down into four discrete steps:

1. First, we extract information about the drag source using the IO_EVENT parameter. If you look at structure FPMGB_S_DRAG_AND_DROP in the ABAP Dictionary, you'll find that it contains a wealth of information about a drag source.

2. Next, we're using the DRAG_SOURCE_INDICES component of the FPMGB_S_DRAG_AND_DROP structure to determine which record was selected in the source list UIBB.

3. Once we determine the index of the source record, we use that index to read from the drag source data table and extract the source data.

4. Finally, we take the extracted source data and copy it over into the form data.

```
method IF_FPM_GUIBB_FORM~GET_DATA.
  DATA ls_drag_result TYPE fpmgb_s_drag_and_drop.
  DATA ls_flight      TYPE sflights.

  FIELD-SYMBOLS <lt_source_data> TYPE STANDARD TABLE.
  FIELD-SYMBOLS <ls_source_rec> TYPE ANY.
  FIELD-SYMBOLS <ls_selected> TYPE rstabix.

  CASE io_event->mv_event_id.
    WHEN if_fpm_guibb_list=>gc_guibb_list_on_drop.
      "Retrieve the selected list record from the drop event:
      io_event->mo_event_data->get_value(
        EXPORTING iv_key   =
          if_fpm_guibb_constants=>gc_guibb_dnd-drag_source
        IMPORTING ev_value = ls_drag_result ).

      IF ls_drag_result-drag_source_data IS NOT BOUND.
        RETURN.
      ENDIF.

      "Read the selected record from the drag source data:
      ASSIGN ls_drag_result-drag_source_data->*
         TO <lt_source_data>.
      LOOP AT ls_drag_result-drag_source_indices
         ASSIGNING <ls_selected>.
        READ TABLE <lt_source_data> INDEX <ls_selected>-tabix
         ASSIGNING <ls_source_rec>.
        IF sy-subrc EQ 0.
          "Copy the selected record to the form data:
          MOVE-CORRESPONDING <ls_source_rec> TO ls_flight.
          cs_data = ls_flight.
          ev_data_changed = abap_true.

          EXIT.
        ENDIF.
```

```
      ENDLOOP.
    ENDCASE.
  endmethod.
```

Listing 9.9: Responding to a Drop Event at Runtime

Even though the code excerpt contained in Listing 9.9 is rather specific to our sample scenario, we can still see a basic pattern for implementing drag-and-drop scenarios. In particular, we can see that the FPM framework makes life pretty easy on us by adding all of the drag source details to the IO_EVENT parameter passed to the target UIBB's feeder class methods. With this information in hand, we can implement the exact data transfer semantics that we want: pure data copy, cut and paste, the shuttle UI pattern, and so on.

Performance Note

At first glance, it may seem that passing all this drag source data around in FPM events is a bad idea performance-wise. Here, it's important to keep in mind that the FPM framework uses reference semantics to pass in the drag source data. Thus, it's not as if we have these large CL_FPM_EVENT instances floating around with huge internal tables nested within. This indirection was evidenced in the code excerpt contained in Listing 9.9. There, we de-referenced the drag source data into a FIELD-SYMBOL and then used index-based access to read[32] the source record.

9.5.2 Overriding Drag-and-Drop Settings

As we observed in the previous section, drag-and-drop scenarios are defined within the GET_DEFINITION() method of GUIBB feeder classes. This implies that drag-and-drop scenarios must be defined up front at design time. That's not to say that we can't apply a few tweaks here and there after the fact though.

The first option we have for adjusting these settings is within a GUIBB configuration. Here, we have the option of changing the drag-and-drop settings specified in the GET_DEFINITION() method. As you can see in Figure 9.19, we can use these settings to disable a drag/drop scenario, adjust the tag values, and so on.

---

[32] It probably goes without saying, but just in case, we highly recommend that you avoid using these data references to modify the source data in any way. If you need want to implement cut-and-paste semantics, the data to be cut should always be removed using an event handler from the source UIBB's feeder class. Indirect referenced-based access can cause all kinds of unexpected problems.

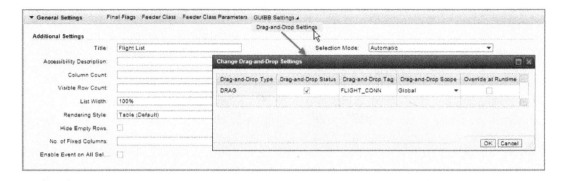

As of the SAP NetWeaver 7.03 release, we also now have the option of changing drag-and-drop scenarios at runtime. Here, we can use the CT_DND_ATTRIBUTES table parameter of the GET_DATA() method in the GUIBB's feeder class to adjust/remove existing drag/drop scenario records or create new ones. Since the CT_DND_ATTRIBUTES table parameter has the same data type as the ET_DND_DEFINITION parameter of the GET_DEFINITION() method, this process should feel pretty straightforward. Indeed, the only real difference in this scenario is that you have to communicate your changes by toggling the EV_DND_ATTR_CHANGED Boolean parameter so that the FPM framework can update its registry of available drag-and-drop scenarios.

9.6   Quick Helps

Despite our best efforts to build an intuitive, easy-to-use UI, there are times whenever we may need to provide users with some additional guidance to help them get up and running. Though there are many ways of achieving this on our own, it turns out that the FPM framework has a standard way of supporting this requirement: *quick helps*.

In a nutshell, quick helps are explanation texts that can be associated with various screens within a floorplan configuration: initial screens, main/substeps, subviews, and so forth. In this section, we'll show you how to provide quick helps with your FPM applications.

9.6.1 Creating Quick Helps

As we noted earlier, quick helps are defined on the level of a floorplan configuration. Within the FPM Configuration Editor tool, we can create a quick help for a given page element by selecting the EXPLANATION button in the toolbar of the OBJECT INSTANCE SCHEMA tab page (see Figure 9.20).

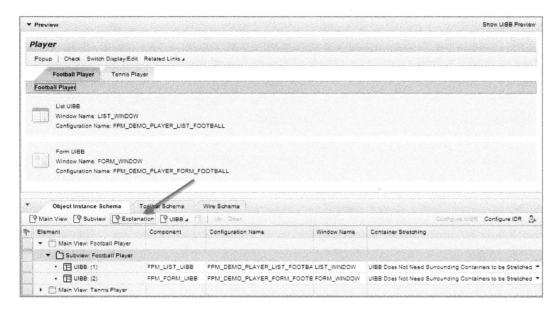

Figure 9.20: Creating an Explanation Text in FLUID – Part 1 © Copyright 2013. SAP AG. All rights reserved

Once the explanation element is created, we can configure its properties on the ATTRIBUTES panel as shown in Figure 9.21. Here, there are two attributes that we can configure:

➢ **Text**

This attribute allows us to specify the quick help text using a free-form text string defined within the floorplan configuration. As you can see in Figure 9.21, whatever we specify here will show up as the quick help text at runtime.

➢ **Documentation Object**

This attribute offers us an alternative approach to defining the quick help text: *documentation objects*. Documentation objects are maintained within the ABAP Workbench using Transaction SE61. Compared with the free-form text approach, documentation objects offer several advantages:

❖ Documentation objects offer better support for styling, long text maintenance, and so on.

❖ Documentation objects are keyed by language, which means that we can implement internationalization (I18N) with our quick help texts if needed.

❖ As standalone objects, documentation objects can be reused in multiple scenarios. Plus, if we need to change the text, we can do so outside of the FPM application(s) and have it apply dynamically at runtime.

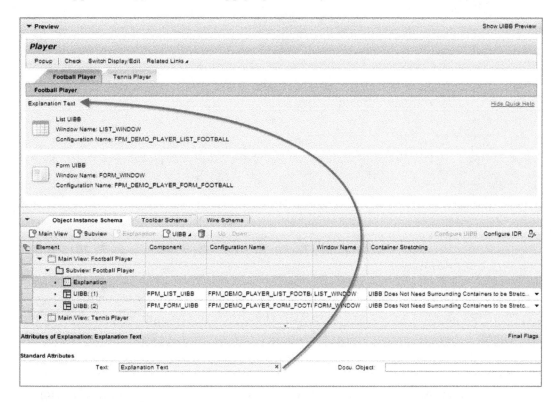

Figure 9.21: Creating an Explanation Text in FLUID – Part 2 © Copyright 2013. SAP AG. All rights reserved

Given the advantages offered by documentation objects, we generally recommend that you define explanation texts using documentation objects wherever possible. This can be achieved by opening up Transaction SE61 and defining a text object of type "General Text" – see Figure 9.22.

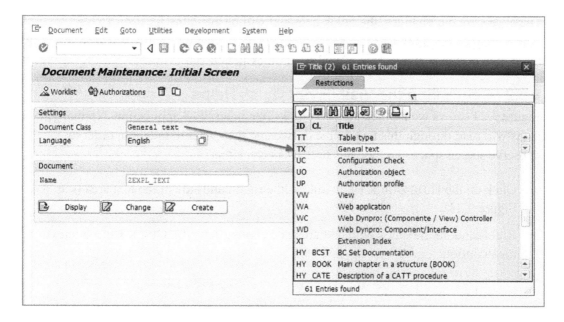

Figure 9.22: Creating a Documentation Object in Transaction SE61 - Part 1

Figure 9.23 shows what the text editor in Transaction SE61 looks like. As you can see, current versions of the SAP GUI embed a Microsoft Word-based editor control into the main editor area so that we can use familiar word processor features to edit the text. Of particular interest here is the STYLES list box which allows us to format various pieces of the text using bold-face font, etc.

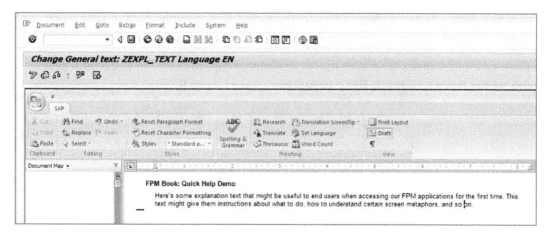

Figure 9.23: Creating a Documentation Object in Transaction SE61 - Part 2

Once we save our changes, the quick help text will be available for users to see whenever they open up the FPM application the next time out. In the next section, we'll learn how users can control the visibility of quick help texts.

9.6.2 Controlling the Visibility of Quick Helps

Figure 9.24 shows what quick help text looks like in an FPM application. Normally, users will read through this text a time or two and then want to hide it in order to conserve screen space. To hide this text, users can either:

➢ Click on the HIDE QUICK HELP link on the right hand side of the text area (see Figure 9.24).

➢ Right-click in the quick help text area and choose the HIDE QUICK HELP context menu option.

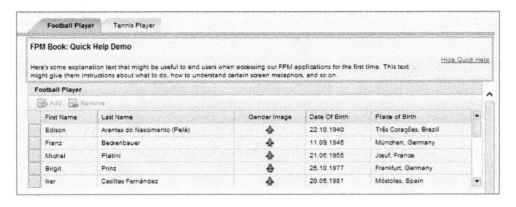

Figure 9.24: Displaying Quick Help Texts - Part 1 © Copyright 2013. SAP AG. All rights reserved

To re-enable the quick help text, users can simply right-click on the target area and choose the DISPLAY QUICK HELP menu option (see Figure 9.25).

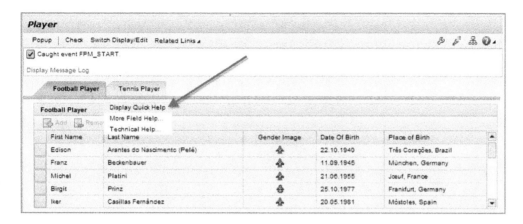

Figure 9.25: Displaying Quick Help Texts - Part 2 © Copyright 2013. SAP AG. All rights reserved

9.7 Summary

In this chapter, we learned about some of the more interactive elements of the FPM framework. These elements are used to put the finishing touches on our FPM application designs so that users have an experience not unlike what they've come to expect in rich client desktop applications.

In the next and final chapter of the book, we'll move beyond custom development concepts and take a look at ways of maintaining and enhancing existing FPM applications – particularly those provided by SAP.

Chapter 10
Enhancement Concepts

Throughout the course of this book, we've explored FPM development concepts mostly from a custom development angle. From a teaching perspective, we found that this viewpoint is ideal for explaining basic concepts since it allows us to see how FPM applications are built from the ground up. In reality though, it's very likely that you'll find that the majority of your time is spent maintaining *existing applications* such as the ones delivered by SAP. This begs the question: how do we enhance existing FPM applications?

In this chapter, we'll explore the myriad of options we have at our disposal for enhancing FPM applications. Here, we'll discover that FPM applications can be enhanced in many ways and at different levels. At first, having all these options can feel overwhelming. However, once you see how the various options are used in some examples, we think you'll find that there's a method to SAP's madness. So without further ado, let's get started.

10.1 Enhancement Options Overview

As we noted earlier, we have quite a few options at our disposal when it comes to enhancing FPM applications. Why so many options you might ask? Well, if we remember that FPM applications are composites which integrate a number of disparate ABAP development objects, it stands to reason that a diverse toolset is required to enhance the various aspects of FPM applications. Some of these tools are specific to FPM development, while others are carry-overs from the underlying WDA framework. Collectively, these tools provide us with the flexibility to enhance pretty much any aspect of an FPM application - a marked improvement over previous UI frameworks in the SAP landscape.

If there's a downside to having all these tools, it's figuring out when to apply them and in what circumstances. To help make sense of all this, we've provided a matrix in Table 10.1 which highlights the various enhancement options in context. Naturally, we'll describe each option in detail in the upcoming sections (you can use the REF. SECTION column as a guide), but we wanted to provide this matrix up front so that you could get a sense for what's possible. You can also use this matrix as a checklist going forward.

Requirement	Enhancement Option(s)	Ref. Section
You want to make wholesale changes to an SAP-delivered FPM application. You want to leverage significant portions of an existing FPM application to create a new application.	Use the Application Hierarchy Browser tool to make a copy of the existing application and then apply changes to the newly-defined floorplan configuration.	4.5
You want to make minor cosmetic changes to the UI (e.g. changing the layout, hiding unused fields, modifying label texts, and so forth).	Use the built-in capabilities of the WDA Configuration Framework to adapt the relevant application components.	10.2.3
You want to apply significant changes to a floorplan/GUIBB configuration.	Use the Enhancement Framework to create an enhancement for the selected configuration. Then, the wholesale changes can be applied to the enhancement configuration in much the same way as if we were building the configuration from scratch.	10.3
You want to tweak the behavior of certain GUIBB instances.	Use the implicit enhancement options provided with the Enhancement Framework to enhance the GUIBB instance's feeder class. - or - Create a sub-class of the GUIBB instance's feeder class and then redefine the relevant callback methods to implement the desired behavior.	10.4

Requirement	Enhancement Option(s)	Ref. Section
You want to apply conditional enhancements. For example, you have a requirement that states that the UI layout should be different for users in the U.S. vs. Europe.	Use Context-Based Adaptations (CBA) to group together related enhancements by *context*.	10.5

Table 10.1: FPM Enhancement Option Matrix

Before we move on to specific enhancement topics, we would be remiss if we didn't draw your attention to another highly useful resource. Out on the SAP SDN, you can find a guide entitled *How to Create, Enhance and Adapt Floorplan Manager Applications* (Günther, et al.) which provides a detailed overview of available enhancement options as well as practical advice regarding their usage. This reference guide is a living document which is updated for each SAP NetWeaver release. Much like the *FPM Developer's Guide* referenced throughout this book, this is another resource that every FPM developer should keep close at hand.

10.2 Working with the WDA Configuration Framework

Since FPM applications are, at the core, WDA applications, we have access to all of the underlying features of the WDA framework. From an enhancement context, this implies that we have the option of tapping into the *WDA Configuration Framework*. In this section, we'll look at all of the powerful features that the WDA Configuration Framework brings to the table.

10.2.1 Conceptual Overview

So what is the WDA Configuration Framework? Well, due to its overall complexity, it's hard to come up with a one line definition which accurately describes what the WDA Configuration Framework is. Therefore, let's attempt to paint a picture by showing you some of the different roles played by the WDA Configuration Framework:

➢ **Design Time Tooling**

At design time, the WDA Configuration Framework can be used to customize WDA components in a couple of different ways:

❖ Though we've sort of glossed over this up to now, the WDA Configuration Framework is actually what's behind the creation/maintenance of WDA component configurations - more on this shortly.

❖ It can also be used to *adapt* pre-existing component configurations (e.g. ones delivered by SAP). In this scenario, the changes we apply are stored separately from the WDA component configuration that we're adapting (in the customizing layer).

➢ **Runtime Environment**

At runtime, the WDA Configuration Framework plays a similar role to a CSS engine on a web browser. Here, it dynamically applies the customizing changes created at design time on top of the standard component configuration settings. This is analogous to a CSS engine applying CSS rules in cascading fashion.

➢ **Personalization Engine**

From an end user perspective, the WDA Configuration Framework is what drives the built-in personalization features used to tweak the UI. Users can leverage these features to hide unused fields, adjust the layout of tables, and so forth.

Figure 10.1 shows you how all these pieces fit together.

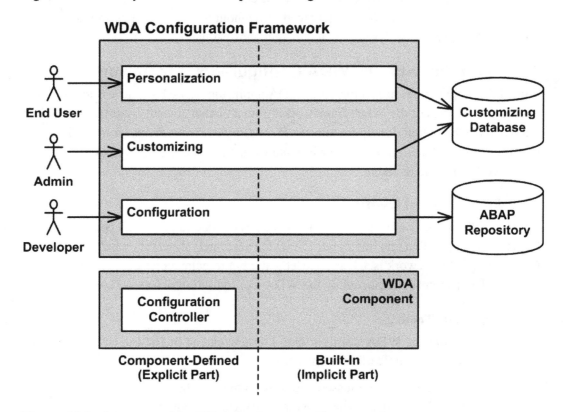

Figure 10.1: Overview of the WDA Configuration Framework

To put these designs into perspective, we'll once again lean on the CSS[33] analogy described earlier. In this comparison, we would equate the configuration settings maintained in WDA component configurations, etc. with the rules maintained in CSS style sheets. At runtime, the WDA Configuration Framework plays the CSS engine role, applying the various configuration settings in cascading fashion as illustrated in Figure 10.2. Here, each layer in the cascade refines the configuration metadata in line with the various customization settings. Once the final settings are determined, the WDA Configuration Framework will dynamically apply the changes during the UI rendering process. In the WDA parlance, this process is described using the term *delta handling*.

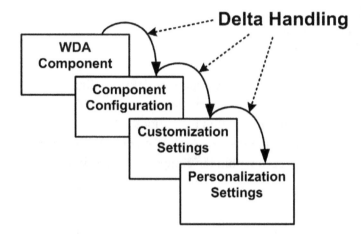

Figure 10.2: Comparing Delta Handling to the CSS Cascade

So, to summarize what we've learned in this section:

➢ The WDA Configuration Framework provides a series of graphical tools which support the customization of WDA components. Conceptually, there are three different layers of customization:

❖ Developers to create component configurations in the ABAP Repository.

❖ Developers can adapt existing component configurations at the customizing layer. These customizing changes are applied at the client level.

❖ End users can further personalize the UI experience by applying cosmetic changes which are unique to their user account.

---

[33] If you're not familiar with CSS technology, you can find a good introduction online at *http://www.w3schools.com/css/css_intro.asp*.

> ➢ At runtime, the settings specified in relevant component configurations, customization, etc. are dynamically applied on top of the default UI. Thus, any enhancements made via the WDA Configuration Framework are considered "modification-free".

10.2.2 Relationship with the FPM Framework

As we noted earlier, we've brushed up against the WDA Configuration Framework many times throughout the course of this book without really noticing it. Indeed, every time we've created a floorplan configuration or configured a GUIBB component, the WDA Configuration Framework has been right there collecting the configuration metadata behind the scenes. Then, at runtime, whenever we launch our FPM applications, the WDA Configuration Framework kicks into overdrive, dynamically applying our changes on top of standard FPM components.

We can match this kind of configuration up with the "component-defined" dimension[34] depicted on the left-hand side of Figure 10.1. This is to say that we're filling in component-specific configuration settings defined within the various FPM components. For example, in Figure 10.3 you can see how the FPM_FORM_UIBB component defines its object schema metadata as WDA context nodes within the component's configuration controller.

---

[34] The "built-in" dimension of the WDA Configuration Framework refers to the built-in configuration capabilities of WDA components. Since the majority of these features are geared towards tweaking WDA UI elements, there's not much relevancy for this feature from an FPM development perspective. Of course, if you happen to be working with a lot of freestyle UIBBs, then that's a different story. In this case, we'd recommend that you check out the SAP Help Library online at *http://help.sap.com*. For your particular SAP NetWeaver release, search on the term *Web Dynpro ABAP Configuration Framework*.

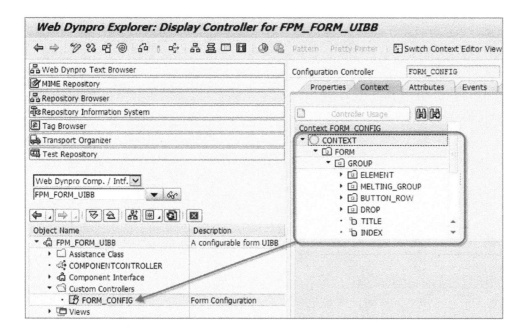

*Figure 10.3: Understanding the Role of Configuration Controllers © Copyright 2013.
SAP AG. All rights reserved*

Once our base-level component configurations are in place, we can fire up our FPM
application and let the WDA Configuration Framework go to work. Here, end users can
tap into the built-in personalization features of the WDA Configuration Framework by
right-clicking on UI elements and selecting from the available USER SETTINGS context
menu options as shown in Figure 10.4.

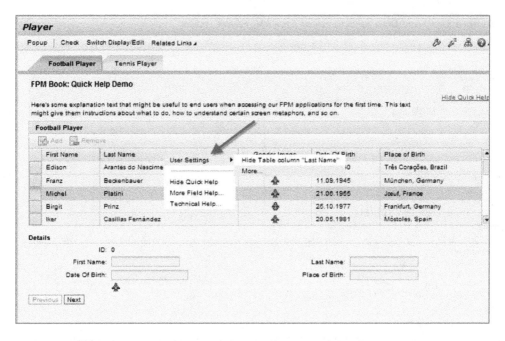

Figure 10.4: Personalizing the UI in an FPM Application - Part 1 © Copyright 2013. SAP AG. All rights reserved

For example, in Figure 10.5, you can see how a user is able to adjust the layout of the FOOTBALL PLAYER table shown in Figure 10.4 by re-arranging the order of table columns. Users also have the option of hiding irrelevant fields or plugging in default values for frequently-used input fields.

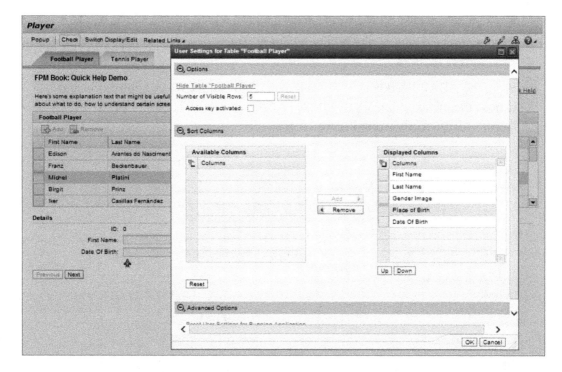

Figure 10.5: Personalizing the UI in an FPM Application - Part 2 © Copyright 2013. SAP AG. All rights reserved

The great thing about the personalization layer of the WDA Configuration Framework is that we don't have to do anything special to turn this feature on. So, if we have one off enhancement requirements from users wanting to apply a cosmetic tweak or two to an FPM application, then personalization may be the way to go. For anything but the most trivial of requirements though, we're going to need to tap into the customizing layer of the WDA Configuration Framework. In the next section, we'll learn how to use this layer to enhance FPM applications on a client-wide scale.

10.2.3 Adapting Existing Configurations

As we learned in Section 10.2.1, the WDA Configuration Framework provides a customizing layer in which we can adapt existing component configurations on a client-wide basis. So, if we need to make changes and/or enhancements to a pre-delivered FPM application, the customizing layer can be a good place to start.

Accessing the Customizing Layer

To access the customizing layer, all we have to do is open up the target FPM application in *administrator mode*. This can be achieved in one of two ways:

➢ If we know the URL of the application, then we can open it up in a browser window/tab and tack on the following query string parameter to the end of the URL: `sap-config-mode=X`.

➢ From the ABAP Workbench, we can open up the target WDA application and choose the menu option WEB DYNPRO APPLICATION → TEST → IN BROWSER - ADMIN MODE as shown in Figure 10.6.

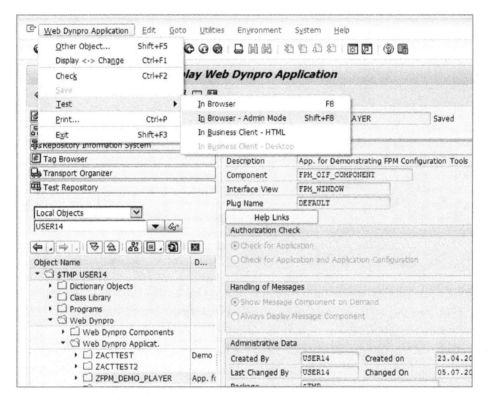

Figure 10.6: Accessing the Customizing Layer to Adapt an FPM Application

Regardless of the path we take, the FPM application will start up in a special *customizing mode*. In more recent SAP NetWeaver releases, we'll see a special banner at the top of the page which is there to remind us that we're operating in customizing mode (see Figure 10.7). For earlier SAP NetWeaver releases, the differences are more subtle, so we have to be careful if we have multiple sessions of the application open in different windows.

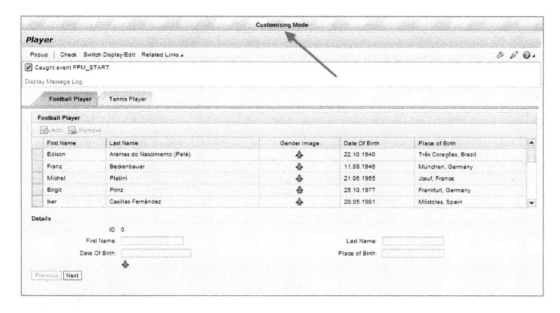

Figure 10.7: Adapting an FPM Application in Customizing Mode - SAP NetWeaver 7.03+ © Copyright 2013. SAP AG. All rights reserved

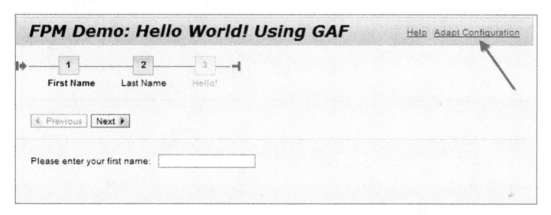

Figure 10.8: Adapting an FPM Application in Customizing Mode - SAP NetWeaver 7.02 © Copyright 2013. SAP AG. All rights reserved

Creating Component Customizations

As we observed in the previous section, launching an FPM application in customizing mode doesn't really effect many changes to the visualization of the application in a browser. However, if you look closely at the top of the page, you'll notice a couple of additional functions on the far right-hand side of the page toolbar[35]. The first button with the little wrench-like icon is the CUSTOMIZE PAGE button. By clicking on this function, we can open up the FPM application's floorplan configuration in customizing mode. The adjacent SHOW CUSTOMIZABLE AREAS toggle button is a new feature in the SAP NetWeaver 7.03 release. When selected, customizable components in the FPM application UI will be highlighted in blue and a wrench-like icon will show up on the right-hand side of the content area (see Figure 10.9). We can click on these icons to jump right into the selected UIBB configurations in customizing mode.

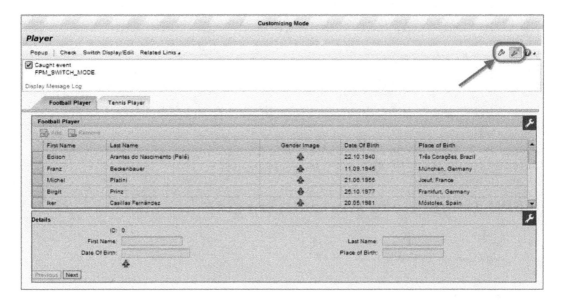

Figure 10.9: Customizing an FPM Application - Part 1 © Copyright 2013. SAP AG. All rights reserved

Regardless of whether or not we select a floorplan component or a UIBB component for customization, the basic customizing steps are the same:

1. First, if we haven't created a customizing record before, we'll be confronted with an error message like the one shown in Figure 10.10. In this case, we simply click on the NEW button to create the customizing record.

---

[35] Prior to the SAP NetWeaver 7.03 release, this functionality was provided via the Adapt Configuration link in the IDR (see Figure 10.8).

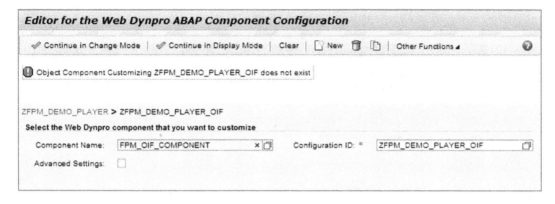

Figure 10.10: Customizing an FPM Application - Part 2 © *Copyright 2013. SAP AG.*
All rights reserved

2. Next, we'll be confronted with a CREATE CUSTOMIZING dialog box like the one
    shown in Figure 10.11. Here, we simply need to fill in the DESCRIPTION field and
    click on the OK button to proceed.

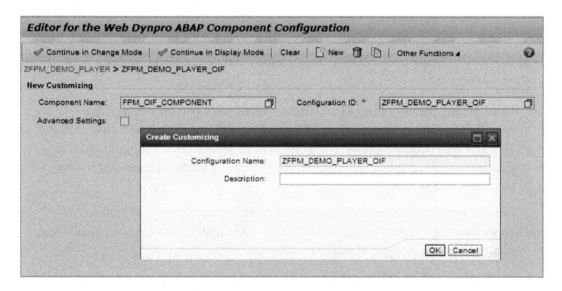

Figure 10.11: Customizing an FPM Application - Part 3 © *Copyright 2013. SAP AG.*
All rights reserved

3. At this point, we'll be prompted to select a customizing transport request to track
    our changes. If you look closely at Figure 10.12, the dialog box shows you that
    the configuration entry will be tracked in table WDY_CONF_USER.

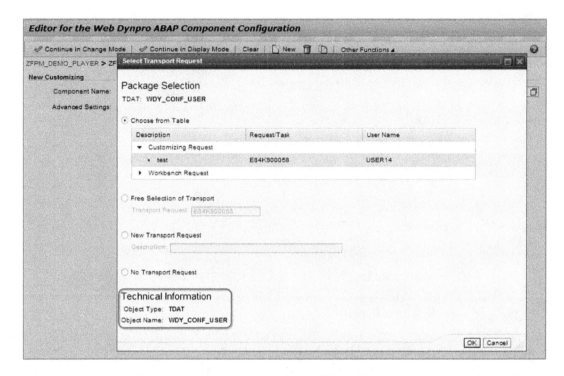

Figure 10.12: Customizing an FPM Application - Part 4 © Copyright 2013. SAP AG. All rights reserved

4. Once we get past all of the administrative stuff, we'll end up at a slightly modified version of the familiar FPM CONFIGURATION EDITOR screen (see Figure 10.13). From here, it's pretty much business as usual from a configuration perspective. We can add/remove UIBBs, switch out feeder classes, add toolbar elements, and so forth[36].

5. Finally, once we're satisfied with our changes, we can hit the SAVE button to apply the customizations. The next time the FPM application runs, we should see our customizations applied automagically.

---

[36] Having said that, we would caution against getting carried away too much here. In the upcoming sections, we'll find that there are some limitations to the customizing approach - particularly from a maintenance perspective. So, our general recommendation would be to limit your changes in the customizing layer to simple changes that are fairly transparent.

Figure 10.13: Customizing an FPM Application - Part 5 © Copyright 2013. SAP AG.
All rights reserved

As we noted earlier, the same customizing process described above also applies to
GUIBB configurations. For example, in Figure 10.14, you can see how we're adjusting
the UI of a form UIBB configuration. Naturally, the same principles would apply if we
needed to tweak a list UIBB, etc.

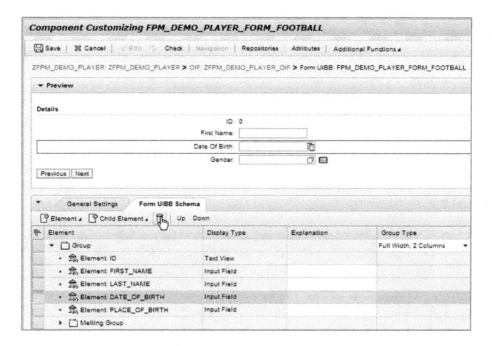

Figure 10.14: Customizing a GUIBB Configuration © Copyright 2013. SAP AG. All rights reserved

Finally, at this risk of sounding like a broken record, we would point out once again that the changes applied at this layer DO NOT affect the underlying component configuration in any way. Rather, the deltas are recorded in customizing records which are accessed by the WDA Configuration Framework at runtime to superimpose our changes on top of the standard configuration. So, while it may feel like a modification inside the FPM Configuration Editor, you can breathe easy knowing that nothing is getting permanently deleted.

Limitations of the Customizing-Based Approach

Throughout the course of this section, we've observed the power of the customizing layer of the WDA Configuration Framework. Within a given customizing record, we have the ability to adapt pretty much any aspect of a selected component configuration. However, as we warned you earlier, it's important to exercise restraint when applying customizations using this tool.

Why, you ask? Well, the short answer here is that adapted configurations can be difficult to maintain long-term. To understand why this is, let's consider an example. Imagine that you adapt an SAP-delivered component configuration using the customizing layer. Then, a short while later, you apply a support pack (SP) upgrade which overlays the standard-delivered component configuration with innovations from SAP. After the SP is applied, you may need to adjust your customizations, but this can be difficult to achieve since there's no way to visually compare the changes[37]. Suffice it to say that version control doesn't really exist in the customizing layer.

Having said all that, we don't want to scare you away from customizations. Indeed, for most run-of-the-mill changes, the customizing layer is the way to go. The types of changes that fall into this category include:

➤ Changing the page title (e.g. in the IDR).

➤ Adding/removing pages/main views/steps to/from floorplan configurations.

➤ Adding custom functions to the page toolbar.

➤ Tweaking forms and lists (e.g. removing unused fields, re-arranging field groups, and so on).

➤ And any other minor, cosmetic tweaks to the UI.

10.3 Working with the Enhancement Framework

As we observed in the previous section, the customizing layer of the WDA Configuration Framework provides us with tremendous flexibility when it comes to adapting existing FPM applications. However, there are a couple of downsides to this approach:

➤ First of all, since the changes are applied in the customizing layer, there is no version history associated with component configurations that are enhanced using this technique. So, it can be difficult to identify what changed and when. Not to mention the fact that there is no concept of reverting back to a previous configuration state.

➤ Once a configuration is defined, it cannot really be turned off. Though this is usually not a problem, there are times whenever it may be helpful to be able to flip the switch on an enhancement.

---

[37] Note: This has changed somewhat in newer SAP NetWeaver releases with the addition of the COMPARISONS panel in the FLUID editor. Here, developers are able to visualize to a certain extent the changes applied in the customizing layer, not to mention enhancements and context-based adaptations.

To get around these limitations, we can enlist the aid of the *Enhancement Framework*. In this section, we'll see how the Enhancement Framework can be used to effectively manage changes to component configurations within the ABAP Repository.

10.3.1 Enhancing Component Configurations

First things first, let's see how to enhance component configurations. As it turns out, this is pretty easily accomplished within the FPM Configuration Editor tool:

1. To begin, we need to open up the target component configuration in the FPM Configuration Editor in display mode. If you happen to be working on a system based on a more recent SAP NetWeaver release, this task is made easier by the built-in technical help feature provided by the WDA framework. Here, when enhancing an existing FPM application, we can simply navigate to the target component configuration using the links provided in the TECHNICAL HELP dialog box shown in Figure 10.15.

Figure 10.15: Enhancing a Component Configuration - Part 1 © Copyright 2013. SAP AG. All rights reserved

2. Next, within the main editor screen, we simply choose the ADDITIONAL FUNCTIONS → ENHANCE menu option as shown in Figure 10.16.

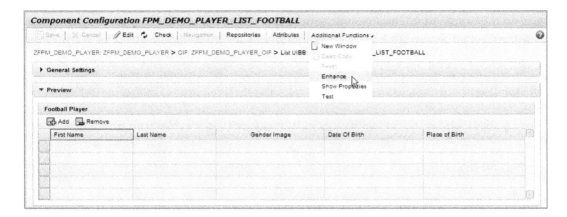

Figure 10.16: Enhancing a Component Configuration - Part 2 © Copyright 2013. SAP AG. All rights reserved

3. This will bring up the CREATE ENHANCEMENT dialog box shown in Figure 10.17. Here, we simply provide a name and optional description for the enhancement implementation and hit the OK button to confirm our changes[38]. At this point, we'll be prompted to fill in typical housekeeping information for ABAP Repository objects: a package assignment, CTS request, and so on.

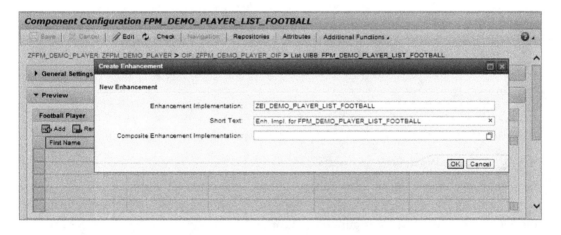

Figure 10.17: Enhancing a Component Configuration - Part 3 © Copyright 2013. SAP AG. All rights reserved

---

[38] If desired, we can also wrap our enhancement implementation up in a composite enhancement implementation using the correspondingly-named field in the CREATE COMPONENT dialog box shown in Figure 10.17.

4. Finally, once we've defined our enhancement configuration, we'll end up in a perspective of the FPM Configuration Editor that looks almost identical to the one used to create component configurations from scratch (see Figure 10.18). From here, we can begin adjusting floorplan configurations, changing form/list layouts, and so on.

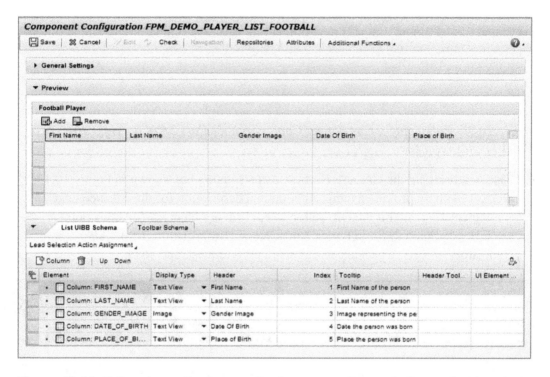

Figure 10.18: Enhancing a Component Configuration - Part 4 © Copyright 2013. SAP AG. All rights reserved

10.3.2 Maintenance Concepts

Now that you have a feel for how enhancements are created for component configurations, let's take a look at what happens behind the scenes while we're making our changes in the FPM Configuration Editor tool.

As we noted earlier, enhancement implementations are stored within the ABAP Repository. To understand what's stored within these enhancement implementation objects, it's helpful to open them up in the ABAP Workbench and look at the XML DISPLAY tab shown in Figure 10.19. Here, we can find what amounts to a delta list of changes applied to the source component configuration. For example, the XML contained in Figure 10.19 describes a change in which we deleted a column from a list configuration. Had we applied additional changes, those changes would be reflected in the XML as well.

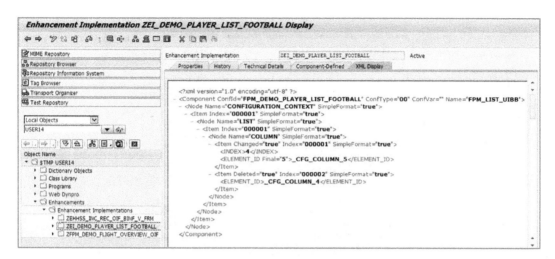

Figure 10.19: Tracking Changes in an Enhancement Implementation © Copyright 2013. SAP AG. All rights reserved

From a developer's perspective, the important take-away from all this is that the enhancement implementation object stores changes in a versionable format. So, over time, we can revert back to prior versions using the familiar version-management features of the ABAP Repository. It's also much easier to compare different versions of an enhancement implementation should two environments get out of sync (e.g. development vs. QA).

Over time, it's possible that the same enhancement implementation may be used and reused multiple times as additional enhancements are made to a given component configuration. In these situations, the development process is the same as the one outlined in 10.3.1; the only difference is that you select the existing enhancement implementation instead of creating a new one (see Figure 10.20). Behind the scenes, any additional changes will be added to the running delta list shown in Figure 10.19.

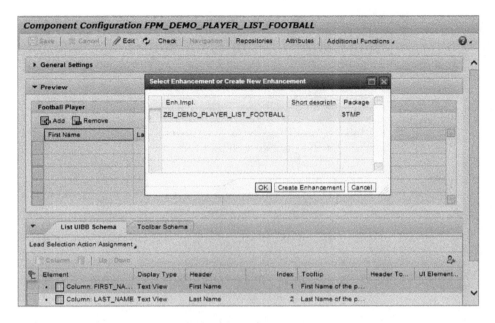

Figure 10.20: Reusing an Enhancement Implementation to Apply Further Changes

10.3.3 Usage Recommendations

From a functional perspective, the enhancement-based approach is almost identical to the customizing approach offered by the WDA Configuration Framework. Indeed, at runtime, the changes applied via enhancement implementations are dynamically applied using the same basic delta handling functionality described for the WDA Configuration Framework in Section 10.2.1.

Given these similarities, you might be wondering when you should apply one technique over the other. To a large extent, the answer is rather subjective in nature. However, as you go to make your decisions, we'd recommend that you consider the following points:

➢ **Version Management**

If you need to keep track of wholesale changes applied by multiple developers, it can be crucial to have the version management capabilities of the enhancement implementations at your disposal just in case you ever need to back out erroneous changes.

➢ **Upgrade Protection**

As of the SAP NetWeaver 7.03 release, both techniques are fully protected against upgrades. Here, any changes applied by SAP will be applied to the source component configuration and any existing enhancements will be dynamically woven in using the delta handling functionality as per usual.

Prior to the SAP NetWeaver 7.03 release though, any corrections/improvements that SAP applies to a component configuration will not picked up by the enhanced component configuration. So, if you're working on an SAP NetWeaver 7.02 system (or earlier), you might prefer to lean towards the customizing approach.

> **Mixing-and-Matching is a Bad Idea**

  Once you decide on an enhancement approach for a given component configuration, we recommend that you stick with that approach if at all possible. Though mixing-and-matching works to some extent, it can cause all kinds of headaches when it comes to troubleshooting problems.

  Along these same lines, we would also recommend against creating multiple enhancement implementations for a given component configuration. Though it's technically possible to create multiple enhancement implementations, it's better to track all the changes in one place so that the configuration remains consistent.

> **Enhancements are Switchable**

  Another potential benefit of going with the enhancement-based approach is that it also allows you to utilize the *Switch Framework* to control when and where enhancements are applied. You can find more information about this feature by performing a keyword search on the term *Switch Framework* in the SAP Help Library.

10.4 Enhancing Application Logic

So far, the enhancement techniques we've considered have been focused on making changes to elements in the UI. This is all fine and well, but what if our requirements call for changes to the underlying application logic? For this task, we need to enhance source code artifacts such as feeder classes, application controller components/classes, and so on. In this section, we'll look at a couple of different ways to accomplish this.

Note

In this section, our focus will be on enhancing FPM-related artifacts. Though freestyle UIBBs certainly have a place in this discussion, the enhancement of regular WDA components extends beyond the scope of this book. You can find detailed information about this process in the SAP Help Library available online at *http://help.sap.com* by searching on the term *Modification-Free Enhancements for Web Dynpro ABAP*. These concepts are also described in *Web Dynpro ABAP: The Comprehensive Guide* (SAP PRESS, 2012).

10.4.1 Using Good Old Fashioned Inheritance

The first technique that we'll look at involves something that should be pretty familiar to developers well-versed in object-oriented programming concepts: *inheritance*. Here, we basically take an SAP-delivered class and extend it by redefining existing methods and/or adding in new functionality. Where possible, this approach provides a clean way of weaving in custom functionality without disturbing the standard code base. Development-wise, the basic procedure is very straightforward:

1. First, we need to identify the feeder class (or application controller class) that we want to enhance and verify whether or not it can be extended. We can determine this by checking the status of the FINAL flag on the PROPERTIES tab of the Class Builder tool (see Figure 10.21). If this checkbox is marked, then we'll have to find another way to enhance the application class.

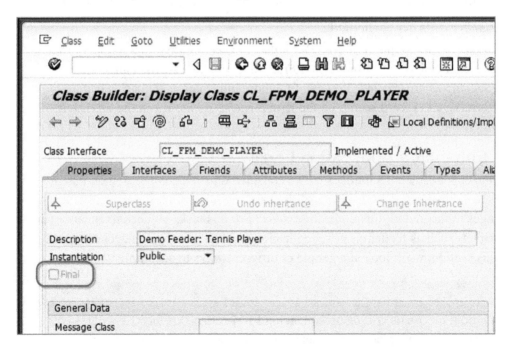

Figure 10.21: Determining if a Feeder Class can be Extended © Copyright 2013. SAP AG. All rights reserved

2. Assuming that the target class is not marked as final, the next step is to move on and create a new custom class that inherits from the target class. This can be

achieved in the ABAP Workbench by simply creating a new class and selecting the CREATE INHERITANCE button as shown in Figure 10.22 and Figure 10.23, respectively.

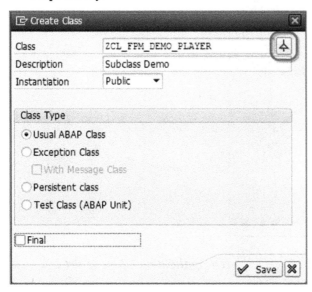

Figure 10.22: Creating a Subclass of a Pre-Delivered Application Class - Part 1

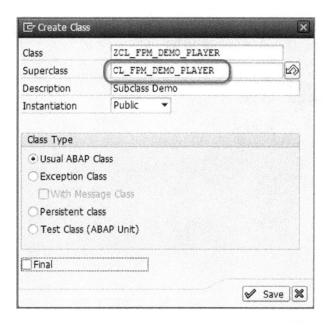

Figure 10.23: Creating a Subclass of a Pre-Delivered Application Class - Part 2
© *Copyright 2013. SAP AG. All rights reserved*

3. Finally, once our subclass is created, we can begin applying the necessary code changes using the Class Builder tool as per usual.

To demonstrate how this works in practice, let's see how we might enhance the event handling logic for the ZCL_FPM_DEMO_PLAYER class created in the screenshots above. To begin, we'll open up the class and redefine the PROCESS_EVENT() method by selecting it and clicking on the REDEFINE button in the toolbar (see Figure 10.24).

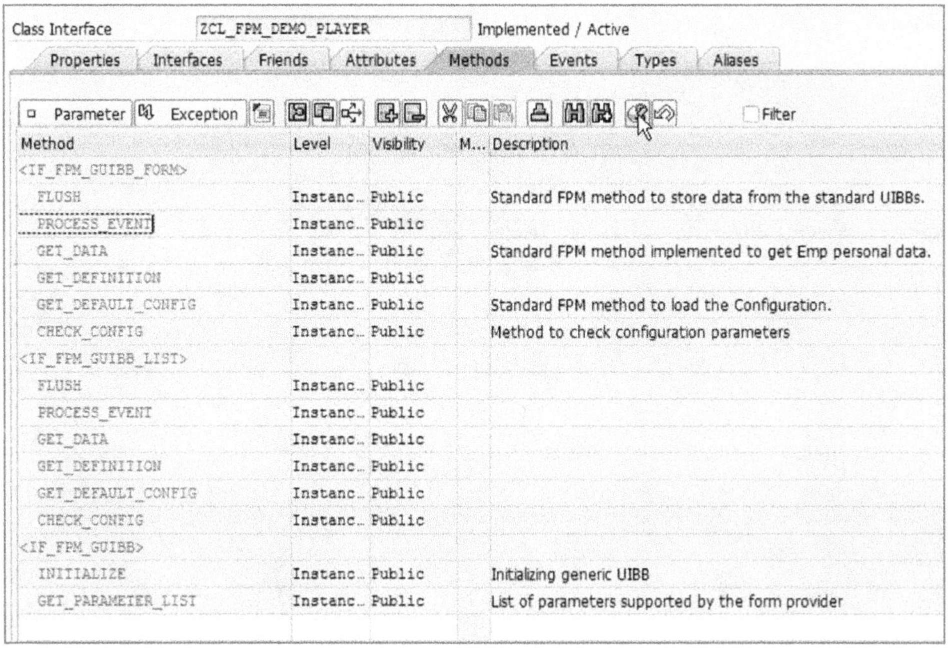

Figure 10.24: Redefining Methods in a Feeder Class - Part 1 © Copyright 2013. SAP AG. All rights reserved

After the method has been redefined, we'll end up at a screen like the one shown in Figure 10.25. Here, you can see that the Class Builder tool has graciously stubbed out a call to the superclass implementation. In almost every case, this will be something that we want to take advantage of. That way, we're not really modifying the existing implementation; we're just adding custom code before/after the standard logic is executed. The code excerpt contained in Listing 10.1 illustrates how this works at the code level.

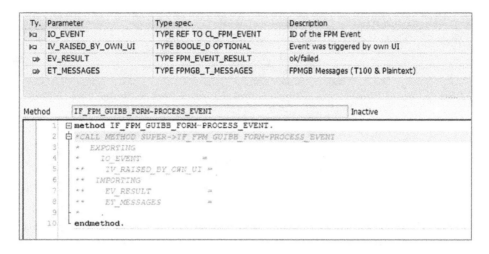

Ty.	Parameter	Type spec.	Description
▶□	IO_EVENT	TYPE REF TO CL_FPM_EVENT	ID of the FPM Event
▶□	IV_RAISED_BY_OWN_UI	TYPE BOOLE_D OPTIONAL	Event was triggered by own UI
□▶	EV_RESULT	TYPE FPM_EVENT_RESULT	ok/failed
□▶	ET_MESSAGES	TYPE FPMGB_T_MESSAGES	FPMGB Messages (T100 & Plaintext)

Method	IF_FPM_GUIBB_FORM~PROCESS_EVENT	Inactive

```
 1  method IF_FPM_GUIBB_FORM~PROCESS_EVENT.
 2  *CALL METHOD SUPER->IF_FPM_GUIBB_FORM~PROCESS_EVENT
 3  *  EXPORTING
 4  *      IO_EVENT             =
 5  **      IV_RAISED_BY_OWN_UI =
 6  **  IMPORTING
 7  **      EV_RESULT            =
 8  **      ET_MESSAGES          =
 9  *    .
10  endmethod.
```

Figure 10.25: Redefining Methods in a Feeder Class - Part 2 © Copyright 2013. SAP AG. All rights reserved

```
METHOD if_fpm_guibb_form~process_event.
  "Delegate most of the processing to the superclass:
  CALL METHOD super->if_fpm_guibb_form~process_event
    EXPORTING
      io_event            = io_event
      iv_raised_by_own_ui = iv_raised_by_own_ui
    IMPORTING
      ev_result           = ev_result
      et_messages         = et_messages.

  "Custom processing goes here..
  CASE io_event->mv_event_id.
    WHEN 'ZCUSTOM_EVENT'.
      "Enhanced event handling goes here...
  ENDCASE.
ENDMETHOD.
```

Listing 10.1: Redefining a Method with Custom Logic

After the relevant code changes are in place, you might be tempted to open up the FPM application and test your changes to see if they're working. However, if you were to do so at this stage, you'd find that nothing's changed. Why? Because the relevant component configurations are still pointing to the superclass. To fix this, we need to enhance the relevant component configuration so that it will point to our new custom subclass. This can be achieved by using either of the enhancement techniques outlined in Sections 10.2 and 10.3.

For example, in Figure 10.26, you can see how we're assigning our custom
ZCL_FPM_DEMO_PLAYER feeder class to an enhancement configuration. Since the
ZCL_FPM_DEMO_PLAYER class is a subclass of CL_FPM_DEMO_PLAYER, we shouldn't have
to change anything else; the subclass should be plug-and-play.

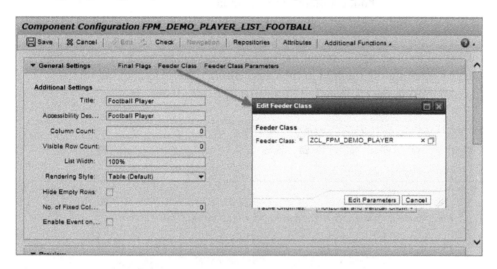

*Figure 10.26: Editing the Feeder Class Assignment © Copyright 2013. SAP AG. All
rights reserved*

Design Note

Before we wrap up this section, we would be remiss if we didn't point out another
important factor which may influence whether or not you want to use inheritance for
your enhancement requirements. As we noted above, the presence of the final flag on a
class is a clear-cut signal that a class has been closed off for extensions. Oftentimes
though, the extensibility of a given class may not be so black-and-white. For example, if
a given feeder/application controller class makes heavy use of private instance attributes,
it's possible that we might not be able to apply the changes we want to make at the
subclass level since these attributes will be cut off scope-wise. Much of this comes down
to basic OO theory, so we won't belabor the point any further except to say that it's
important to bear in mind that some classes were never designed with extension in mind,
so tread carefully.

10.4.2 Implicit Enhancements

If the class we need to enhance is marked as final, or unsuitable for extension, the next
option that we can look at involves the use of *implicit enhancement spots* that are
provided with the Enhancement Framework. In this section, we'll see how this

functionality can be used to apply modification-free enhancements to standard-delivered code.

To demonstrate how implicit enhancement spots work[39], let's take a look at an example. Imagine that we want to enhance a method in a standard-delivered feeder class. Here, the steps required to implement this change are as follows:

1. First, we need to open up the target method in *enhancement mode*. This can be achieved by opening the method in the Class Builder tool and clicking on the ENHANCE button in the toolbar (see Figure 10.27).

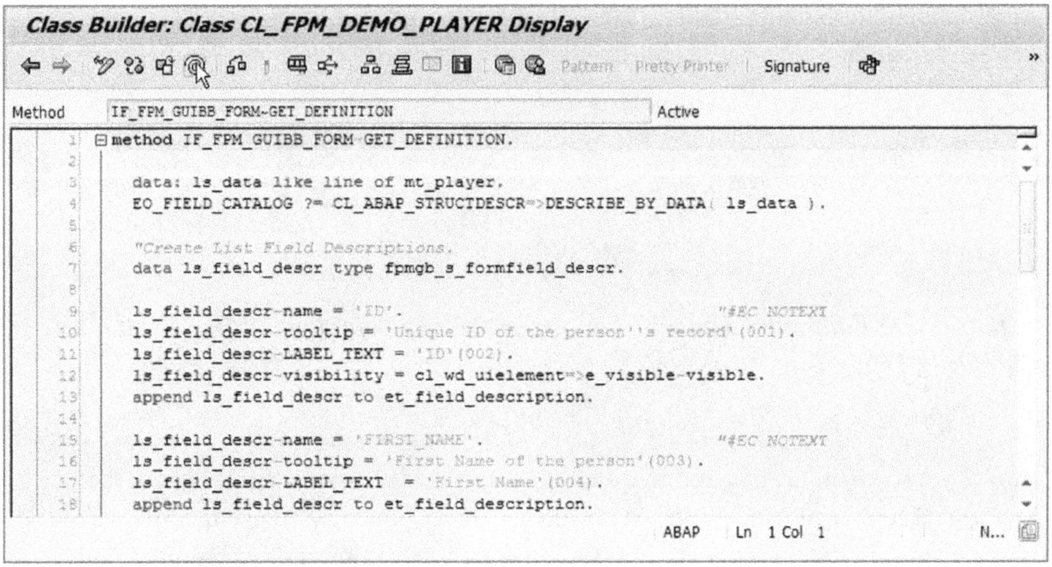

Figure 10.27: Defining an Implicit Enhancement - Part 1 © Copyright 2013. SAP AG. All rights reserved

2. Next, we need to visualize the implicit enhancement options available for us. This can be achieved by selecting the menu option EDIT → ENHANCEMENT OPERATIONS → SHOW IMPLICIT ENHANCEMENT OPTIONS (see Figure 10.28).

---

[39] For a more thorough treatment on implicit enhancement options and the Enhancement Framework in general, we would recommend that you visit the SAP Help Library and perform a keyword search on the term *Enhancement Framework*.

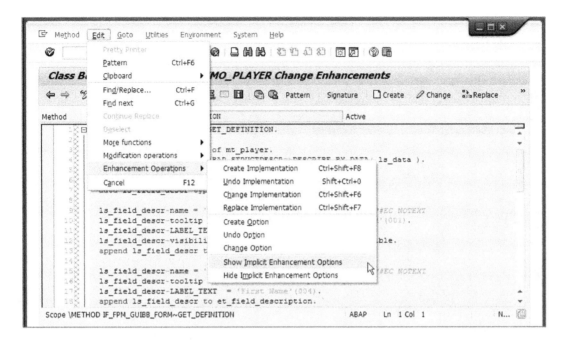

Figure 10.28: Defining an Implicit Enhancement - Part 2 © Copyright 2013. SAP AG. All rights reserved

3. In the case of a method definition, we have two implicit enhancement spots at our disposal: one at the beginning of the method and one at the end. Within the source code editor pane, we can access these implicit enhancement spots by right-clicking on the quoted lines that show up directly after the METHOD statement and before the ENDMETHOD statement. Then, in the context menu, we can select the menu option ENHANCEMENT OPERATIONS → CREATE IMPLEMENTATION (see Figure 10.29). Depending on our requirements we can use either or both of these implicit enhancement spots to apply the necessary logic enhancements.

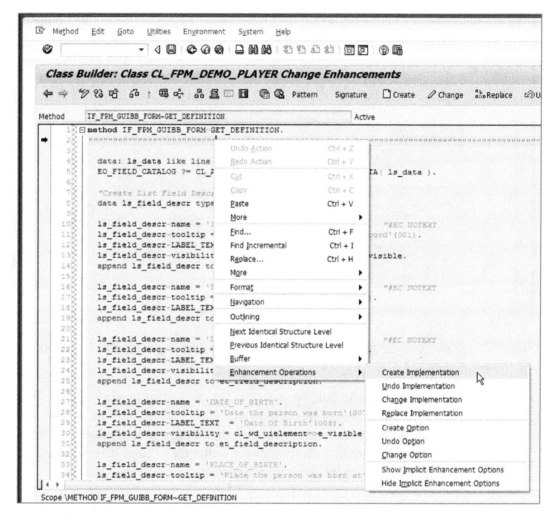

Figure 10.29: Defining an Implicit Enhancement - Part 3 © Copyright 2013. SAP AG. All rights reserved

4. During the enhancement implication creation process, we'll be presented with the CHOOSE ENHANCEMENT MODE dialog box shown in Figure 10.30. Here, we'll want to select the CODE button in order to apply code-level changes.

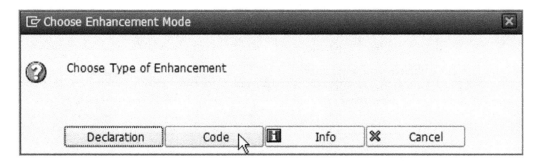

Figure 10.30: Defining an Implicit Enhancement - Part 4 © Copyright 2013. SAP AG. All rights reserved

5. Next, if there are no existing enhancements applied to the class in question, we'll encounter the CREATE ENHANCEMENT IMPLEMENTATION prompt shown in Figure 10.31. Here, we simply define the new enhancement implementation and hit the enter key to confirm our changes.

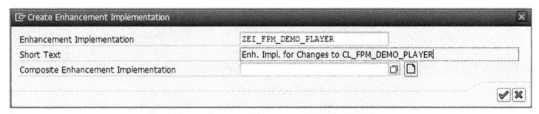

Figure 10.31: Defining an Implicit Enhancement - Part 5 © Copyright 2013. SAP AG. All rights reserved

6. Finally, after the enhancement implementation is created, we'll end up with a new ENHANCEMENT...ENDENHANCEMENT block like the one shown in Figure 10.32. Within this block, we can add in the necessary enhancement logic using ABAP code as per usual.

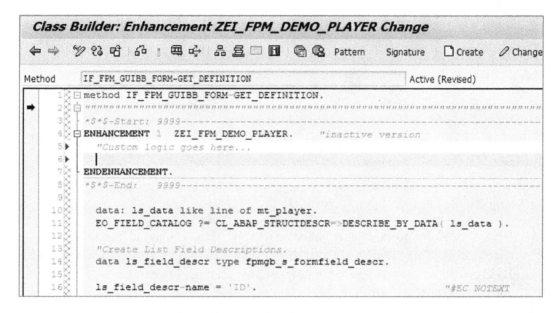

Figure 10.32: Defining an Implicit Enhancement - Part 6 © Copyright 2013. SAP AG. All rights reserved

10.4.3 Enhancing Application Controllers

The enhancement methods outlined in Section 10.4.1 and 10.4.2 work well whenever we need to make changes to ABAP Objects classes. However, as we learned in Chapter 8, a considerable amount of application logic often goes into application controllers based on WDA components. Therefore, in this section, we'll see how to apply enhancements to application controller components.

To some extent, the enhancement process for WDA controller methods is similar to the process outlined in Section 10.4.2 in that we're leveraging the Enhancement Framework to drive the changes. The primary difference in this context is that the enhancement options for WDA controller methods are more pronounced. To put these differences into perspective, let's look at how such enhancements are applied step-by-step:

1. To begin, we open up the target WDA component's component controller in the ABAP Workbench as shown in Figure 10.33. If an enhancement implementation doesn't exist already, then we can create one by clicking on the ENHANCE button in the application toolbar. This will take us through the same enhancement implementation creation process demonstrated throughout the course of this chapter.

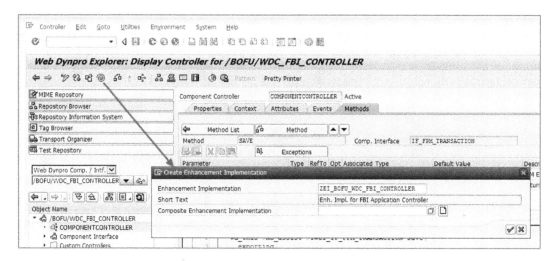

Figure 10.33: Enhancing an Application Controller - Part 1 © Copyright 2013. SAP AG. All rights reserved

2. Once the component controller is opened up in enhancement mode, we'll see that a number of new functions are provided on the METHODS tab (not to mention the other tabs). For example, let's say we need to enhance the SAVE() method highlighted in Figure 10.34. In this case, we can choose between three different functions: PRE-EXIT, POST-EXIT, and OVERWRITE EXIT. We can use the pre/post exits to add code before/after the existing method implementation in a similar fashion to what we demonstrated in Section 10.4.2. The OVERWRITE EXIT function is more involved, allowing us to completely replace the existing implementation with one of our own.

Method	Method T...	Comp. Interface	Pre-Exit	Post-Exit	Overwrite Exit	Enh.Impl.
OVERRIDE_EVENT_GAF	Method	▼ IF_FPM_GAF_CONF_EXIT	▯	▯	▯	
OVERRIDE_EVENT_OIF	Method	▼ IF_FPM_OIF_CONF_EXIT	▯	▯	▯	
OVERRIDE_EVENT_OVP	Method	▼ IF_FPM_OVP_CONF_EXIT	▯	▯	▯	
SAVE	Method	▼ IF_FPM_TRANSACTION	▯	▯	▯	
WDDOAPPLICATIONSTAT...	Method	▼	▯	▯	▯	
WDDOBEFORENAVIGATION	Method	▼	▯	▯	▯	
WDDOEXIT	Method	▼	▯	▯	▯	
WDDOINIT	Method	▼	▯	▯	▯	
WDDOPOSTPROCESSING	Method	▼	▯	▯	▯	

Figure 10.34: Enhancing an Application Controller - Part 2 © Copyright 2013. SAP AG. All rights reserved

3. Finally, regardless of the function that we choose, we'll end up at an editor screen like the one shown in Figure 10.35. Here, we can add in our custom ABAP changes just like we would if we were creating the application controller from scratch.

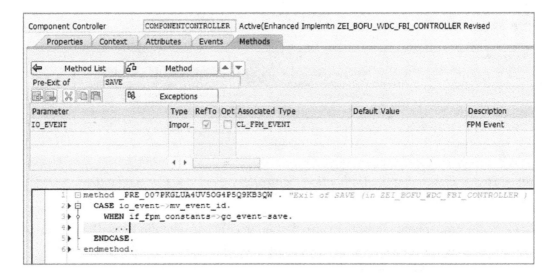

Figure 10.35: Enhancing an Application Controller - Part 3 © Copyright 2013. SAP AG. All rights reserved

10.5 Context-Based Adaptations

So far, the enhancement techniques that we've considered have been rather static in nature. This is to say that we implement our changes at design time and they are indiscriminately applied at runtime regardless of context. Though this approach generally works for 90% or more of the run-of-the-mill enhancement requirements, there are times whenever we need to apply enhancements on a more conditional basis. Recognizing this, SAP elected to expand the FPM enhancement toolkit to include a functionality called *Context-Based Adaptations* (CBAs). In this section, we'll take a look at CBAs and see how they can be used to handle more complicated enhancement requirements.

10.5.1 Conceptual Overview

As the name suggests, context-based adaptations are adaptations that are applied to an FPM application based on a certain *context*. Here, the term *context* could be used to describe a number of different application scenarios:

> If we're customizing a global application, the context might refer to the user's location and logon language.

> For applications with a diverse user base, the context might refer to different user roles (e.g. managers vs. regular employees).

> For transaction editor applications (e.g. sales order editors), the context might vary based on the selected transaction type.

Collectively, a context and the related adaptations that we define against it create a sort of *application variant*. If you've spent much time working with classic Dynpro transactions in the SAP GUI, then you might equate CBAs with transaction/screen variants in that environment. Basically, these variants allow us to reuse a given FPM application in a variety of settings. Figure 10.36 illustrates this phenomenon for an HR application which is adapted using an adaptation context based on the user's role assignments.

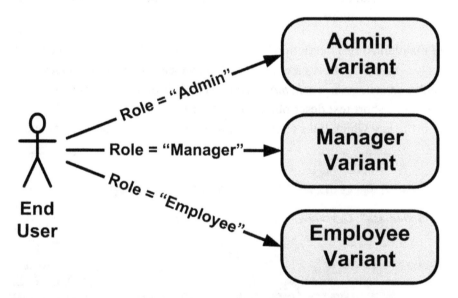

Figure 10.36: Using CBAs to Create Application Variants

Comparatively speaking, CBAs offer a much more streamlined approach than previous alternatives. Prior to the introduction of the CBA concept, the two common strategies for context-based enhancements involved the following:

> Copying the source FPM application multiple times - once per application scenario. Then any scenario-specific tweaks were applied to the application copies. Besides the obvious overhead involved in creating so many applications, the major downside

to this approach is that it separates the application copies from the standard code base. So, if SAP introduces any break fixes and/or enhancements to the standard application, we may have to manually copy them into our custom application(s).

➤ The other alternative involves the use of an AppCC controller to dynamically swap out UIBBs at runtime based on context details. As you might expect, this can get messy in a hurry.

OK, enough about theory; let's move on to more practical matters. In the next section, we'll get things started by looking at how to define the *adaptation context*.

10.5.2 Defining an Adaptation Schema

As we noted in the previous section, the context for adapting an application can be pretty much anything we put our minds to. On a practical level though, we eventually have to model an adaptation context in such a way that it can be used to drive adaptations within the FPM application. This can be achieved by defining an *adaptation schema* within the view cluster FPM_VC_ADAPT_SCHEMA.

View clusters are maintained in Transaction SM34. Figure 10.37 shows the main editor screen for the FPM_VC_ADAPT_SCHEMA view cluster. Here, we can see that the top level element in an adaptation schema is a *schema*. A schema definition consists of a 10 character identifier and a short text description. In Section 10.5.3, we'll see that this schema identifier is the key which links an FPM application with an adaptation context.

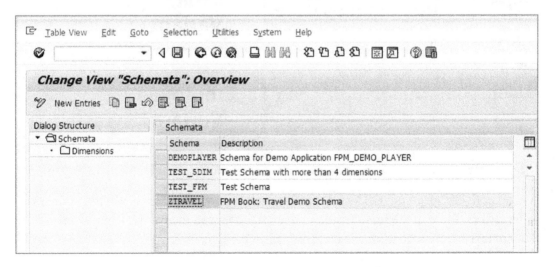

Figure 10.37: Defining an Adaptation Schema - Part 1 © Copyright 2013. SAP AG. All rights reserved

In order to give an adaptation schema depth, we must assign to it one or more *dimensions*. A dimension definition consists of a name, a data element, and an index which assigns a weight to the dimension. In Figure 10.38, you can see how we've defined a dimension called USER_GROUP for a demo schema we created called ZTRAVEL. At runtime, these dimensions will be used to determine when to apply specific adaptations. In the upcoming sections, we'll see how this schema can be used to adapt the look-and-feel of different screens based on a user's group assignment(s).

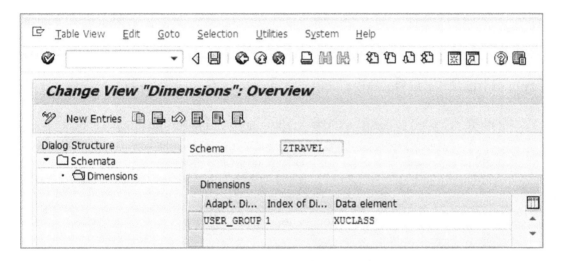

Figure 10.38: Defining an Adaptation Schema - Part 2 © Copyright 2013. SAP AG. All rights reserved

Before we wrap up our discussion on adaptation schemas, we should point out an important design point: adaptation schemas should be flexible enough to support an entire application area. This is to say that you shouldn't need to create separate application schemas for individual scenarios within an application area. In the upcoming sections, we'll see that it's much easier to work with only one schema from a configuration perspective.

10.5.3 Defining an Adaptable Wrapper Application

Now that you have a feel for how adaptation schemas are defined, you might be wondering how these schemas are linked with FPM applications. In this section, we'll explore this relationship and see how CBAs are applied without modifying the source FPM application.

In order to adapt an existing FPM application, we must define a *wrapper* application which extends the existing application to include information about the adaptation context. Depending on the underlying floorplan of the FPM application in question, our wrapper application will be based on one of three different WDA component types:

➢ FPM_ADAPTABLE_OIF for OIF applications

➢ FPM_ADAPTABLE_GAF for GAF applications

➢ FPM_ADAPTABLE_OVP for OVP applications

Once we identify the target wrapper component, the process of creating the wrapper application is pretty straightforward. To demonstrate this[40], let's see how to create a wrapper application around the standard-delivered FPM_QAF_CREATE_REQUEST application used to book flight trip requests for employees. Then, in the next section, we'll use this demo application to illustrate the CBA configuration process.

1. First off, we need to define a CBA wrapper application for the target application in the ABAP Workbench. Since the target application is based on the OIF floorplan type, we'll base our application on the FPM_ADAPTABLE_OIF component as shown in Figure 10.39.

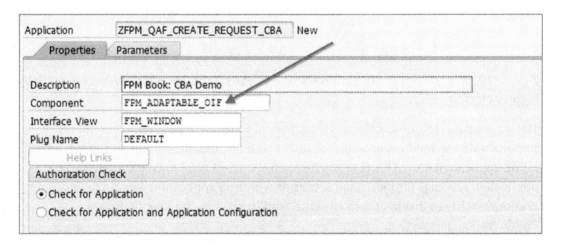

Figure 10.39: Creating an Adaptable Application Wrapper - Part 1 © Copyright 2013. SAP AG. All rights reserved

---

[40] For demonstration purposes, we'll be showing you how to perform these tasks manually. However, once you become comfortable with the concepts, you can use the ACT tool introduced in Chapter 4 to speed things along.

2. An optional next step is to define a series of application parameters which correspond with the dimensions identified in the target application schema. For our flight creation example, we're going to be working with an adaptation context based on a user's group assignment. So, in Figure 10.40, you can see how we've defined a parameter called USER_GROUP. At runtime, this parameter will be used to apply adaptations based on user group assignments (e.g. travel agents vs. administrators, etc.).

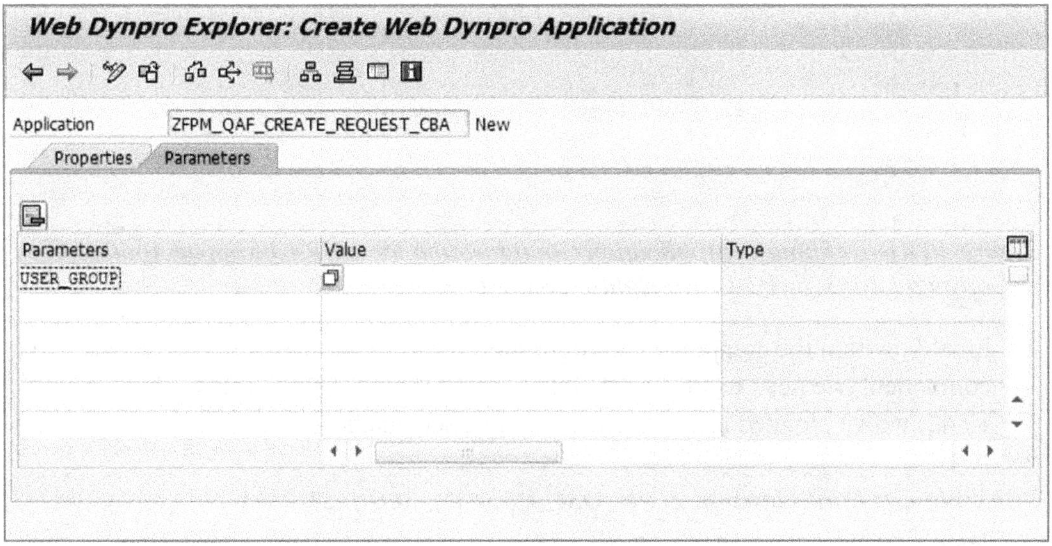

Figure 10.40: Creating an Adaptable Application Wrapper - Part 2 © Copyright 2013. SAP AG. All rights reserved

3. After the wrapper application is saved, the next step is to create an application configuration for it. Here, we define a WDA application configuration as per usual. However, this time, we have a little more work to do. As you can see in Figure 10.41, in addition to the source floorplan configuration, we also have to specify a component configuration for the adaptable component.

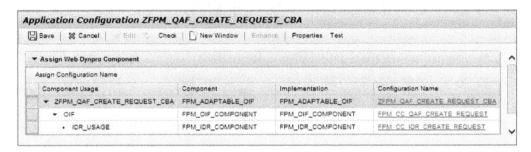

Figure 10.41: Defining an Application Configuration for a CBA Wrapper Application

4. Finally, within the component configuration for the `FPM_ADAPTABLE_OIF` component, we need to specify the adaptation schema. As you can see in Figure 10.42, we've plugged in our `ZTRAVEL` sample schema here.

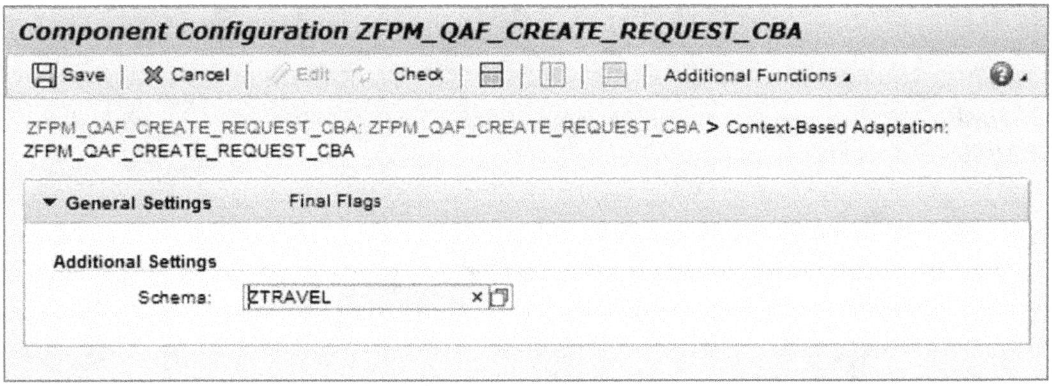

Figure 10.42: Configuring the FPM_ADAPTABLE_OIF Component © Copyright 2013.

Once our wrapper application is saved, we can fire it up and see that it behaves just like the standard-delivered application it encapsulates. With this foundation in place, we're now ready to define our CBA configurations. In the next section, we'll see how this works.

10.5.4 Creating a CBA Configuration

As we noted in the previous section, CBA wrapper applications start off on an even footing with the standard applications they are designed to enhance. From here, we can use this baseline as a springboard for applying our context-based adaptations. As you might expect, this is a task that we perform using the FPM Configuration Editor tool.

To demonstrate CBA configurations, we'll adapt the flight creation request application developed in the previous section to hide customer address/contact information from travel agents who are not authorized to see this data. This process is outlined as follows:

1. To begin, we need to open up the application configuration created for our CBA wrapper application and navigate to the target floorplan configuration (in display mode). From here, we can either begin adapting the overall floorplan layout or navigate to specific UIBBs that we want to tweak by following the FLUID navigation links. For the purposes of our example, we'll proceed with the latter and navigate to the form UIBB with the configuration name FPMGB_CC_QAF_CREATE_REQ_PER.

2. After we arrive at the form editor screen, we need to click on the ADAPTATIONS & COMPARISONS button in the toolbar to access the CBA adaptations panel shown in Figure 10.43.

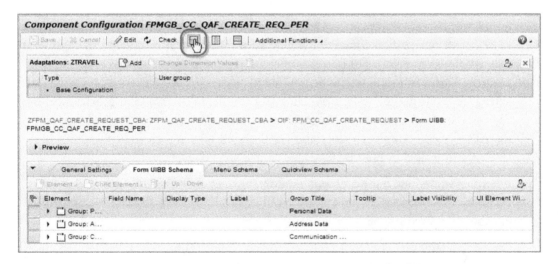

Figure 10.43: Applying a CBA Configuration © Copyright 2013. SAP AG. All rights reserved

3. As you can see in Figure 10.43, the ADAPTATIONS panel contains a table of configuration records which correspond with particular adaptation instances. By

default, there is only a base-level configuration which is identical to the source application. From here, we'll want to create new configuration records by clicking on the ADD button in the toolbar (see Figure 10.44).

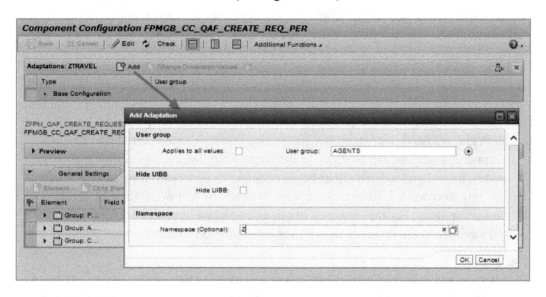

Figure 10.44: Creating a New Adaptation Record © Copyright 2013. SAP AG. All rights reserved

4. In the ADD ADAPTATION dialog box, we can plug in specific dimensional values to define the adaptation context in which we want to apply the enhancements against. For the purposes of our example, we'll plug in a user group called AGENTS. This user group would be applied to any travel agent users that will be accessing the flight requests application (e.g. on the GROUPS tab in Transaction SU01). Also note that we could specify multiple user group values by clicking on the ADD VALUE button (i.e. the button with the little plus icon adjacent to the USER GROUP field in Figure 10.44).

5. After we've defined our adaptation context, we can click the OK button to confirm our selections. At this point, we'll be prompted to assign a development package, CTS request, and so on.

6. Once the adaptation context is defined, we can begin editing the UIBB content as per usual. Getting back to our travel agents example, you can see how we're removing the contact information from the customer details form in Figure 10.45. Note that when we save our changes, the changes are applied against an auto-generated component configuration created in relation to our adaptation record.

This is evidenced by the cryptic component configuration name shown at the top of Figure 10.45.

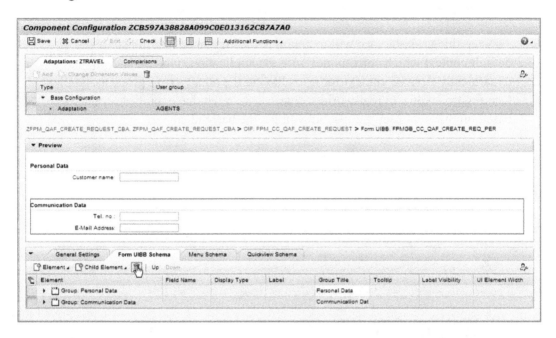

Figure 10.45: Adapting a Form UIBB Using CBAs © Copyright 2013. SAP AG. All rights reserved

7. Finally, after all of our changes are saved, we can re-start the CBA wrapper application to see the changes. This time, however, we will want to specify the value AGENTS for the USER_AGENT application parameter that we created in conjunction with our CBA wrapper application. Now, if you compare/contrast our adapted application with the standard application, you can see that the CBA wrapper application hides customer contact information from travel agents as expected.

10.5.5 Deriving the Adaptation Context Dynamically

Hopefully by now you can see the power of CBAs compared to legacy techniques for applying dynamic enhancements. Of course, a contrived example like the one described in the previous sections barely scratches the surface of what's possible with CBAs. After all, in real world scenarios, it's unlikely that the application context would be derived exclusively off of application parameters. Instead, we would like to be able to derive the adaptation context dynamically based upon user input, a user's preferences/locale, etc. As you might expect, these types of scenarios require some custom ABAP development.

To demonstrate how this works, let's see how we could rework the flight example we've been working on to dynamically derive the adaptation context based on a user's group assignments at runtime. Here, the steps required are as follows:

1. To keep things simple, we will maintain two different adaptation contexts: a default context which corresponds with the application standard and a dynamically-derived context for users having the AGENTS user group assignment (see Figure 10.46). In real-world scenarios, we might have multiple contexts based on different user groups, but you get the basic idea.

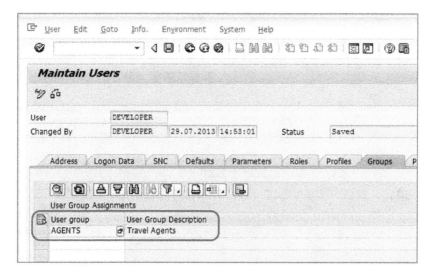

Figure 10.46: Keying on a User's Group Assignment © Copyright 2013. SAP AG. All rights reserved

2. Since we already defined the AGENTS context in the previous section, we just need to define the default context that will be accessed initially whenever we fire up our CBA wrapper application. As you can see in Figure 10.47, we can use the APPLIES TO ALL VALUES checkbox to define the default context.

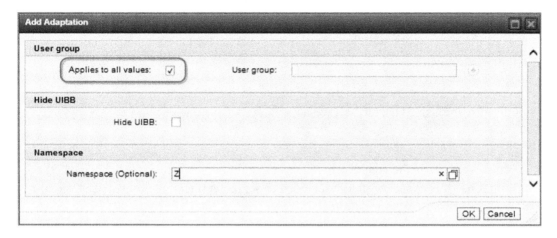

Figure 10.47: Defining a Wide-Open Adaptation Context © Copyright 2013. SAP AG. All rights reserved

3. Next, within both of our adaptation records, we need to replace the standard feeder class with our own feeder class as shown in Figure 10.48 - more on this in a moment.

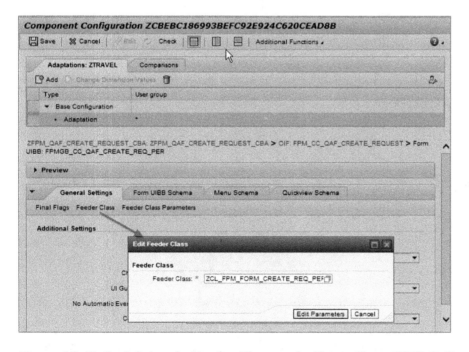

Figure 10.48: Redefining the Feeder Class on the Target Form UIBB © Copyright 2013. SAP AG. All rights reserved

4. Finally, once we save our changes in the FPM Configuration Editor, all that's left is to fill in the application logic within our custom feeder class to dynamically set the adaptation context.

For the most part, programmatically setting the adaptation context is a fairly straightforward task. Basically, all we have to do is raise one of two FPM events:

➤ `FPM_ADAPT_CONTEXT`

This event resets the adaptation context on a global level (i.e. across UIBBs). We might use this event on an initial screen to set the application context after the user selects certain key information.

➤ `FPM_ADAPT_CONTEXT_LOCAL`

This event resets the adaptation context locally within a given UIBB.

For the purposes of our demonstration, we'll use the local event type since we only want to adjust the layout of a single UIBB within our application. Listing 10.2 shows how we're raising this event within the overridden GET_DATA() method of our custom feeder class[41].

```
method IF_FPM_GUIBB_FORM~GET_DATA.
  DATA lo_fpm TYPE REF TO if_fpm.
  DATA lo_event TYPE REF TO cl_fpm_event.
  DATA lt_return TYPE STANDARD TABLE OF bapiret2.
  DATA lt_groups TYPE STANDARD TABLE OF bapigroups.
  DATA lv_group TYPE string.

  FIELD-SYMBOLS <ls_group> LIKE LINE OF lt_groups.

  "Let the parent class do its thing:
  CALL METHOD me->mo_super->if_fpm_guibb_form~get_data
    EXPORTING
      io_event               = io_event
      iv_raised_by_own_ui    = iv_raised_by_own_ui
      it_selected_fields     = it_selected_fields
      iv_edit_mode           = iv_edit_mode
      io_extended_ctrl       = io_extended_ctrl
    IMPORTING
      et_messages            = et_messages
```

---

[41] Note: You can find a complete implementation for our custom feeder class in the provided source code bundle. Since the standard-delivered content from SAP used a feeder class that was marked as final (class CL_FPM_FORM_CREATE_REQ_PER), we had to use composition techniques to encapsulate the standard functionality into our pseudo subclass.

```
    ev_data_changed           = ev_data_changed
    ev_field_usage_changed    = ev_field_usage_changed
    ev_action_usage_changed   = ev_action_usage_changed
  CHANGING
    cs_data                   = cs_data
    ct_field_usage            = ct_field_usage
    ct_action_usage           = ct_action_usage.

CHECK cl_fpm_factory=>get_instance( )->mo_adaptation_manager
    IS BOUND.

CHECK io_event->mv_event_id NE
        if_fpm_constants=>gc_event-adapt_context_local.

"Also check to see if we've already set the adaptation context:
IF me->mv_user_name EQ sy-uname.
  RETURN.
ELSE.
  me->mv_user_name = sy-uname.
ENDIF.

CALL FUNCTION 'BAPI_USER_GET_DETAIL'
  EXPORTING
    username = me->mv_user_name
  TABLES
    return   = lt_return
    groups   = lt_groups.

READ TABLE lt_groups ASSIGNING <ls_group>
      WITH KEY usergroup = 'AGENTS'.
IF sy-subrc EQ 0.
  lv_group = <ls_group>-usergroup.
ENDIF.

"If we get to here, then we need to set the adaptation context.
"This can be achieved by raising an FPM event as follows:
CREATE OBJECT lo_event
  EXPORTING
    iv_event_id =
      if_fpm_constants=>gc_event-adapt_context_local
    iv_adapts_context = abap_true.

lo_event->mo_event_data->set_value(
  EXPORTING
    iv_key = 'USER_GROUP'
    iv_value = lv_group ).

lo_event->mo_event_data->set_value(
```

```
    EXPORTING
      iv_key = if_fpm_constants=>gc_event_param-source_config_id
      iv_value = me->ms_instance_key-config_id ).

  lo_event->mo_event_data->set_value(
    EXPORTING
      iv_key =
        if_fpm_constants=>gc_event_param-source_config_type
      iv_value = me->ms_instance_key-config_type ).

  lo_event->mo_event_data->set_value(
    EXPORTING
      iv_key = if_fpm_constants=>gc_event_param-source_config_var
      iv_value = me->ms_instance_key-config_var ).

  lo_event->mo_event_data->set_value(
    EXPORTING
      iv_key =
        if_fpm_constants=>gc_event_param-source_instance_id
      iv_value = me->ms_instance_key-instance_id ).

  lo_fpm = cl_fpm_factory=>get_instance( ).
  lo_fpm->raise_event( lo_event ).
endmethod.
```

Listing 10.2: Dynamically Setting a Local Adaptation Context

As you can see in Listing 10.2, the logic we've encoded within our GET_DATA() method is pretty straightforward:

➤ First, we check to see if our feeder class is operating in an SAP NetWeaver system based on release 7.03 or newer. If not, we won't try to access any CBA-based functionality as this would simply result in a lot of unnecessary event processing.

➤ Next, we have a check in place to ensure that we only process the local context change event once. Without this check, we would enter into an infinite loop situation since the GET_DATA() method is invoked any time an event is triggered - including the FPM_ADAPT_CONTEXT_LOCAL event.

➤ If we get past the first two checks, we also have a logic gate that checks to see whether or not we've already adjusted the adaptation context. In this particular case, we need only set the context one time since the executing user will not change during an application session. Of course, if our adaptation context was based on data the user was keying in, then the nature of this check would need to change.

➢ Once we determine that a context change is in order, we read the user's group assignments using BAPI_USER_GET_DETAIL.

➢ Finally, we raise the FPM_ADAPT_CONTEXT_LOCAL event, passing in the user's group assignment as well as certain metadata about the current UIBB configuration. If you're wondering where we got this information, rest assured that we didn't conjure it from thin air. Rather, we simply cached these values within the INITIALIZE() method, which is passed this information by default by the FPM framework during the UIBB instantiation process.

Now, if we fire up our application and set a break point in the GET_DATA() method of our custom feeder class, we can see how the context gets adjusted dynamically based on the group assignments of the logged-on user. Had we wanted to set this context on a more global level, we could have raised the FPM_ADAPT_CONTEXT event within an application controller. Indeed, regardless of where we put the code, the logic is basically the same in either case.

10.6 Summary

In this chapter, we learned how to enhance pre-existing FPM applications using a variety of techniques. We learned how to tap into the customizing layer of the WDA Configuration Framework, how to enhance FPM development objects using the enhancement framework, and even how to apply conditional enhancements with CBAs. Collectively, these tools provide us with the flexibility we need to handle pretty much any enhancement request that might come our way.

About the Author

 **James Wood** is the founder and principal consultant of Bowdark Consulting, Inc., an SAP NetWeaver consulting and training organization. With over 12 years of experience as a software engineer, James specializes in custom development in the areas of ABAP Objects, Java/JEE, SAP NetWeaver Process Integration, and the SAP NetWeaver Enterprise Portal.

Before starting Bowdark Consulting, Inc. in 2006, James was an SAP NetWeaver consultant for SAP America, Inc. and IBM Corporation, where he was involved in multiple SAP implementations. He holds a Master's Degree in Software Engineering from Texas Tech University. He is also the author of *Object-Oriented Programming with ABAP Objects* (SAP PRESS, 2009), *ABAP Cookbook* (SAP PRESS, 2010), *SAP NetWeaver Process Integration: A Developer's Guide* (Bowdark Press, 2011), and *Web Dynpro ABAP: The Comprehensive Guide* (SAP PRESS, 2012). To learn more about James and the book, please check out his website at http://www.bowdark.com. You can also contact him directly via e-mail at jwood@bowdark.com.

Index